The construction of personality

The Author
Until recently, Sarah E. Hampson was a lecturer in psychology at Birkbeck College, University of London. She is now at the Oregon Research Institute in the USA, where she is conducting research in personality and social cognition. She has served on the editorial boards of the *British Journal of Social Psychology*, the *European Journal of Personality*, and *Personal and Individual Differences*. She was the founding secretary of the European Association for Personality Psychology, established in 1984.

D0424231

Introductions to Modern Psychology

General Editor: Max Coltheart
Birkbeck College, University of London

The construction of personality

An introduction

Second edition

Sarah E. Hampson

London and New York

First published in 1982 by
Routledge
Second edition published in 1988 by
Routledge
11 New Fetter Lane, London EC4P 4EE

Published in the USA by
Routledge
29 West 35th Street, New York, NY 10001

Reprinted 1990

Set in Baskerville
by Columns of Reading
and printed in Great Britain
by T.J. Press (Padstow) Ltd, Padstow, Cornwall

Library of Congress Cataloging in Publication Data
Hampson, Sarah E., 1951–
    The construction of personality.

(Introductions to modern psychology)
    Bibliography: p.
    Includes indexes.
    1. Personality.   2. Personality–Research.
I. Title.   II. Series
BF698.H333 1988   155.2   87-12875

British Library CIP Data also available

ISBN 0-415-00255-9 (c)
     0-415-00256-7 (ppr)

Contents

Acknowledgments

First edition

A number of people have read some or all of this book at different stages in its preparation and their reactions have been invaluable. I am especially indebted to Max Coltheart for his help with the entire manuscript and to Camilla Mower White who also commented on all the chapters. In particular, I would like to thank Paul Harris for his candid comments. I am also grateful to Mary Boyle, Gordon Craig, Peter Dowrick, Daphne Loasby, Angus McLachlan and the third and fourth year Birkbeck psychology undergraduates in 1979–80 for their evaluations of various chapters, and I would like to thank Carol Machen and Patricia Caple for their assistance with typing.

Second edition

I would like to thank Lewis Goldberg, David Good, Dean Peabody and Nico Smid for their thoughtful suggestions for revisions, and Hazel Sparey for typing the manuscript. In addition, help from Helen, Frank and Larry at various stages in the preparation of this book has been indispensable.

Some of this book was written while I was at the Oregon Research Institute, Eugene, Oregon, USA, and partially supported by grant MH39077 from the National Institute of Mental Health, USA, and also by a grant from the British Academy.

The figure from *Dimensions of Personality* edited by H. London and J.E. Exner (1978), is adapted on page 19 with kind permission of John Wiley & Sons.

1 The concept of personality

A definition of personality

Personality has different meanings for theologians, philosophers, and sociologists, and within psychology it has been defined in many ways (Allport, 1937). Rather than give examples of the diversity of the definitions, which tends to be confusing rather than illuminating, we will begin by considering just one definition of personality considered acceptable by many psychologists today (Block, Weiss and Thorne, 1979): personality refers to *'more or less stable, internal factors that make one person's behaviour consistent from one time to another, and different from the behaviour other people would manifest in comparable situations'* (Child, 1968, p.83).

In a few words, this definition manages to encompass all the major assumptions of a generally accepted definition of the concept of personality. These assumptions are that personality is *stable, internal, consistent* and *different*.

Stability

The definition begins by stating that the personality is more or less stable. It is not assumed that personality is entirely stable but rather that it can, to a limited extent, undergo changes. Such a view allows for the possibility of long-term personality growth and change over the life-span and short-term fluctuations in personality from day to day. Nevertheless, these instabilities are regarded as relatively superficial when compared with the underlying core of continuity

1

implied by the personality concept. The assumption of stability corresponds to our everyday experience: friends and acquaintances do not present radically different personalities on every fresh meeting, but instead are likely to be approximately the same from occasion to occasion. Even when we are taken by surprise by an old friend's dramatic new image, we are usually able to fit the new and old selves into a coherent whole, and to be reassured that deep down the person is still the same.

Internality

Next, the definition states that personality is *internal*. Personality cannot be observed directly; it can only be measured indirectly by making observations of that which is available externally. For example, on the basis of a personality test, a psychologist will infer the level of the underlying personality trait presumed to determine responses on that test. Similarly, we make inferences about the personalities of our friends and acquaintances on the basis of observations of their behaviour.

Consistency

The definition goes on to state that personality makes one person's behaviour consistent from one time to another. The assumption that behaviour is consistent is one of the most controversial issues in personality (see chapter 4). Consistency over time refers to the similarity between a person's behaviour on two different occasions. Everyday life is full of examples of consistency, from trivial daily routines such as the order in which you do your morning toilette to more weighty matters such as which way you vote in a general election. Personality is assumed to explain behavioural consistency because it is assumed to be a major determinant of behaviour and, since personality remains relatively stable, the behaviour it determines will be consistent.

Individual differences

Finally, the definition states that personality makes a

person's behaviour *different from the behaviour other people would manifest in comparable situations*. It is a major assumption underlying the personality concept that there are individual differences in behaviour which are large enough to warrant investigation: people respond to the same situation in different ways. For example, even in such a constrained situation as a lecture, students' behaviour will vary from sleep to furiously energetic note taking. Individual differences in response to the same situation are assumed to be the product of variations in personality.

The emphasis on traits

The definition refers to stable, internal *factors* of personality, and personality psychologists differ substantially in how they conceptualise these 'factors' or elements. Indeed, the question as to what is the basic element of personality has been an enduring point of controversy (e.g. Fiske, 1974). At various times, rivals to traits have included instincts, motives, goals, desires, beliefs, and attitudes (Alston, 1975). Recently, goals (e.g. Pervin, 1983), and motivational states (e.g. Apter, 1984) have been favoured as alternatives to traits. Nevertheless, the majority of past and present research in personality has centred on the trait concept.

As with definitions of personality, definitions of traits abound. We shall be examining specific uses of the term when particular theories are described (see chapters 2 and 3). Despite differences in detail, traits are generally seen as 'broad, enduring, relatively stable characteristics used to assess and explain behavior' (Hirschberg, 1978, p. 45). One of the main differences between definitions of traits concerns whether the trait is considered to be a summarising concept serving descriptive purposes (e.g. Buss and Craik, 1983) or whether it is also endowed with causal potency (e.g. H.J. Eysenck and M.W. Eysenck, 1985). Both points of view accept that traits are inferred from observations of past behaviour and provide a convenient way of describing consistent behavioural patterns. Both points of view also assume that the occurrence of similar behaviours in the future may be predicted from patterns of past behaviour. However, some theorists prefer a descriptive but non-causal view of traits because they regard it as tautological to argue that a trait is inferred from the same behaviours that it is also assumed to have caused.

Regardless of a theorist's position on the nature of traits, it is generally agreed that traits are manifested in behaviour. This is the trait's advantage over many other person concepts. Alston (1975) argued that whereas other person concepts can be attributed to an individual in the absence of direct behavioural evidence, this is not true of traits. For example, it makes no sense to claim that a person is very sociable but never talks to people, whereas it is reasonable to say that a person has a *need* to be sociable but never talks to people. Thus, given that traits are a kind of person concept which is usually reflected in behaviour, this makes them accessible for research purposes.

An alternative to the personality *trait*, which enjoyed popularity in the past and is presently receiving renewed attention, is the personality *type* (e.g. Gangestad and Snyder, 1985). A type theory of personality assumes that all individuals can be allocated to one of a limited number of types. Although not a scientific theory of personality (Startup, 1985), the astrological theory of star signs is a good example of the type approach since it assumes that everyone falls into one of twelve mutually exclusive personality types. Types differ from traits primarily in that a person cannot be described as possessing a type to varying degrees; the person either is or is not a member of the type. Traits, on the other hand, are dimensions that are believed to be normally distributed throughout the population and therefore are characteristic of all people, but to varying degrees. The main criticism against types is that there is an arbitrariness and simplicity about them which does not match our intuitions. Personality is a rich and complicated concept, and individual differences cannot be adequately captured by slotting people into a few all-or-none categories.

Perspectives on personality

This book is organised around three different perspectives on personality, which have generated three kinds of personality theory: explicit theories of personality from the personality psychologists' perspective; implicit theories of personality from the lay person's perspective; and the perspective from the standpoint of the self, which is concerned with the theories people have about their *own* personalities.

The distinction between explicit and implicit theories refers to the distinction between psychologists' theories of personality derived from formal investigations versus lay persons' theories or systems of beliefs about personality derived from everyday experience (Sternberg, 1985). Explicit theories constitute one way of looking at personality: the personality theorist's perspective, in which the actual manifestations of personality in observable behaviour are studied. Implicit theories provide another viewpoint: the lay perspective, in which people's beliefs about personality are the object of study. The self perspective refers to both the scientific and lay theories developed to study the way people perceive and understand themselves.

A similar distinction to explicit versus implicit theories was made by Wiggins (1973) in his separation of external from internal personality data, and by Buss and Craik (1983), who distinguished between manifested and conceptual personality. Research into external, manifested (i.e. explicit) personality is typically conducted in the context of real individuals by observing their patterns of actual behaviour. The focus is on the personalities of the individuals under investigation. In research into internal, conceptual (i.e. implicit) personality, the focus is on the knowledge and beliefs about personality held by the individuals under investigation.

Explicit personality and the personality theorists' perspective

Psychologists have studied personality by observing behaviour and developing formal theories to account for their observations. Personality theories typically consist of propositions concerned with three main areas: the structure, dynamics and development of personality (Hall and Lindzey, 1978). Propositions about personality structure are meant to specify more precisely the nature of the internal factors making up personality; the study of personality dynamics is concerned with what drives the structure to result in behaviour; and personality development has to do with the origins of the mature structure and its dynamics.

The three areas described by personality theories may be illustrated by reference to Freud's theory of personality (which is dealt with in more detail in chapter 9). First, the id, ego, and superego are the three interrelated systems which make up the structure of personality. Second, they are regarded as being in constant competition for control of psychic energy, which is the basis of the Freudian account of dynamics. Finally, Freud proposed that personality develops predominantly as a sequence of three stages which is completed around the age of 5 years. These are the oral, anal, and phallic stages, their names deriving from the part of the body assumed to provide the major source of gratification during the particular stage. Other personality theories, such as Eysenck's and Cattell's, are based on more objective observations of normal populations.

Part One of this book is concerned with explicit theories. A selection of explicit personality theories is presented in chapters 2 and 3, and in chapter 4 the most challenging issue for explicit theories – behavioural consistency – is discussed.

Implicit personality and the lay perspective

The implicit approach refers to the study of widely shared beliefs about personality which are not generally made explicit, but which remain implicit and form the basis of lay or everyday theories of personality, theories which we all use in an informal and often unconscious way (Bruner and Tagiuri, 1954). Lay theories have become embodied in the language of personality description. For example, we might be telling friends about a person we had recently met and describe this new person as 'warm' and 'friendly'. Our friends would have no difficulty in understanding this description and would probably infer that were they also to meet this person it would be easy to strike up a conversation, since the person would be likely to be 'sociable' as well. In short, we tend to believe that certain personality characteristics like 'warm', 'friendly', and 'sociable' go together, and we use these beliefs to make additional inferences about personality on the basis of limited information. These beliefs help us to simplify and organise our social world by enabling us to categorise people in terms of their personality characteristics in ways which then allow us to make predictions about their future behaviour. Lay personality theory is a form of general knowledge comparable to our knowledge about other aspects of the animate and inanimate environment. One does not need to be a biologist to know that dogs can bite, or a chemist to know that paper dissolves in water.

General knowledge about personality is of interest to personality psychologists for at least two reasons. First, in order to understand social behaviour it is necessary to understand the informal personality theories people use to categorise one another and to make predictions about additional characteristics and behaviour. Second, the existence of the lay perspective raises the question of how it relates to the personality theorists' perspective. They are both concerned with the same subject matter, but how far are they the same? These issues will be considered in chapter 6. Part Two reviews research into implicit personality and compares implicit and explicit theories.

The self perspective

The final approach to personality that we shall be considering is the combination of both explicit and implicit personality that arises in the concept of the self. Psychologists have been concerned with the origins of our self-awareness (Mead, 1934) and the form in which our self-perceptions are structured (Rogers, 1959). One of the most interesting issues raised in connection with the concept of the self is the extent to which our self-perceptions are accurate. Although we may think that no one knows us better than we do ourselves, there is evidence to suggest that this self-knowledge is not as accurate as we would like to believe. The self is discussed in chapter 7.

These three approaches are not the only standpoints from which observations about personality can be made; theologians, philosophers, and sociologists all have their own perspectives from which to think about and study personality. However, the three perspectives to be described here incorporate the main areas of psychological research into personality. Traditionally, these three approaches have not been given equal weight in personality textbooks. Accounts of implicit personality and the self are more commonly found in social psychology texts. However, the intention is to show that the understanding of personality is enhanced by a consideration of all three perspectives.

The construction of personality

The combined study of explicit and implicit personality, and the self, is necessary because personality is a social construction. Therefore, it is important not only to study what the actor displays to others (explicit personality) but also how the actor is construed by observers (implicit personality) and how the actor construes her or himself (the self perspective).

The social constructivist approach is 'principally concerned with explicating the processes by which people come to describe, explain, or otherwise account for the world (including themselves) in which they live' (Gergen, 1985, p. 266). This approach has been influential in sociology for some time (e.g. Berger and Luckmann, 1971), and is now having an impact on social psychology (Gergen and Davis, 1985; Landman and Manis, 1983). By emphasising that personality is the product of a person's behaviour and the manner in which that behaviour is construed by others and by the self, this book may be said to be adopting a social constructivist approach to personality.

Social constructivism alerts us to the absence of an

objective existence which is typical of many of the phenomena studied in psychology. Our knowledge of the world must always be indirect, since we only have access to reality via our sense organs and our minds. Thus we bring pre-existing categories to bear upon the world which make our experience meaningful, but at the same time prevent us from ever knowing what the 'raw' experience of the world is like. In addition, there are many topics of psychological investigation which are composed of both our indirect experience of their objective aspects and the social significance that we have attached to them. For example, schizophrenia, childhood, and ageing (Gergen, 1985) are all psychological concepts which are composed of behaviours and physical character-istics that take place in the real world, but which we see as distinct categories because we imbue those behaviours and physical characteristics with particular significance and meaning. We could choose to ignore them, or to value them differently, as has happened at other times in our history and in other cultures. In that case, the 'phenomena' would no longer exist since they do not have any significance in the absence of social recognition. Phenomena such as schizo-phrenia, childhood, and ageing are therefore social artifacts; they are creations of a culture.

Personality is also a social artifact (Hampson, 1984). We attach meaning and significance to behaviour by using it to infer underlying personality characteristics. Regardless of the terms that we use to conceptualise personality (e.g. goals, motives, instincts, traits), we are using concepts that are derived in part from our indirect perception of reality (in this case, the person behaving in a certain way in a certain situation), and in part from social knowledge.

The social construction of personality involves the combin-ation of explicit and implicit personality and the self. It is described more fully in chapter 8. Part Four describes two applications of the constructivist approach. In chapter 9, the discussion of personality over the life-span tries to show how the three perspectives work together to produce the impression of an enduring personality. In chapter 10, we shall see how these perspectives contribute to the concept of a criminal personality.

Part One

Explicit Personality: The Personality Theorist's Perspective

2 Single-trait theories

Personality is typically regarded as internal and hence not directly accessible. It is made manifest in a person's behaviour and appearance; these provide the outward signs from which the internal elements of personality may be inferred. This inference process is not always accurate; for example, the nineteenth-century criminologist Lombroso believed that the criminal personality could be inferred from a variety of physical characteristics such as long arms and flat noses. The long arms were not for reaching into pockets, nor were the flat noses a consequence of such behaviour; both were regarded as inherited features indicative of a reversion to animals lower down the evolutionary scale such as the apes. However, Lombroso's outward signs of criminality turned out to be nothing more than the physical concomitants of severely subnormal intelligence. Another example of inferring personality from behaviour is Freud's view that relatively trivial and usual behaviours, like slips of the tongue or forgetting people's names, reveal volumes about a person's underlying conflicts. But although Freud's interpretations of everyday behaviours may be fascinating, they are virtually impossible to put to the test.

Despite the dangers, the assumption that outward signs may be used for the inference and assessment of personality remains the hallmark of scientific approaches to the study of personality (Wiggins, 1973). It is assumed that carefully selected samples of behaviour may be used to measure a person's position on the underlying personality dimensions believed to give rise to the overt behaviour.

13

Interest in personality measurement developed as a result of successful attempts to measure another dimension of individual variation: intelligence. Since personality measurement started out with many of the assumptions and techniques that had proved successful in mental testing, it is worth mentioning these before moving on to personality proper.

Origins of personality measurement

Measurement of intelligence

Mental testing was first introduced at the beginning of this century by Binet in France. His goals were pragmatic: to find tests that would discriminate among children in schools in Paris, so that the duller ones could be identified and sent for special education (Herrnstein, 1973). Binet was not primarily concerned with the nature of intelligence, but instead with producing ways of testing it that were sensitive to the range of individual differences in ability. If he did not understand the nature of intelligence, how could he be sure that his tests were measuring it? His approach relied on the fact that it is generally agreed that as children grow older they become more intelligent and within each age-group some children are more precocious than others. Binet used these two sources of information about intelligence as the yardstick against which to measure the success of his tests: they had to distinguish the younger children from the older ones and, within one age group, they had to distinguish the children the teachers thought were bright from the children regarded as dull.

Although Binet's approach to intelligence testing was pragmatic, subsequent researchers were not content to let the nature of intelligence remain an enigma. They noticed that intelligence appeared to be composed of a number of different abilities, such that a person might be more able in some areas than others. These different facets of intelligence were identified by discovering groups of intercorrelated subtests each measuring specific abilities.

The statistical technique for isolating separate groups of subtests is factor analysis (Harman, 1967), which will be described in more detail in the next chapter. The pioneers of factor analysis in mental testing were Spearman and Thurstone. Spearman (1927) argued that intelligence involves two kinds of factors: a *general factor* (which enters into all subtests) and a *specific factor* (restricted to the particular ability being measured by the subtest). Thurstone (1947) proposed several general factors which enter into the correlations between subtests, and he developed a more sophisticated form of factor analysis to demonstrate the plurality of general factors.

Similarities between measuring intelligence and measuring personality

Personality testing has the same aims as intelligence testing: to distinguish between individuals and to make predictions about their performance in other settings. One of the major problems for personality testing is the lack of an obvious yardstick or criterion against which to assess the ability of the test to measure what it claims to be measuring. There are hundreds of ways of discriminating among people, from their body weight to their taste in light reading, and the problem is to decide which of these outward signs may be taken as an index of personality. Unfortunately the natural yardstick of age, which is appropriate for intelligence testing, is not relevant so far as personality testing is concerned.

Although personality probably does change with age, it does not appear to do so in any straightforward way. We cannot say that 7-year-olds are 'less' extraverted than 9-year-olds. Nor is there an obvious group of experts, such as teachers, who might agree on a rank ordering of people in terms of personality characteristics. Instead, other less satisfactory criteria have to be used, as we shall see later in the chapter.

Personality testing inherited the technique of factor analysis for unravelling the structure of personality, and thus also inherited the technique's capacity to produce different solutions for the same data. The final solution looks different depending on, for example, the choice of items put into the analysis and the level in the hierarchy of factors with which the researcher chooses to work. These issues will be examined more closely when the work of Eysenck and Cattell is considered.

To summarise, personality and intelligence have a number of features in common. They are both psychological components of the individual which can be measured to reveal individual differences. Factor analysis has been used to investigate the structure of the psychological components assessed by intelligence and personality tests. Intelligence is fortunate in having both a natural criterion (age changes) and teachers' expert opinions against which to validate its tests; but those interested in measuring personality are not so lucky.

Single-trait theories

Single-trait theories are concerned with the role played by one particular part of the personality structure in the determination of behaviour. The most influential single-trait theories have been those which describe traits that enter into a wide variety of behaviours. Some well-known examples of such traits are Authoritarianism (Adorno, Frenkel-Brunswick, Levinson and Sanford, 1950), the Achievement Motive (McClelland, Atkinson, Clark and Lowell, 1953), and Repression versus Sensitisation (Byrne, 1964). The ambitions of a single-trait investigator studying one aspect of personality are far more humble than those of the multi-trait investigator, who hopes to describe personality in its entirety.

When discussing the personality theorist's perspective, the terms 'trait' and 'dimension' will be used interchangeably. Both refer to an internal characteristic which is capable of distinguishing between individuals in the sense that it is believed to be present to a greater extent in some people than in others. The two single-trait theories and their associated measures to be presented here involve the traits of Field Dependence-Independence (FD-I) and Locus of Control, respectively. These particular theories have been chosen because of the vast amount of research they have generated (approximately 3,000 studies between them – ample testimony to their popularity and influence). Reviews of these and other single-trait theories are to be found in Blass (1977) and in London and Exner (1978).

Field dependence-independence

FD-I is a dimension of individual variation which characterises an aspect of information processing. The relatively field-dependent person is readily influenced by the environment and tends to incorporate information non-selectively. In contrast, the field-independent person relies more on internally generated cues and is more discriminating in the selection of environmental information. FD-I has been the subject of extensive investigation by Witkin and his colleagues (Witkin, Lewis, Hertzman, Machover, Meissner and Wapner, 1972; Witkin, Dyk, Paterson, Goodenough and Karp, 1974). It forms part of Witkin's general theory of the development of perception and cognition in which he proposes that development involves the gradual shift away from the interpretation of the environment in a relatively global, unstructured manner towards a more complex interpretation in which the environment is perceived as consisting of many independent elements forming a detailed organisation. FD-I is sometimes referred to as a 'cognitive style' variable, since it is concerned with individual differences in information processing; but this does not mean that its relevance is limited to tasks we typically regard as cognitive, such as remembering telephone numbers or problem solving. The environment is also rich in social information, and this too requires selective attention and processing. It is thus not surprising that FD-I has been investigated in relation both to the more cognitive kinds of behaviours and to social behaviours.

Origins of the concept of FD-I

It is helpful to look into the historical origins of the FD-I dimension in order to understand the nature of this ubiquitous trait. It shares, along with penicillin and North

America, the distinction of having been discovered by accident. Originally, Witkin and his co-workers were investigating the factors involved in the perception of verticality in visual stimuli. In particular, they were studying the relative importance of external cues about verticality (such as the presence of other vertical lines in the environment) and internal cues about verticality (cues made available by the mechanisms of balance in the body). They devised several ingenious tests by which they could separate the influences of these external and internal cues: the rod and frame test, the rotating room test, and the embedded figures test.

In the rod and frame test (RFT) the cues available in the external environment are distorted by having the subject sit in a darkened room and adjust a luminous rod set in a luminous frame. Nothing can be seen but the rod and the frame. The frame can be tilted so that if the subject, when asked to set the rod to vertical, relies on external cues, then the rod will be lined up parallel with the frame since that is the only external information available. If the subject relies on internal cues then the rod will be set vertically, and hence at an angle to the frame. Subjects who behave in the former way may be described as field-dependent; those who behave in the latter way may be described as field-independent.

The RFT holds internal cues constant and manipulates external cues. A more elaborate testing apparatus, the rotating room test (RRT), was devised to study the effects of varying internal cues independently of external cues. In the RRT the subject's task is to set his or her own body position so that it is upright. The subject is seated in a box-like room which is suspended from an arm onto a circular track. The room is then spun round on the horizontal track, causing its occupant to be subjected to gravitational and centrifugal forces which distort the mechanisms of balance inside the body. The chair in which the subject is seated is adjustable and while the room is being spun round the subject is asked to adjust the chair, and thus him or herself, to the upright. Reliance on internal cues in this situation would result in error since these cues are distorted by the forces resulting from the motion of the room.

Although, with an inventive battery of these and other

tests, Witkin was able to separate the effects of internal and external cues in perceiving the vertical, his hope of discovering which of the two was more important was never realised because the results were swamped with individual differences. Some people consistently relied on internal cues whereas others relied on external cues. These individual differences were so marked that Witkin decided to explore them further, and therefore he abandoned his research on the perception of the visual vertical. Instead, he and his colleagues set about investigating the generality of these individual differences and testing hypotheses about their underlying psychological basis. One of their first discoveries was that a test of a person's ability to differentiate within the visual field, the embedded figures test (EFT), was highly correlated with the RFT and the RRT. The EFT requires the subject to locate a simple geometric shape within a complex pattern (see Figure 2.1).

In addition to providing results confirming that Witkin and his colleagues were studying a general perceptual dimension, the EFT also provided a paper-and-pencil

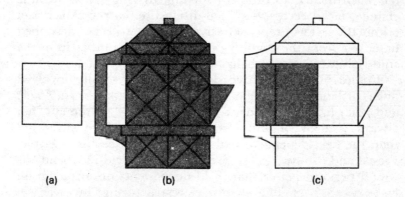

(a)   (b)   (c)

FIGURE 2.1 *An example of an item of the type used in the Embedded Figures Test (adapted from Goodenough, 1978, p. 175). The task is to find the square (a) within the coffee pot (b). The solution is shown in (c)*

measure of FD-I, which is more convenient to administer than the RFT or RRT. Several reliable individual and group forms of the EFT for use with adults and with children have been developed (Jackson, Messick and Myers, 1964). Some tests purporting to measure FD-I, such as the Hidden Picture Test, have low reliability and validity (Karp, 1977), so the FD-I researcher must take care in choosing a sound test.

Differences between FD and FI individuals

The development of measures of FD-I has been helped by the existence of objective criteria in the form of the original tests by which it was first observed. Any subsequent measure had to correlate with the original tests to demonstrate that it was measuring the same variable and, in this way, the early perceptual tests formed the keystones around which the dimension has been built. Armed with reliable measures, FD-I researchers have ventured into a wide range of territories looking for differences between field-dependent and field-independent people. These explorations have led them into extremely diverse areas; for example, the dimension has been related to problem solving, driving skills, attitude change, facial recognition, self-disclosure, career choice and criminality. Two representative studies will be described here, one from the cognitive domain and the other from the study of interpersonal behaviour.

Studies in the cognitive domain have typically involved different kinds of problem-solving tasks (Witkin *et al.*, 1974) and the field-independent person usually, although not always (Nebelkopf and Dreyer, 1973), is more successful than the field-dependent person in such tasks. For example, Frank and Noble (1984) predicted that field-independents would perform better than field-dependents on an anagram task because of the cognitive restructuring involved in successful anagram solution. They found that field-independents solved both easy and difficult anagrams significantly faster than did field-dependents. This result cannot be explained by differences in verbal intelligence, since the groups did not differ significantly on this factor.

Another cognitive skill with which FD-I has been associated is reality monitoring in memory, which is the ability to recall whether information originated from an external or internal source. For example, if you are given the following sentence to read: 'For breakfast I scrambled some *eggs*', then the word *eggs*, like the rest of the sentence, originates externally. However, if you are asked to read the sentence: 'For breakfast I scrambled some . . .', and you have to supply the most natural last word, then *eggs* originates internally. Durso, Reardon and Jolly (1985) compared field-independent and field-dependent subjects' reality monitoring using this kind of sentence. The subjects read sentences in half of which the last word, although obvious, was missing and they were required to generate it. On a subsequent recognition test, the subjects judged whether the test words were ones which had been given at the end of sentences, or ones the subjects had generated, or ones which were entirely new. Field-dependent subjects made more confusions between given and generated words (i.e. external versus internal memories) than did field-independent subjects. Further experiments demonstrated that field-dependents were as good as field-independents in distinguishing between two external memories and between two internal memories. Therefore, field-dependents appear to have a specific rather than a general memory deficit: they have difficulty maintaining the distinction between self and other as the origin of information.

Studies in the social domain have tested the hypothesis that field-dependent people are more responsive to the social stimuli provided by others in the environment than are field-independent people. Clearly such sensitivity could either be advantageous or disadvantageous, depending on the situation. When sitting an examination, sensitivity to the appearance of the other candidates would be distracting rather than helpful, whereas when conducting a job interview the behaviour and appearance of the candidate is of prime importance. Witkin and Goodenough (1977) reviewed a wide range of studies on field dependence and interpersonal relations, and concluded that field-dependent people make use of information provided by others in the environment only under certain conditions: when the situation is ambiguous and the source of information is regarded as helpful. Under the same conditions, field-independent people do not make use of the social information.

The attention to social stimuli characteristic of field dependence can be measured in terms of the amount of time spent looking at others. In a study by Ruble and Nakamura (1972), looking at the experimenter was compared in field-dependent and -independent children aged around 8 years. There were two tasks. In the first task, the child had to assemble a puzzle, and in one condition on the first trial the experimenter also assembled the puzzle in front of the child. Field-dependent children were found to look at the exper-imenter's face more than field-independent children. However, looking at the experimenter did not improve their perform-ance on the next trial. Presumably, watching how the experimenter solved the problem, rather than looking at her face, would have been helpful in this situation. In the second task the field-dependent children's tendency to look at the experimenter worked to their advantage. It was a concept formation task in which, on each trial, the child had to select the correct instance out of a choice of three. In one condition, the experimenter provided social cues as to which was the correct instance (she looked at it and leaned slightly towards it). Field-dependent children did better than field-independent children in this condition, where looking at the exper-imenter's face did provide relevant social cues.

From the extensive research into the characteristics of relatively field-dependent and -independent adults and children, separate portraits of the two extremes can be drawn. Field-independent people emerge as possessing the necessary qualities to be effective in the cognitive domain: they possess a clear view of the distinction between self and other, and an ability to analyse the environment into its components and make use of this information selectively. According to Witkin and Goodenough (1977), such individ-uals are not particularly popular and are described by others as ambitious, inconsiderate and opportunistic. They tend to be found in occupations such as engineering, architecture, experimental psychology and science teaching (Goodenough,

1978). In contrast, field-dependent people possess qualities resulting in superior effectiveness in interpersonal relations. They are sensitive to others in the environment and are regarded by others as popular, friendly, considerate and warm (Witkin and Goodenough, 1977). They tend to be found in occupations such as social work, clinical psychology and elementary school teaching (Goodenough, 1978).

Studies of FD-I demonstrate how the two extremes of the dimension are favoured differentially in different contexts within the same culture. It has also been observed that similar effects occur on a wider scale: it has been hypothesised that some cultures would favour field independence while others would favour field dependence. More specifically, it has been suggested that 'loose' societies of hunters and gatherers, where autonomous action is encouraged, would be more field-independent than 'tight' societies of farmers and herders which depend on a close-knit, highly ordered social structure (Witkin and Berry, 1975). Two contrasting societies were selected by Berry (1966) for study: the Eskimos of Baffin Island and the Temne of Sierra Leone. The Eskimos are hunters and live in family groups, they encourage independence in their children, and are relatively lax over discipline; this is a 'loose' society. The Temne are farmers, they place a strong emphasis on their rule-governed society and bring up their children strictly, encouraging them to be dependent; this is a 'tight' society. Using the RFT and the EFT, Berry (1966) found, as predicted, that the Eskimo people were more field-independent than the Temne.

Distinguishing between FD-I and intelligence

Some investigators, notably Vernon (1972), have claimed that FD-I is indistinguishable from intelligence. Since certain performance subtests of the Wechsler intelligence scales do correlate with FD-I, it can be argued that FD-I is not a dimension in its own right, but merely a spatial aspect of intelligence. Developmental studies have shown that between the ages of 8 and 17 years there is a steady increase in field independence as measured by the RFT (Witkin, Goodenough and Karp, 1967), and these changes are found cross-culturally. Such findings support the view that FD-I is indistinguishable from intelligence, since intelligence also increases with age.

However, work on sex differences in FD-I conflicts with the intelligence hypothesis. Women tend to perform less well than men on spatial tasks (Maccoby and Jacklin, 1974) and, since performance on spatial tasks is correlated with FD-I (Vernon, 1972), it is reasonable to expect sex differences in FD-I; and such differences have been found. On the EFT, females from 12 years upwards are more field-dependent than males (Maccoby and Jacklin, 1974), although interestingly there is some evidence that under 12 years girls are more field-independent than boys (Coates, 1972; Immergluck and Mearini, 1969). On the RFT, the majority of studies show females as more field-dependent than males. Since there is probably no sex difference in intelligence, the findings suggesting if anything a trend towards higher IQ in females (Jensen, 1971; Maccoby and Jacklin, 1974), the association between females and field dependence goes against the hypothesis that FD-I is merely measuring intelligence.

Why, then, does field independence increase with age, if it is not because of the increase in intelligence with age? Witkin considers FD-I to be one aspect of a more general concept of cognitive differentiation, and he considers that cognitive differentiation increases with age; as we mature, we become more able to differentiate between aspects of the environment, and hence more field-independent. Witkin's view is supported by the findings that although certain cultures have been found to be relatively field-dependent (e.g. the Temne), the age change towards greater field independence is found universally. It seems that maturation is accompanied by an increase in psychological differentiation (i.e. field independence), although some cultures foster more differentiation than others.

However, there is an alternative explanation of the apparently universal age trend towards greater differentiation and hence field independence. In intelligence tests, and in the RFT and RRT, the better and more sophisticated strategy is typically the field-independent strategy. It could be argued that, as children get older, what they learn is to adopt the better strategy, and hence they only appear to be growing more field-independent. If appropriate tests were to be devised where being field-*dependent* were the better strategy, then developmental changes towards increasing field dependence might also be observed. Such tests should not prove too difficult to construct since we already know of certain contexts (such as interpersonal relations) where the relatively field-dependent person performs better. In the cross-cultural work, FD-I was measured using tests where the better strategy is to be field-independent. Although age changes towards greater field independence were generally observed, some societies (e.g. the Temne) were found to be less field-independent than others (e.g. the Eskimos). It could be argued that the Temne have more experience with problems where the better strategy is to be field-dependent than is the case for the Eskimos or Western societies. Therefore the Temne are less knowledgeable about situations where the field-independent strategy is more successful, and so perform less well on tests requiring the field-independent strategy. Nevertheless they are not entirely ignorant of the field-independent strategy and their ability to apply it correctly does improve, as is indicated by the developmental change towards increased field independence, even though it is less marked than in other cultures.

If tests favouring the hypothesised developmental change towards increased field dependence were to be used in cultures such as the Temne, changes towards greater field dependence might be observed. Witkin has argued that development involves increasing psychological differentiation, which results in increasing field independence. The alternative argument is that development involves the acquisition of knowledge about good strategies, and these may be either field-independent or -dependent. The alternative interpretation does not succeed in making a clear distinction between FD-I and intelligence since the ability to acquire and apply knowledge about good strategies is presumably an aspect of what is meant by intelligence.

Summary

FD-I contrasts two approaches to the processing of information: field dependence, which emphasises the role of external cues and the non-selective intake of information, versus field independence, which emphasises the role of internal cues and a more discriminating processing of input. Although it is generally found that people become more field-independent as they mature, it is possible to distinguish between relatively field-dependent and field-independent individuals in both children and adults. Behavioural differences between such groups have been demonstrated for a wide variety of social and cognitive tasks. In the main, field-dependent people function more effectively in the former, whereas field-independent people are more successful in the latter. The main criticism of the concept of FD-I is that it is so similar to intelligence that there is nothing to be gained by studying it in addition to intelligence. To counter this criticism, there is evidence that there are groups that can be distinguished on the basis of FD-I but not in terms of intelligence (e.g. women are more field-dependent than men but no less intelligent). Such evidence indicates that FD-I is worthy of study in its own right as an aspect of personality. Indeed, FD-I has been one of the most extensively studied personality traits, and it has been implicated in a diversity of behaviours. The next section discusses another extensively studied trait: internal versus external locus of control.

Internal versus external locus of control (I-E)

Theoretical background

Consider the following situation: imagine you have been learning to drive and your driving test is due shortly. Would you approach the test with the attitude that passing or failing is primarily determined by how well you have prepared for the test? Or would you regard passing or failing as having very little to do with how much preparation you had put in and far more to do with factors beyond your control, such as how heavy the traffic is on that day, or whether the examiner is in a good mood?

If you regard your performance on a driving test as the result of your own effort, then you see the locus of control in the situation (control over whether you pass or fail) as being with you. If you regard passing or failing as being predominantly out of your hands, then you see the locus of control depending upon chance or fate (e.g. how heavy the traffic is) or upon powerful others beyond your influence (the driving examiner). The former point of view would be typical of someone with *internal* locus of control, the latter of someone with *external* locus of control.

The concept of I-E was first proposed by Rotter (1966), and it forms a relatively small part of a more extensive personality theory incorporating many of the principles established in the psychology of learning. This theory is known as *social learning theory* (Rotter, 1954; Rotter, Chance and Phares, 1972). Rotter proposed that the degree to which people believe their lives to be under their own control is an important dimension of individual variation. People who are relatively internal believe they are responsible for their destiny, whereas people who are relatively external believe that the good and bad things that happen to them are determined by luck, chance or powerful others. In Rotter's social learning theory I-E is regarded as a characteristic attitude towards the world, referred to as a *generalised expectancy*. The expectancy about the locus of control over rewards and punishment generated by a person's position on the I-E dimension will influence the way that person perceives most situations, and hence will partially determine how the person will behave.

Rotter regards generalised expectancies as only one of the factors which determine the way a person behaves in a particular situation. Since he is a social learning theorist, he believes that behaviour is a function of reinforcement, but generalised expectancies have important modifying effects on the expected relation between behaviour and reinforcement. First, people have to believe that they have the capability to perform the necessary behaviour to earn the reinforcement, and also to regard the reward as worth the effort, before they will act. Second, and even more important, they have to expect that when they behave appropriately they will actually receive the desired reward. Whether or not a behaviour occurs depends on these three conditions being met: a person must have the capacity to produce the behaviour, must regard the reward as desirable, and must expect that the reward will be received if the behaviour is produced.

Rotter and his colleagues investigated the role of expectancy in the laboratory (Phares, 1957; James and Rotter, 1958; Rotter, Liverant and Crowne, 1961), and their findings confirmed that subjects are influenced by reinforcement only to the extent that they perceive it as contingent on their own behaviour. Given the empirical evidence confirming the importance of expectancy, it seemed reasonable to hypothesise that individuals might differ in their generalised expectancy about the locus of control of reinforcement, and Rotter (1966) developed the first scale to measure the I-E dimension.

Measurement of I-E

Rotter's (1966) I-E scale consists of twenty-nine items each comprising a pair of statements lettered *a* and *b*. The respondent is asked to choose the statement from each pair which he or she believes more strongly. Twenty-three of the items measure I-E while the remaining six are fillers consisting of statements unrelated to locus of control. The filler items are included to make the dimension being measured by the test less obvious to the respondent. Two examples of the sort of items appearing in the test are:

> I more strongly believe that:
> 1*a* Whether I make a success of my life is entirely up
>   to me;
> 1*b* Success is a matter of being lucky enough to be in
>   the right place at the right time.
> 2*a* Pressure groups can influence government decisions;
> 2*b* The government is beyond the influence of the ordinary
>   person.

These items do not appear in the actual test and were composed for illustrative purposes only. 1*a* and 2*a* are intended as examples of typical internal statements; 1*b* and 2*b* are intended as examples of typical external statements.

Producing a questionnaire is not simply a matter of sitting down and writing out a series of items that appear to relate to the dimension the investigator is studying. (However, see Burisch, 1984, for an alternative point of view.) Test construction is a technical subject described in detail in more specialised texts (e.g. Anastasi, 1982). To give an introduction to the process of constructing a personality questionnaire, the steps involved in the development of Rotter's I-E scale will be described.

The first stage in questionnaire construction is to write a pool of items that by guesswork and from previous research would seem likely to measure the dimension. The next stage is to give these items to a representative sample of people for whom the test is intended and to carry out a detailed analysis of their responses. First, each item has to be checked to see by what percentage of the sample it was endorsed. Items with which everyone agrees, and those with which everyone disagrees, are useless, since they do not distinguish between respondents (which, after all, is the aim of the questionnaire). In developing the I-E scale, Rotter discarded every item with which more than 85 per cent or less than 15 per cent of the sample agreed.

The next stage in developing a questionnaire is to make sure that the test is internally consistent. The internal consistency of a scale refers to the extent to which *each* individual item is measuring the same dimension as is measured by the scale as a whole. At this stage, the investigator is concerned with constructing a test that measures reliably, and internal consistency is one requirement for a reliable test. Internal consistency may be measured in a number of ways, but the general principle is that the responses to individual items should correlate reasonably highly with the total scale score. Although internal consistency should be high, it is unlikely that measures of internal consistency will yield correlations of 1.0. A scale consisting of the same item repeated twenty times would produce perfect internal consistency (unless the respondents were playing games – which well they might given such a dull scale); but personality dimensions are expressed in a variety of behaviours so scales usually have a corresponding variety of items. Hence internal consistency does not have to be extremely high for the scale to be acceptably reliable. Rotter (1966) cites reliability coefficients ranging from .65 to .79 for the I-E scale, which is acceptable for a scale purporting to measure a dimension entering into a wide range of behaviour.

Having produced an internally consistent set of items, the scale constructor's worries are far from over. The next task is to check for the influence of response biases (Berg, 1967). There are two of particular importance: *acquiescence response set* and *social desirability*.

Acquiescence response set refers to the tendency of respondents to agree with a relatively large proportion of the items ('Yeasayers') or to reject a relatively large proportion ('Naysayers') (Couch and Keniston, 1960). It can be overcome by writing items which require a 'yes' or 'no' answer in such a way that the maximum total scale score on the whole scale consists of 'yes' responses to half the items (positively keyed items) and 'no' responses to the other half (negatively keyed items). The intention is that respondents will be forced to consider each item carefully: to some respond 'yes' and to others respond 'no'. Yeasayers and naysayers who did not pay attention to the wording of the items would be recognised because they would have total scale scores of zero, as a result of the positively and negatively keyed items cancelling each other out. Since Rotter's I-E scale is composed of items in which a forced choice between alternative statements is required, it avoids the acquiescence problem. However, a similar response set could occur if respondents adopted a strategy of always endorsing either the *a* or the *b* statement. As a control for this, the response corresponding to external locus of control is the endorsement of the *a* part of the item for exactly half of the items.

Social desirability response bias refers to the tendency to agree with items referring to positively evaluated behaviour or beliefs and to reject those which are negatively evaluated, regardless of whether the respondents really are the paragons of virtue they make themselves out to be (Edwards, 1957). The tendency to make socially desirable responses is so pervasive that psychologists have studied it as a personality dimension in its own right (Millham and Jacobson, 1978). Some individuals are particularly prone to this bias, whereas others are comparatively immune. There are several questionnaires for measuring this, one of the most popular being the Marlowe-Crowne Social Desirability Scale (Crowne and Marlowe, 1960). Using such a scale it is possible to measure the extent to which a person tends to make the socially desirable response when answering questionnaires. By giving subjects both the personality scale under construction *and* the Marlowe-Crowne scale, and then correlating scores on each of the items of the personality scale with the total scores on the social desirability scale, it is possible to determine the extent to which responses on the personality scale are being influenced by social desirability. Rotter (1966) selectively rejected individual items with high social desirability correlations. However, the scale as a whole has been criticised on the ground that there is a substantial correlation with social desirability: the internal response is recognised as the desirable one (Nowicki and Duke, 1974). In the driving test example given at the beginning of this section, the internal response (the belief that passing is dependent on the testee's own efforts through adequate preparation) certainly has a socially desirable ring to it.

Rotter (1975) has countered this criticism with the point that social desirability is not a property inherent in a questionnaire, but is rather the product of the total testing situation. It is possible to devise test situations in which the socially desirable response on the I-E scale would be to endorse the external items: for example, if it was the selection test for entry into the higher echelons of an occult society. In more down-to-earth circumstances, there are ways of reducing the likelihood of contamination from social desirability by adjusting aspects of the test situation (such as not requiring subjects to give their names). However, this may encourage the respondents to contaminate their responses in other ways; for example, subjects are more likely to submit spoiled response sheets under conditions of anonymity. The best the test constructor can do is to ensure that each item has a reasonably low correlation with social desirability and pass the problem on to the tester, who must use ingenuity to make the test situation evaluatively neutral.

Having constructed a scale which was internally consistent and relatively free from response bias, Rotter then had to demonstrate a further aspect of its reliability: test-retest reliability. If a person completes the same test on two separate occasions, the two sets of responses should be highly correlated. Correlations for I-E scores obtained from the same subjects on two different occasions range from as high as .84 to as low as .26 (Phares, 1978). Low test-retest reliability can be explained as being the result of experiences of relevance to I-E during the test-retest interval. However, there is a limit to which a score on a dimension can vary from one occasion to another beyond which it becomes meaningless to regard the dimension as a more or less stable aspect of personality. Therefore, consistently low test-retest correlations are a cause for concern. Fortunately, with correlations as high as .83, the I-E scale is acceptably reliable.

Having established that a test is a reliable measure, it is next necessary to demonstrate that it is valid. Test validity refers to the degree to which the test actually measures what it claims it measures. It is determined in studies which seek behavioural differences between groups selected on the basis of their test scores. Unlike intelligence, with its objective age-related criterion, the I-E scale has to demonstrate that it measures what it claims to measure by showing that predicted behavioural differences between internals and externals do in fact occur. We shall be considering a limited selection of the hundreds of studies which have a bearing on the I-E scale's validity in the next section.

The investigation of I-E

Research into locus of control can be divided into three categories: the study of different components of I-E, the characteristics of relatively internal and relatively external people, and investigations of the interplay between I-E and other determinants of behaviour. Much of this research involves making comparisons between subjects identified by measures of I-E as tending to believe that the locus of control is internal and those tending to believe that the locus of control is external. As a shorthand these two groups will be referred to as 'internals' and 'externals', but it should be remembered that I-E is a continuum and there are no internal or external *types*, but rather only degrees of internality and externality.

Rotter's original scale was designed to measure a generalised expectancy relevant to a wide variety of situations. However, the breadth of the original I-E construct suggests that it may be subdivided to reveal components of I-E interesting in their own right. There are two ways in which narrower distinctions subsumed by the broad locus of control dimension may be made. The first is situational: a measure of I-E may be developed to assess locus of control beliefs pertaining to a specific subset of situations. For example, the Health Locus of Control Scale was developed to measure I-E beliefs with respect to health-related behaviour (Wallston, Wallston and DeVallis, 1978), but it has not always been successful at predicting health-relevant activities (e.g. Schifter and Ajzen, 1985). There is also a measure of locus of control for affiliation and behaviour in social interactions (Lefcourt, von Baeyer, Ware and Cox, 1979). Internal affiliation beliefs are associated with active listening and socially skilled behaviour in social interaction (Lefcourt, Martin, Fick and Saleh, 1985).

The second way of subdividing I-E involves the fractionating of the construct itself into different components. One such multidimensional measure of I-E assesses two components of external beliefs – control by powerful others and control by chance – in addition to measuring internal beliefs (Levenson, 1974). This measure revealed a strong relationship between believing in control by chance and experiencing bouts of depression in a six-month follow-up study of college students (Burger 1985). Another subdivision of I-E measures the extent to which people believe in internal locus of control for successful outcomes and external locus of control for failures. The significance of this distinction has been investigated in children using the Intellectual Achievement Responsibility Questionnaire (Crandall, Katkovsky and Crandall, 1965) which contains two subscales, one measuring the strength of belief that success is contingent on one's own efforts, the other that failure is due to one's lack of effort.

Morris and Messer (1978) used these scales in their study of children's academic task persistence. Highly internal and highly external children were allocated in a two-by-two design to either a self-reward or an external-reward condition on a teaching machine task. Under conditions of self-reward the children decided how many points to give themselves for a right answer whereas in the external-reward condition the children were allotted points by the experimenter. Morris and Messer predicted that under conditions of self-reward the internals would work harder, whereas under conditions of external-reward the externals would work harder. However, the predicted interaction between locus of control and type of reinforcement did not occur. The subjects were then reclassified so that the internal group consisted only of those children who scored highly on both internal subscales (they believed they controlled the positive as well as the negative events in their lives), and the external children had low scores on both scales. When the data were analysed with the subjects classified in this way, the predicted interaction was obtained. When the distinction between the subscales was ignored in the original analysis no significant results were obtained, because the high scores would have included some subjects with internal beliefs with respect to either success or failure, but not both.

The characteristics of internal and external people have been explored in a large number of studies (for reviews, see Lefcourt, 1982; Phares, 1976, 1978; and Strickland, 1977). Investigations reported by Phares (1978) into the relationship between I-E and demographic variables suggest that there are no sex differences in I-E, that whites tend to be more internal than blacks, and that middle-class subjects tend to be more internal than working-class subjects. Phares also reports that there is no substantial relationship between intelligence and I-E.

From the research summarised by Phares (1978) relating I-E to a wide variety of behaviours, a distinct picture of the internal as compared with the external person emerges. The internal person is more likely to be receptive to aspects of health care such as weight watching, giving up smoking, taking exercise and carrying out prophylactic measures such as going to the dentist regularly. In part, this behaviour is a result of the internals' superior knowledge about such things, since internals are characterised by their efforts to seek out information which enables them to exert greater control over their environment. Their desire for self-determination is reflected in their greater resistance to social influence and attempted attitude change. In the area of mental health, internals are generally found to be better adjusted and less anxious than externals, and external beliefs are symptomatic of a number of psychiatric disorders such as depression and schizophrenia. In short, the internal individual, in contrast to the external, is independent, achieving and masterful.

The internal person conforms to the American ideal (Sampson, 1977). Sampson describes the prevailing cultural ethos in the USA as one of 'self-contained individualism', by which he means that people are encouraged to be independent as opposed to interdependent, and to focus on self-enhancement and self-sufficiency instead of surrendering individuality in the pursuit of the wider goals of the community.

Sampson draws attention to the danger of mistaking products of the prevailing cultural ethos for fundamental principles. For example, the concept of psychological androgyny (S.L. Bem, 1974, 1981) is currently a popular research topic. Androgynous people are those who attribute to themselves both stereotypically feminine and masculine characteristics, behaviours and beliefs. In a culture such as ours, where self-contained individualism is highly valued, psychological androgyny is desirable since it avoids dependence on members of the opposite sex. However, in cultures where interdependence is valued, androgyny may not be regarded as an important psychological concept.

The same argument applies to locus of control. Internal locus of control is necessary for successful self-contained individualism and hence, in our culture, locus of control is regarded as being an important psychological concept. However, it may be quite irrelevant in other societies. Of course, the possibility that a phenomenon is culture-specific does not automatically render it unworthy of study; but investigators need to be cautious in the claims they may make about the significance and generalisability of their findings. In this regard, a recent longitudinal study of locus of control has demonstrated the susceptibility of the I-E dimension to cultural factors (Doherty and Baldwin, 1985). The study reveals a substantial increase in externality (of more than one standard deviation) in women over the period from the late 1960s to the late 1970s, whereas men's externality remained stable. Doherty and Baldwin (1985) speculate that this sex difference may be explained by the rise of feminism during this period and the increasing awareness among women of their lack of control over their lives.

It is a disappointing feature of studies of the characteristics of internal and external people that they are so mundane from a theoretical point of view. Elaborating the network of correlations between personality dimensions and a range of behaviours smacks of butterfly collecting. More interesting are those studies which have sought to investigate the role of I-E within the context of Rotter's formulation for the prediction of social behaviour.

In just such an investigation, Karabenick and Srull (1978) studied the relations between I-E, situational variables, and cheating, with college student subjects. They were interested in the effects of expectancy on reinforcement value. The experimental task consisted of solving a series of line puzzles. The subject was required to trace a line figure onto a blank piece of paper without lifting the pencil from the paper or retracing over any of the lines. There were twelve such figures, only two of which were possible to trace in accordance with the rules, the remainder being unsolvable. The subjects were not informed that only two of the puzzles could be solved. They were told to mark their successful attempts with an X, the number of unsolvable figures marked in this fashion therefore providing an index of cheating. The subjects were allowed as many tries at each figure as they liked.

The subjects were preselected on the basis of their I-E scores in such a way that half the group were highly internal and half were highly external. Some of the subjects were told that the task was a measure of intelligence and involved skill, and some were told that performance on the task was entirely unrelated to ability. Cheating was measured by totalling the number of unsolvable figures marked with an X. The experiment manipulated locus of control of the subjects' beliefs and also the locus of control in the situation; this permitted a comparison of the effects of congruence versus incongruence between these two variables. Congruent conditions were those in which externals were told that the task was one of chance and internals were told that it was one of skill; incongruent conditions were the reverse. The dependent variable was frequency of cheating, which provided an index of the reinforcement value of success.

The analysis of cheating frequency showed a marked congruence effect. Internals cheated more under skill conditions and externals cheated more under chance conditions (see Table 2.1).

Table 2.1 Mean frequency of cheating (out of a maximum of 12) for the two locus of control groups under the two task conditions (Karabenick and Srull, 1978)

Group	Task condition	
	Skill	Chance
Internal	1.3	0.4
External	0.3	1.6

Reinforcement value (indexed by cheating) was a function of I-E and task conditions, with congruence between I-E and task conditions resulting in higher reinforcement value. Karabenick and Scrull offered the following interpretation of the congruence effect: internals cheat to conform to their status on the internal dimension of ability, whereas externals cheat to maintain their belief in their status as fortunate individuals.

At the beginning of this chapter, in discussing the applications to personality of techniques developed for measuring intelligence, two problems were raised: the question of an appropriate criterion against which to validate a personality measure and the problem of how best to conceptualise the trait (i.e. how many components are involved). For the broad dimension of I-E there can no longer be any doubt about its validity in light of the sheer bulk of favourable studies in which predicted differences between internal and external people have been found. Research into I-E can now afford to branch out beyond the validation stage and to investigate how I-E, in the context of social learning theory, can help in the understanding and prediction of behaviour.

The issue of the components of I-E still remains. Should subscales be developed to measure different facets of the dimension? The issue here is a familiar one in personality measurement: if a scale measures a broad dimension applicable to a wide variety of situations, its powers of prediction are less than if its relevance is narrowed down to a more limited range. However, the narrowly applicable scale will only be predictive within a restricted set of situations, and therefore will lack wider utility (Cronbach and Gleser, 1957).

Rotter argued that I-E is a generalised expectancy that remains invariant across situations. The development of subscales detracts from its generalisability, although they may enhance prediction in specific situations. The more general-isable I-E scale and the more context-specific subscales each have their own part to play in different types of research.

Conclusions

To conclude this chapter on single-trait theories, some of the advantages and disadvantages of this approach to personality will be considered. Given the complexity of personality, it is a sensible strategy to restrict research to one aspect at a time, as the single-trait approach is doing. However, such a piecemeal approach is inevitably unsatisfactory, since no single-trait theory can provide a complete explanation of behaviour. Despite the vast amount of data each theory has generated, no single-trait theory can be said to have had anywhere near the impact on psychology that, say, Freud's much more general personality theory can claim.

Why are single-trait theories flourishing? One explanation lies not in the intrinsic merits of the dimensions themselves, but in the change in emphasis of current personality research. As we shall see in chapter 4, there is a growing interest in investigating the joint effects of personality and situational variables in efforts to understand and predict behaviour. Single-trait theories provide measures of discrete aspects of personality which can be varied relatively easily, whereas the more general multi-trait approaches to personality, to be considered in the next chapter, make the manipulation of personality variables much more difficult.

3 Multi-trait theories

Introduction

Multi-trait theories are designed to describe the entire personality. Their purpose is to locate the constellation of traits that make up the structure of personality and to devise appropriate measures of each of these traits. This approach assumes that we all share the same personality structure, although people differ from each other because we are each characterised by our own particular combination of trait scores. Hence the multi-trait approach captures both the underlying similarity between human beings and the surface differences; or, to use Allport's terminology, it is able to make both nomothetic and idiographic statements about personality (Allport, 1937). It is surprising that, although the subject matter of the various multi-trait theorists has been the same (they have all been studying personality), they have nevertheless produced different models of personality structure. These differences, and the possible reasons for them, will be one of the main discussion points of this chapter.

The discussion will be restricted to the two best-known multi-trait theories: Eysenck's and Cattell's. Although there are several other multi-trait theories (e.g. Guilford and Zimmerman, 1956; Comrey, 1970), the personality tests devised by Eysenck and Cattell are widely used today, and it is helpful to understand something of the theories behind them. Also, Eysenck's and Cattell's approaches to the study of personality differ from each other in a number of interesting ways. The most obvious difference is that Eysenck regards three traits as adequate for describing the structure of personality whereas Cattell insists on at least sixteen.

The multi-trait approach, in contrast to single-trait approaches, has a characteristic methodology which remains fundamentally the same from theorist to theorist. Multi-trait theories are all attempts to represent the whole personality, they all originate from similar databases, and they all use the same method of statistical analysis.

The database of multi-trait theories

Personality is inferred from behaviour, and multi-trait theorists have developed three techniques of data collection, each of which measures a different form of behaviour: questionnaires, ratings and objective tests.

Probably the best known technique is the questionnaire. The rationale behind the use of questionnaires is that the best way to find out about an individual's personality is to ask that person. Respondents are required to answer questions about their behaviours, feelings, thoughts and opinions. These responses provide the investigator with a limited sample of people's behaviour, namely their self-observations. These data are prey to distortions resulting from the respondent's inaccurate self-observations, which may be deliberate, or may be due to genuine ignorance or misunderstanding of the meaning of the items or to people's misperceptions of themselves. We have already seen how a great deal of care is taken in the construction of reliable questionnaires to attempt to overcome these problems. Nevertheless, the basic limitation of the questionnaire is unavoidable: it only measures the respondents' views of themselves.

The second technique for collecting personality data is by observers' ratings of other people's behaviour. A group of observers is given a list of items describing various behaviours such as 'keeps their room neat and tidy' or 'takes the lead in group discussion', and they rate their allotted ratees on these items. Ratings avoid the problem of self-distortion encountered in questionnaire data, but have their own inherent sources of bias and error. Raters are not mechanical recording devices, but human beings and therefore subject to distortions and inaccuracies. The main problem with ratings is that the items are difficult to frame in an unambiguous way. For example, different raters will have different personal standards of neatness and tidiness and whereas one rater might consider the ratee's room obsessionally immaculate, another might consider it only moderately tidy. What exactly is meant by 'takes the lead in discussion'? Would a ratee who did most of the talking count as taking the lead, or one who made occasional but effective comments which redirected the conversation? Raters may only see one side of the ratees' personality. For example, the ratees may be scrupulously tidy at home (perhaps because they know they are being rated), while their desk at work is a disaster area; they may be vociferous in group discussions but, when left alone with someone of the opposite sex, be reduced to speechlessness. Would it be correct to rate such people as 'tidy' and 'dominant'? Designers of rating scales are aware of these problems and are often as skilful as questionnaire constructors in their efforts to overcome them. Nevertheless, the problems of the idiosyncrasies of raters and their limited exposure to ratees are ultimately unavoidable.

Aware of the inherent inaccuracies in questionnaire and rating data, some investigators (notably Cattell) have turned their attention to the third technique of data collection: the use of objective tests. These are samples of behaviour obtained under laboratory conditions which make it impossible for the subjects to know exactly what is being assessed and thus to have any distorting influence on their responses. The behaviours measured in this way may be physiological. For example, Eysenck has developed a lemon-drop test which discriminates between introverts and extraverts in terms of the amount of saliva they produce when lemon juice is placed in their mouths: introverts generally produce more saliva than extraverts (S.B.G. Eysenck and H.J. Eysenck, 1967). Other objective tests measure cognitive behaviours (such as solving puzzles or making up captions for cartoons) and visual motor co-ordination (such as the pursuit rotor test). Although objective tests overcome the problems of distortion encountered in the other two types of personality data, they confront the investigator with a new set of problems. In practical terms, they may be inconvenient to transport and administer, requiring elaborate apparatus; but more important, it may be difficult to demonstrate precisely what aspect of personality they are measuring. However, irrespective of the techniques used to collect personality data, the next step is to try to make sense of the material. The most commonly used method for doing this is a statistical technique known as factor analysis.

Factor analysis

Factor analysis can be applied in the same way to any of the three forms of personality data. It will be discussed here as it is applied to rating data.

Let us imagine that an investigator was interested in personality in the classroom, and collected ratings on twenty items of behaviour (A-T) on fifty ratees. The ratees were schoolchildren and the items were classroom behaviours such as asking questions (item A), volunteering for jobs (item B), whispering to friends (item C), getting on with studying (item D), and so on down to item T. The observers' ratings of these behaviours form the raw data, which can be set out in a table in which the twenty columns are the rated behaviours and the fifty rows are the ratees (see Figure 3.1a). The numbers in the body of the table would be the average of the ratings given to each child by the observers on each of the twenty items.

The first step in factor analysis is to produce a correlation matrix. This is done by correlating each item with every other. A correlation measures the degree to which items covary: thus there will be a large positive correlation between items A and C if the children who were rated highly on A were also rated highly on C, and the children who had low ratings on A also had low ratings on C. For example, the children who asked lots of questions (A) were probably the ones who whispered to their friends (C), whereas the ones who got on with studying (D) neither asked questions nor whispered. So there will be a high correlation between A and C, but not between A and D nor between C and D.

The correlations are arranged in a matrix in which both the columns and the rows are the item names and the body of the matrix contains the correlation coefficients, which can vary between +1.0 through 0 to −1.0 (see Figure 3.1b). The correlation matrix is the clay from which the mathematical procedures of factor analysis will mould a representation of personality.

(a) Raw data

Ratees	*Items* A B C D . . . T
1	
2	
3	
4	
.	
.	
.	
50	

(b) The correlation matrix

Items	*Items* A B C D . . . T
A	
B	
C	
D	
.	
.	
.	
T	

(c) Results of factor analysis showing positive high loading items

Factor I	Factor II
A	B
C	D
E	F

(d) Results of factor analysis showing positive and negative high loading items

Factor I	Factor II
A+	B+
C+	D+
E+	F+
G−	H−
I−	J−
K−	L−

FIGURE 3.1 *The stages involved in factor analysing rating data*

Factor analysis is a mathematical technique for extracting the underlying dimensions ('factors') of the correlation matrix, but it is not necessary to understand mathematics in order to appreciate, in general terms, what factor analysis does with the correlation matrix. (For a simple explanation of the mathematical technique involved see D. Child, 1970.) The procedure discovers how best to reduce the large number of correlations (in our example it would be 190) to a much smaller number of factors by picking out the clusters of items which, as indicated by the correlations, are closely related and therefore measuring the same underlying characteristic. These clusters are composed of items which are intercorrelated. For example, items A, C, E and G in our example might be intercorrelated in the sense that each correlates strongly with every other: A correlates with C, and C with E, and E with G, and A with E, etc. Given this pattern of intercorrelations between items A, C, E and G, it can be inferred that these four items are measuring basically the same thing (the same 'factor') and hence the four different measures have been reduced to a single underlying dimension.

When the calculations are complete, the results consist of a number of basic factors which represent the clusters of similar items. Let us assume there are only two factors in our example (see Figure 3.1c). In addition to determining the number of factors, the analysis also calculates the degree to which the items are related to the factors. Every item's relationship to each factor is calculated in the form of a correlation known technically as a 'factor loading'.

The identification and naming of factors is based on inspection of the factor loadings and figuring out what the high loading items have in common. In our example, Factor I has high loadings from items A (asking questions), C (whispering to friends) and E (participating in group games). These items all appear to be measuring an outgoing approach to the child's relationships with his or her peers, so we could identify this factor as 'sociability'. The high loading items on Factor II are B (volunteering for jobs), D (getting on with studying) and F (tidy desk) so this factor could be identified as 'conscientiousness'.

Since factor loadings consist of correlations, they can be positive or negative. A high negative factor loading is just as informative as a high positive factor loading. In our example, the items strongly related to the factors were assumed to have high positive loadings. However, what if some of the items had high negative loadings? Let us assume that three further items have high negative loadings on Factor I: these are G (plays on own during break), I (blushes and stammers when answering the teacher's questions) and K (participates in individual as opposed to team sports). Such a pattern came about because all those children with high ratings on A, C and E had low ratings on G, I and K, and vice versa. In this case, Factor I would be identified as a bipolar factor and named 'sociable-withdrawn' (see Figure 3.1d). Similarly, Factor II would be identified as a bipolar factor and named 'conscientious-slapdash' if there were items with high negative loadings such as H (spills ink), J (loses pens and pencils) and L (late returning library books). The investigator would conclude from this hypothetical example that the broad spectrum of classroom behaviour is characterised by two underlying dimensions: 'sociability' and 'conscientiousness'.

Whereas the basic techniques of factor analysis remain constant, there are certain variations favoured by some users but not others, and these are often the cause of dispute. As we shall see in the following sections, the different variations favoured by Eysenck and Cattell have resulted in two rather different representations of personality.

H.J. Eysenck's personality theory

Eysenck's application of factor analysis to personality data has led him to propose that personality is adequately described by three factors: extraversion–introversion, neuroticism–stability and psychoticism–normality. He arrived at this tripartite view of the structure of personality as a result of a series of factor analytic studies in which he tested hypotheses about the nature of personality.

The structure and measurement of personality
On the basis of extensive psychological and philosophical

reading, Eysenck observed that similar descriptions of particular human personality types kept occurring (H.J. Eysenck, 1953). From the days of Greek philosophy to twentieth-century psychiatry, there has been a tendency to categorise people. The Greeks used four categories: melancholic, choleric, sanguine and phlegmatic. These were 'types' in the sense that people were pigeonholed into one of them; a person could not be described as having a bit of each.

Another way to conceptualise the differences between people is in terms of dimensions. The concept of dimension differs from the concept of type in that people can be located at any point along a dimension, whereas whether one belongs to a certain type is an all-or-none matter. Eysenck was influenced by Kretschmer's theory of the psychoses (Kretschmer, 1948) in which it is proposed that normal and abnormal people can be arranged along a dimension or continuum of psychosis ranging from schizophrenia at one extreme to manic depression at the other. Schizophrenics and manic depressives would be placed at these extremes and normal people would be placed at the mid-point of the dimension.

Eysenck was also influenced by Jung's theory of personality (Jung, 1923). Jung proposed that people tend either towards extraversion, directing their energies outwards, or to introversion, directing their energies towards their inner mental state. Jung applied this conceptualisation to neurotic disorders and proposed that neurotics liable to hysterical symptoms were extraverted, whereas neurotics liable to anxiety were introverted.

Eysenck's theory of the structure of personality manages to encompass all these views (see Figure 3.2). He favours a dimensional as opposed to a typological approach. Initially (Eysenck, 1953), he hypothesised that two dimensions only would suffice to describe the variation in human personality: introversion–extraversion and neuroticism–stability. More recently (H.J. Eysenck and S.B.G. Eysenck, 1976) he has proposed the addition of a third dimension, psychoticism.

The two dimensions, introversion–extraversion and neuroticism–stability, yield four quadrants which correspond to the four Greek types. Kretschmer's dimension was regarded by Eysenck as corresponding to the introversion–extraversion dimension. Jung's two varieties of neurosis, anxiety and hysteria, correspond to neurotic introversion and neurotic extraversion or the Greek types of melancholic and choleric.

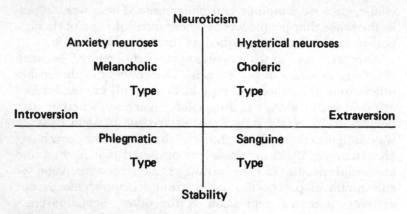

FIGURE 3.2 *Hypothesised human personality dimensions encompassing earlier conceptualisations*

In his early studies, Eysenck set out to test this hypothetical two-dimensional structure using rating data obtained from an abnormal population. Eysenck (1944) tested the hypothesis that neurotic patients could be conceptualised in terms of these two dimensions such that hysterical patients would be highly extravert and neurotic, whereas anxious patients would be highly introvert and neurotic. In a military hospital, he collected psychiatrists' ratings on thirty-nine rating scales (covering present behaviour and past life history) of 700 patients suffering from various forms and degrees of neurotic disorders. Some examples of the scales are: 'dependent', 'sex anomalies', 'headaches', 'degraded work history' and 'narrow interests'. The scales were intercorrelated and factor analysed.

The factor analysis resulted in two main factors with high loadings from two different subsets of the thirty-nine scales. Eysenck's hunch that two dimensions would be adequate to describe the data was confirmed, and consideration of the scales most strongly associated with each of the factors led to the identification of one factor as neuroticism–stability and the other as introversion–extraversion. All the high loadings on the neuroticism factor were positive, and included scales such as 'badly organised personality', 'dependent' and 'little energy'. Introversion–extraversion proved to be a bipolar factor, with high positive loadings from scales such as 'anxiety', 'depression', 'obsessional tendencies', 'sex anomalies', 'narrow interests' and 'degraded work history'.

From these results Eysenck concluded that two factors alone were sufficient to give an adequate description of personality. The neuroticism–stability factor accounted for items referring to severity of the disorder while the introversion–extraversion factor accounted for items which distinguished between the two major forms of neurosis, anxiety and hysteria.

The next step was to attempt to find independent criteria to support the claims about the identity of each of the two personality factors (Eysenck, 1947). We have already discussed the problem that the natural criterion of age changes used in the validation of intelligence tests is not available in personality. The other criterion for intelligence was teachers' expert opinion, and Eysenck made use of this type of criterion in his personality study.

Eysenck obtained expert psychiatric opinion as to what type of neurosis each of his subjects was suffering from, and validated his dimensions against these opinions. By locating the high loading scales on each factor and working back to each subject's score on these scales, he could classify them according to his dimensions as neurotic introverts or neurotic extraverts. Eysenck predicted that neurotic introverts would include subjects diagnosed as anxious, obsessional or depressed, whereas neurotic extraverts would include subjects diagnosed as hysterical or psychopathic. This is what he found. The technique of comparing the results of factor analysis with an independent classification is known as criterion analysis. Since the dimensions agreed with the criterion, Eysenck could be confident that they were a meaningful way of classifying people. Further studies, involving literally thousands of normal and abnormal people, have subsequently shown that these two factors emerge repeatedly when different samples are tested, they are normally distributed throughout the population, and there are important behavioural differences between introverts and extraverts and neurotic and stable individuals selected on the basis of these dimensions (H.J. Eysenck and M.W. Eysenck, 1985).

The typical high scorer on extraversion is a sociable person who thrives on human company and seeks out exciting activities. He or she is restless, impulsive and optimistic. In contrast, the low-scoring introverted person prefers the company of books to people and is orderly, restrained and serious. The high scorer on neuroticism is characterised by a variety of somatic and interpersonal difficulties reflecting tension and anxiety, whereas the low scorer, the normal person, does not have these difficulties.

Eysenck's initial studies used rating data; later he and his colleagues investigated the factor structure of questionnaire data, and devised a series of questionnaires to measure extraversion–introversion and neuroticism. The current version is the Eysenck Personality Inventory (EPI) (H.J. Eysenck and S.B.G. Eysenck, 1964).

Recently, Eysenck has expanded his conceptualisation of personality structure to include a third factor, psychoticism (H.J. Eysenck and S.B.G. Eysenck, 1968; S.B.G. Eysenck and H.J. Eysenck, 1968; H.J. Eysenck and S.B.G. Eysenck, 1976). Psychoticism is claimed to measure an aspect of personality not subsumed by the extraversion and neuroticism dimensions, and may be summarised as the individual's predisposition to psychotic breakdown. There is now a questionnaire, the Eysenck Personality Questionnaire (EPQ), to measure all three personality factors – extraversion, neuroticism and psychoticism (H.J. Eysenck and S.B.G. Eysenck, 1975).

Some of the items measuring psychoticism are 'Do you enjoy hurting people you love?', 'Do you worry a lot about catching diseases?' and 'Would it upset you a lot to see a child or animal suffer?' (S.B.G. Eysenck and H.J. Eysenck, 1968). High scorers on this dimension have not necessarily experienced a psychotic breakdown. Eysenck considers both neurotic and psychotic disorders to be the result of predisposing personality characteristics and precipitating environmental events. However, studies of criterion groups indicate that criminals and schizophrenics have high psychoticism scores. Although there is some evidence of a low positive correlation between neuroticism and psychoticism (S.B.G. Eysenck and H.J. Eysenck, 1968), the three factors are relatively independent, and therefore it is possible for a given individual to have any combination of high or low scores on the three factors.

The hierarchical nature of personality

According to Eysenck, the structure of personality may be described with only three factors. But how can three scores adequately summarise all the complexities that go into making up a person's individuality? Eysenck's chief critic, Cattell, argues that this conceptualisation is far from adequate. Adopting a non-critical frame of mind for the moment, let us consider Eysenck's theoretical account of how human personality reduces to just three factors (Eysenck,

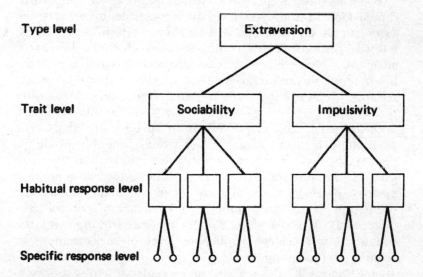

FIGURE 3.3 *Eysenck's hierarchical model of personality (adapted from Eysenck, 1947)*

1947). This is achieved by adopting a hierarchical model (see Figure 3.3).

At the lowest level are specific responses. These refer to particular pieces of behaviour such as talking to the person in front of you in the bus queue or reading a book on the train. At the next level are habitual responses. These are composed of clusters of specific responses. The third level consists of traits. These are characteristics inferred from observable behaviour. Any number of different habitual responses may all be explained by a single underlying trait. For example, in Figure 3.3, 'sociability' subsumes 'being friendly to strangers', 'going to parties' and 'participating in team games'. Above the trait level, at the top of the hierarchy, comes the type level. Types consist of clusters of related traits. Thus extraversion has several subcomponents, sociability and impulsivity being the two major ones (S.B.G. Eysenck and H.J. Eysenck, 1963). Although Eysenck refers to the top of the hierarchy as the 'type' level, extraversion, neuroticism and psychoticism are dimensions, not types, and hence everyone possesses all three to varying degrees.

By knowing a person's score on one of the three dimensions at the type level it is possible to predict the extent to which he or she will be characterised by the traits, habitual responses and specific responses which the dimension subsumes. However, predictions become less reliable at the lower levels of the hierarchy (e.g. specific responses are less reliably predicted than are habitual responses). Measuring the subcomponents of extraversion will result in more accurate prediction of behaviour in specific situations. For example, a measure of sociability would probably predict a person's behaviour at a party more accurately than the more general measure of extraversion. The issue of generality versus specificity has already been encountered in the discussion of the subcomponents of locus of control (see chapter 2). Eysenck, like Rotter, prefers working with the broader, more widely applicable level of measurement to relying on subcomponents.

The hierarchical model corresponds to the processes involved in factor analysis. Questionnaires and ratings consist of items drawn from habitual and specific response levels. When these items are intercorrelated and factor analysed they yield factors corresponding to the trait and type levels. The factors that emerge from analysing the intercorrelations between items are called first-order factors. These may then be intercorrelated and factor analysed to form second-order factors. It is tempting, but wrong, to equate the trait level with first-order factors and the type level with second-order factors. In Eysenck's analyses, extraversion, neuroticism and psychoticism all emerge from the factor analysis of *items*, and therefore are first-order factors. As we shall see later on, Cattell has argued that the way Eysenck uses factor analysis has led him mistakenly to regard these three dimensions as first-order factors when actually they are second-order factors.

The physiological basis of personality

So far we have seen how Eysenck's conceptualisation of personality consists of underlying dimensions inferred from observations of behaviour (rating data) or self-report (questionnaires). As such, these dimensions have the status of hypothetical constructs. That is, the dimensions are not directly observable but are implied by the data and have been validated by criterion analysis and proved to be useful in explaining and predicting behaviour. However, Eysenck has developed a theory of the physiological basis of personality which gives the dimensions a physical reality (H.J. Eysenck, 1967). He has proposed that the extraversion –introversion dimension is related to the activity of a particular part of the brain, the ascending reticular activating system (ARAS). The level of activity in the ARAS determines the arousal level in the higher brain centres, which in turn influences the amount of cortical control exerted over the lower brain centres. The extravert is one whose level of arousal is low, whereas the introvert is continuously over-aroused. Hence the extravert's desire to seek, and the introvert's desire to avoid, additional (arousing) stimulation.

The hypothesised physiological basis of neuroticism is the autonomic nervous system (ANS). The neurotic is believed to possess a changeable or labile ANS which is highly sensitive to stimulation. The subjective experience of fear and anxiety has a number of familiar, unpleasant autonomic components, such as butterflies in the stomach, increased heart rate and sweating. A neurotic person with a sensitive ANS is more prone to such autonomic reactions than is the normal individual. These reactions can become associated with neutral stimuli through the process of conditioning, and Eysenck claims that the neurotic person is liable to accumulate an excess of unnecessary conditioned emotional reactions. (For further physiological details, see Powell, 1979.)

The psychophysiological structures implicated in extraversion and neuroticism are said to explain most of the observed differences between introverts, extraverts, neurotics, and stable individuals. As yet, a physiological basis for psychoticism has not been proposed. Eysenck claims that one of the most significant psychological differences between introverts and extraverts is the relative ease or difficulty with which they acquire conditioned responses. This difference was demonstrated by Franks (1956, 1957), who studied eyeblink conditioning.

Franks's experiment was a classical conditioning paradigm, in which a puff of air to the eyeball (the unconditioned stimulus) causing the eye to blink (the unconditioned response) was paired with a buzzer (the conditioned stimulus). After repeated pairings, subjects blinked on hearing the buzzer in the absence of the puff of air. This blink is a conditioned response. It was found that introverts acquired the conditioned response after fewer pairings of buzzer and air-puff than did extraverts, and also that introverts required more trials to extinguish the response than extraverts. The psychophysiological explanation for these observed differences in conditionability is that since introverts are at a higher level of arousal than extraverts, their nervous systems are more ready to form the necessary associations.

The psychophysiologically based differences in conditionability are believed to explain why neurotic introverts acquire a surplus of conditioned anxiety responses. Eysenck regards this surplus as being the basis of neurotic anxiety, obsessional, and depressive neuroses. The conditionability differences are also proposed as an explanation for neurotic extraverts being deficient in certain learned characteristics: such deficiencies are in turn used to explain hysteria and psychopathy. For example, one such learned characteristic, Eysenck argues, is the conscience (H.J. Eysenck, 1977).

Psychopaths are people who do not feel guilt or remorse for their antisocial behaviour. Eysenck claims that psychopaths are highly neurotic, extraverted, and psychotic, and their behaviour is antisocial because they have failed to acquire (via conditioning) the constraints of a conscience. The conscience is seen as a product of socialisation, and is composed of conditioned anxiety responses to antisocial acts. Psychopaths, since they are extraverts and hence under-aroused, are constitutionally inferior in their ability to acquire the constraints of a conscience. The neuroticism dimension also plays a part since when the level of neuroticism is extremely high it can interfere with learning because of the excessive fear and anxiety provoked by the learning experience. Therefore psychopaths, who are highly neurotic, are particularly difficult to condition. However, attempts to test Eysenck's theory using criminal populations have failed to find convincing evidence that offenders are more extraverted than non-offenders, although there is some evidence that they are more neurotic and more psychotic (see chapter 9).

If it is the case that the Eysenckian personality dimensions are the product of distinct psychophysiological structures, then there should be a significant genetic factor in personality. With the aid of colleagues expert in genetical analysis, Eysenck has been determining the relative contributions of heredity and environment to extraversion (e.g. Eaves and Eysenck, 1975). A popular method is to correlate the trait scores within pairs of identical and fraternal twins (Loehlin, 1977). In a review of the twin study data, Shields (1976) concluded that extraversion scores for identical twins correlated around .50, whereas for fraternal twins the correlation can be as low as .20. In addition, studies of adopted children and correlations between relatives have indicated that there is a genetic component to both extraversion and neuroticism (Fulker, 1981).

Eysenck's theory of the psychophysiological structures underlying extraversion and neuroticism is highly speculative and has received only mixed support (Claridge, 1967). For example, the theory predicts that extraverts will differ from introverts on the classic measure of cortical arousal, the electroencephalogram (EEG). However, numerous studies have failed to yield consistent differences between introverts' and extraverts' EEGs (Gale, 1973). There remain many conceptual problems which have not been adequately dealt with – for example, what are the precise mechanisms by which cortical arousal and autonomic lability affect conditioning? Are these the same or different for operant versus classical conditioning? A revised statement is needed incorporating recent developments in physiological psychology and learning theory.

This need has been partially met in a modification of the theory proposed by Gray (1970, 1972). He argued that the diffuse arousal functions of the ARAS should be replaced with two separate physiological systems in the brain, one connected with punishment, the other with reward. Gray reviewed the evidence for a general factor of conditionability and observed that introverts are only found to condition better than extraverts under certain situations. Introverts are the more susceptible to conditioning where punishment and frustrative non-reward are involved, whereas extraverts are more susceptible to conditioning when rewards are positive. To accommodate these differences in conditioning, Gray proposed that introverts have the more sensitive punishment system and extraverts have the more sensitive reward system. Neuroticism may involve both systems, with highly neurotic people being sensitive to both reward and punishment.

A study by Nagpal and Gupta (1979) supported Gray's hypothesis. Subjects were selected on the basis of their extraversion and neuroticism scores to form four groups consisting of those scoring high on both dimensions, low on both dimensions, high on extraversion but low on neuroticism, and low on extraversion but high on neuroticism. They were assigned at random to either a punishment condition (electric shock for errors) or reward condition (verbal praise for correct responses) in a verbal operant conditioning task. The analysis of the conditioning scores showed that the neurotic extraverts conditioned more readily than the three groups in the reward condition, whereas the neurotic introverts conditioned more readily than the other groups in the punishment condition.

More recent research suggests that extraverts and introverts may differ not only in their sensitivity to punishment, but also in how they respond to it. For example, Nichols and Newman (1986) demonstated that extraverts responded more quickly than introverts after punishment on a pattern-matching learning task, and Pearce-McCall and Newman (1986) demonstrated that extraverts' expectations for success on a learning task were raised by the experience of punishment during an initial training session, whereas introverts' expectations were lowered by the same experience. These findings suggest that it is extraverts' style of responding, rather than their insensitivity to punishment, that results in their inferior learning.

Gray's conceptualisation of the physiological basis of conditioning is superior to Eysenck's on two counts. First, it takes into account recent physiological findings. Second, it utilises a more sophisticated view of conditioning in line with recent developments in learning theory (Mackintosh, 1974), where conditioning is regarded as a process of learning about relations between events rather than the automatic strengthening of stimulus-response relations through reinforcement. (For more detail on Gray's theory, see Gray, 1983, 1985).

When Eysenck embarked on his investigations, he studied the ways in which people throughout the ages had classified one another. He believed that these classification systems, although developed in a non-scientific way, would nevertheless reflect an accumulated wisdom based on observation and experience, and would therefore provide sound hypotheses for a scientific study of personality. He set out to test this hypothetical picture of the major dimensions by which people's personalities could be distinguished. From his investigations he concluded that personality may be described by three broad dimensions and he postulated their biological bases.

In contrast, Cattell's investigations began in a different way and, at first sight, it looks as though the two theories have produced two entirely different personality structures. The next section discusses how this came about, and then presents a reconciliation of the two views.

Cattell's personality theory

Cattell differs from Eysenck both in his approach to the study of personality and in his findings. Methodologically, Cattell favours an atheoretical approach in which factor analysis is used in an exploratory way to discover personality factors. Eysenck, on the other hand, used factor analysis to test previously formulated hypotheses about likely personality factors. The end result of the extensive work of Cattell and his colleagues in several different countries is a complex personality structure involving at least twenty traits and a massive supporting personality theory embracing areas often ignored by other personality theorists (such as ability, motivation, emotion and learning). As in the discussion of Eysenck's theory, the intention here is to outline Cattell's approach and summarise the main findings. A more detailed account and a comparison between Cattell and several other multi-trait theorists is available in Cattell and Kline (1977).

The structure and measurement of personality

The first stage in Cattell's methodology was to devise a technique whereby every possible aspect of personality would be included in the investigation, with the eventual aim of reducing this mass of non-selective material to more manageable proportions. For his starting point Cattell chose the English vocabulary of personality description. His rationale was that all the significant dimensions of variation in human personality would have found their way into the language, and therefore the complete set of adjectives used to describe personality, known as personality traits, would encompass the whole personality or, as Cattell terms it, the 'personality sphere'.

The English vocabulary of personality description was first identified by Allport and Odbert (1936). From their survey of a standard English dictionary, they found 18,000 words which could be used to describe personality and around 4,500 which they regarded as used specifically for personality description. Cattell's first task was to reduce this huge number of adjectives to a more workable size by removing all the synonyms. By this process, the list was reduced to 160 traits, to which were added eleven traits from the psychological literature. Cattell regarded these 171 traits, or personality variables, as representing the personality sphere. The complete list is given in Cattell (1946).

The list was still too large to form the basis for a rating study, so Cattell surveyed the findings from previous rating studies which had used some or all of the variables from this list to discover which traits were found typically to covary. As a result of pooling the results of fourteen such studies he was able to locate clusters of traits which tended to covary and he selected a single variable to represent each cluster. These variables, thirty-five in all, were used as the scales in his rating study.

Cattell calls rating data 'L data' (life data) and, in his early studies, it was collected in the following manner (Hammond, 1977). Members of groups of up to sixteen people, who had known each other for at least six months, would rate one another on the scales (thus each person was both a rater and a ratee). To control for the fact that individuals differ from one another in their propensity to use extreme versus middle-of-the-road judgments, Cattell required each rater to use the various points of the rating scale in a fixed proportion. For example, the mid-point of each scale could be used 30 per cent of the time. The ratings across the raters were summed so that each ratee's score on a scale was the total of the fifteen raters' ratings. These ratings were then subjected to factor analysis to discover the number and identity of the underlying dimensions. Cattell and his colleagues carried out several such investigations and concluded that around sixteen factors were necessary to describe personality as revealed by these data (Cattell, 1957).

Why is it that Cattell's rating studies resulted in around sixteen underlying dimensions whereas Eysenck's initial rating studies only resulted in two? The reason for this discrepancy lies in the contrasting ways Cattell and Eysenck use factor analysis (Cattell, 1966). There are two stages in the calculation of a factor analysis at which the investigator has to make a decision. The first decision concerns the number of factors to be extracted from the correlation matrix, and the second concerns the particular technique for arriving at the final solution. Eysenck and Cattell disagree on procedure at both these decision points, thus producing different results.

In deciding how many factors should be extracted, the investigator tries to avoid erring on the side of too many or too few: too many factors will leave nearly as complicated a picture as was given by the original correlation matrix, and too few means that some important dimensions may have been lost by being subsumed under a more general dimension. To use a simple analogy, the Left-Right dimension fails to capture all the variations between the political parties to be found in, for example, the European Assembly. On the other hand, to have as many dimensions as there are parties would not be helpful in trying to understand the major dimensions of political belief. The aim of factor analysis is to achieve a midway position which results in a manageable number of factors locating dimensions of psychological interest. Although there are various tests that can be applied to the date to indicate, in an objective way, the appropriate number of factors to extract (Harman, 1967), there is still room for the subjective element to enter into the decision. Cattell, who regards the structure of personality as a complex edifice, favours working with more factors than do most other investigators.

The second decision point concerns the choice of technique used to achieve the final calculation of the factor loadings (the correlations between the items and each factor from which the psychological identity of the factors is inferred). The final solution is achieved via a set of procedures known as rotation, and factor analysts become extremely heated in their arguments over the best methods of rotation. Their arguments are highly technical and will not be gone into in any detail here (see Cattell and Kline, 1977, for a more thorough discussion). For the present purposes, rotation may be seen as a form of fine tuning in which factors are delicately adjusted in order to ensure that they have located as accurately as possible the clusters of intercorrelations in the original correlation matrix. The different techniques of rotation are of two kinds: orthogonal and oblique.

In orthogonal rotations, the factors produced will be independent of one another. Eysenck has generally favoured orthogonal solutions (H.J. Eysenck and S.B.G. Eysenck, 1969), which has meant that extraversion, neuroticism and psychoticism are treated as independent factors referring to separate areas of personality: knowing a person's score on one of them does not enable you to predict their score on the others. Cattell, on the other hand, has favoured oblique solutions where the factors are correlated (i.e. they are not entirely independent of one another but refer to related areas of personality). Cattell prefers oblique solutions because he believes in the interconnectedness of personality.

Factors are rotated either orthogonally or obliquely until they have been located in the optimal position as defined by the principles of simple structure which correspond to the principles of parsimony. Simple structure has been achieved when the number of zero factor loadings has been maximised. A solution in which each factor's loadings are either high or near to zero means that only a few of the factors are involved in accounting for the variance associated with each variable. Such a solution is more parsimonious than a solution in which all the factors are implicated in every variable. Cattell argues that simple structure can only be achieved by using oblique rotation, and advocates that the final adjustment of the factors be done by visual inspection of the solution rather than by mathematical procedures alone.

Having located the factors present in rating data, Cattell and his colleagues went on to investigate the personality structure revealed by the two other sources of data: questionnaires and objective tests. Cattell (1957) discussed the relative merits of ratings, questionnaires and objective tests, which he called L, Q and T data respectively. He assumed that all three databases would tap the same underlying personality structure, although there might be some minor variation, since some aspects of personality may only be expressed in one kind of data. For example, a person's hopes and aspirations could be measured in a self-report questionnaire but would be much harder to infer from observing their overt, day-to-day behaviour (L data). Also, the techniques for measuring the different data have their particular distortions (called 'instrument factors') which may influence the appearance of the structure revealed in each domain. For example, a person's tendency to give the socially desirable response (to 'fake good') may distort Q data, and a rater's idiosyncratic definition of the item being rated may distort L data. As it turns out, there is considerable agreement between the factor structure found in L and Q data, but T data appear to be tapping a rather different aspect of personality, as we shall see below.

As a result of extensive investigation of questionnaire data (involving several thousand subjects) sixteen factors, including an intelligence factor, have been found repeatedly. These well-substantiated Q factors are set out in Table 3.1, which also shows which of these Q factors are the same as the factors in L data.

A glance at Table 3.1 shows that Cattell has invented the words used to label many of the factors and, although other words have been used in addition to these inventions, the preponderance of words like threctia, harria and zeppia create something of a barrier between Cattell and his students. The rationale for these invented names is that the factors refer to what Cattell calls source traits, and these are dimensions underlying the surface traits and it is the surface traits to which we refer with our large vocabulary of trait language. As source traits had not been discovered before Cattell's investigations, there were no appropriate names for them in the language; hence, he had to invent them.

Cattell has developed a widely used questionnaire for measuring Q factors called the Sixteen Personality Factor questionnaire (16PF) (Cattell, Eber and Tatsuoka, 1970).

Table 3.1 Factors found in L and Q data (adapted from
Cattell and Kline, 1977, pp. 112–19)

Factor	Description			
A	Sizia (reserved) *v.* Affectia (outgoing)	L	Q	
B	Intelligence	L	Q	
C	Dissatisfied emotionality *v.* Ego strength	L	Q	
D	Excitability	L	—	Q+
E	Submissiveness *v.* Dominance	L	Q	
F	Desurgency *v.* Surgency	L	Q	
G	Superego	L	Q	
H	Threctia (shy) *v.* Parmia (adventurous)	L	Q	
I	Harria (tough-minded) *v.* Premsia (tender-minded)	L	Q	
J	Zeppia (zestful) *v.* Coasthemia (individualistic)	L	—	Q+
K	Boorishness *v.* Mature socialisation	L	—	Q+
L	Alexia (trusting) *v.* Protension (suspicional)	L	Q	
M	Praxernia (practical) *v.* Autia (unconventional)	L	Q	
N	Natural forthrightness *v.* Shrewdness	L	Q	
O	Self-confident *v.* Guilt-prone	L	Q	
P	Sanguine casualness	—	—	Q+
Q1	Conservatism *v.* Radicalism	—	Q	
Q2	Group dependency *v.* Self-sufficiency	—	Q	
Q3	Strength of self-sentiment	—	Q	
Q4	Ergic tension	—	Q	
Q5	Group dedication with sensed inadequacy	—	—	Q+
Q6	Social panache	—	—	Q+
Q7	Explicit self-expression	—	—	Q+

There is a supplement to the 16PF for the assessment of the
Q factors only discovered recently (shown as Q+ factors in
Table 3.1). Versions of the 16PF have been developed to
study the structure of children's personality, and tests for
ages ranging from the pre-school child to the adolescent are
now available (Dreger, 1977). All these questionnaires are
suitable for use on normal populations. In contrast to
Eysenck, Cattell regards the abnormal personality as being
qualitatively different from the normal personality (Cattell,
1973). Although the 16PF is able to discriminate between
neurotics and normals, additional factors are needed for the
discrimination of psychotics, who are regarded as possessing
personality traits not present in normal and neurotic
populations. Cattell and Kline (1977) present twelve abnormal factors, seven of which are related to depression.

So far we have only considered two sources of information about personality: behaviour ratings (L data) and self-report questionnaires (Q data). Cattell and his colleagues have also devoted a great deal of research effort to the investigation of personality via objective tests (T data). An objective test, as defined at the beginning of the chapter, is one in which a person is required to respond to a miniature life situation which is presented in such a way that the person is unaware of what the test is actually measuring and therefore cannot 'fake good'. The rationale behind objective tests lies in the assumption that all behaviour is potential personality data, from handwriting to nose blowing. The choice of miniature life situations is restricted only by practical limitations of portability, administration time and the ingenuity of the researcher. There are now over 400 objective tests, and over 2,000 different measures may be derived from them (Cattell and Warburton, 1967). Several objective tests are usually administered in one session, making up what is termed an objective test battery. Some instances of the more zany objective tests, selected from the examples given by Cattell and Kline, are blowing up a balloon (which identifies timid, inhibited people), reading backwards (which is difficult for rigid people) and selecting the funnier of the two jokes (which reveals a person's repressed impulses). There are also more familiar tests, such as physiological measures and reaction times.

Theoretically, T data are regarded as measuring the same personality sphere as L and Q data. Therefore the same personality structure should emerge when T data are factor analysed. Minor differences are to be expected due to instrument factors, but the same essential structure should be there. The results so far have been less clear than had been predicted. Twenty factors have been located and replicated, but the correspondence between these factors and those found in L and Q data is yet to be fully established.

Motivation

For Cattell, the structure and measurement of personality does not stop at describing temperament and ability, but also includes dynamics or motivation: personality is composed of both the way we do things (temperament and ability) and why we do things (motivation). Motivation is regarded as having two aspects requiring separate investigation and measurement: its strength and the goals involved (Cattell and Child, 1975).

Motivational strength refers to the degree of interest a person displays in particular activities. For example, some people regard cooking as an unavoidable chore while others find it a never-ending delight. Cattell was interested in discovering whether a person's strength of interest in an activity could be broken down into various components. Some interests may be equally strong and yet reflect different aspects of motivation. Thus the person who is keen on cooking may also be an enthusiastic worker for a charity. These two different interests, the former tending towards hedonism and the latter towards selflessness, suggest that motivation is multi-dimensional.

Cattell studied motivational strength using objective tests. When the scores were factor analysed, three main dimensions of motivational strength emerged. They corresponded approximately to the Freudian concepts of id, ego, and superego. For example, imagine a couple buying a house. Their strength of interest in the purchase could be impulsive: they see a charming house and desire to own it. In this case the id component is predominant. Alternatively, the house may fulfil all the criteria of the appropriate choice for the couple: it is the right size, in the right area and the price is reasonable. Interest in the purchase in this case is predominantly ego-based. A third possibility is that the house represents a sound investment and the buyers know that purchasing property is a sensible hedge against inflation and is something they ought to do, even though it is much less trouble to rent a place. Here, the superego component is at work. Usually, house buying involves all three components to varying degrees. In brief, motivation consists of three components: id interest (I want), ego interest (I choose to want) and superego (I ought to want).

So much for motivational strength, but what about the goals of motivation? Cattell calls the ultimate goals of motivated behaviour the 'ergs'. These are roughly comparable to instincts (e.g. food seeking, sex, gregariousness). While ergs are culturally universal because of their biological origins, the means by which ergs can be satisfied will vary from culture to culture. In our society areas such as sport, occupation, religion and the home are all mediums for erg satisfaction. These culture-specific activities through which ergs are satisfied Cattell called sentiments. A single sentiment, such as a sport, may be involved in the satisfaction of a number of different ergs, such as gregariousness, pugnacity and possibly even sex (if one of the aims of taking physical exercise is to develop an attractive physique). The complex connections between all the different sentiments and the ergs to which they are related are termed the 'dynamic lattice', a much simplified version of which is shown in Figure 3.4. Such a lattice can be constructed for a particular culture or, more specifically, for a particular individual. It will tell the investigator what a person's interests are and what basic ergs these interests are satisfying.

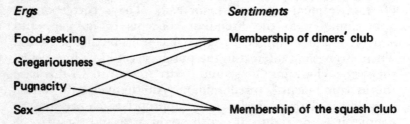

FIGURE 3.4 *A simplified representation of a part of a dynamic lattice*

   Temperament, ability and motivation factors make up the key elements of Cattell's theory of the structure of personality; they form what may be regarded as its relatively fixed base. However, people change from day to day and year to year, and a complete personality theory needs to be able to accommodate these short- and long-term fluctuations. Cattell has studied relatively short-term moods and states, and concludes that anxiety is the most important aspect of these transient conditions (Cattell and Scheier, 1961). More permanent changes in personality structure are the result of maturation and learning experiences, and Cattell has begun to develop an account of how learning affects the relatively fixed elements of the personality structure to bring about enduring changes.

We have now seen how Cattell's conceptualisation of personality describes the basic structure of personality, its dynamics, and the temporary and more permanent changes it can undergo. Cattell attempts to draw together all these separate influences bearing on behaviour in a single equation. The behaviour specification equation sets out the components of a particular behaviour specifying the level of involvement of traits, ergs, states, learning factors and situational variables. What began as a simple formula has expanded over the years, in pace with the theory, to an unwieldy and impractical series of algebraic terms, some of which refer to concepts as yet unmeasurable. The specification equation is no longer a succinct and useful description of behaviour. Perhaps the same is true of Cattell's theory as a whole: in an effort to be all-embracing it has itself become too vast to encompass.

An integration of Cattell and Eysenck

Superficially, Cattell and Eysenck have arrived at two different conceptualisations of personality structure, the former's comprising twenty-three traits (from L, Q and T data) and the latter's a mere three. Since both have been investigating the same subject matter it would appear that one of them must be wrong. However, happily for them both, it can be shown that the two conceptualisations are not irreconcilable.

The issue can be resolved by a closer examination of the different ways the two theorists have used factor analysis. The factors obtained in the initial analysis of personality data are called first-order factors. As has already been described, Cattell favours oblique factors. Because they are correlated, the twenty-three oblique factors resulting from Cattell's analyses can themselves be intercorrelated and factor analysed. As a result of this process, a smaller number of so-called second-order factors may be obtained. When this is done with Cattell's twenty-three first-order factors several second-order factors emerge, but the two most important are exvia-invia and anxiety. Second-order factors can be identified by their high loadings on first-order factors, which for exvia-invia are sociable (A), surgent (F), adventurous (H) and dependent (Q2), and for anxiety are weak ego strength (C), timid (H), suspicious (L), guilt-prone (O), low self-sentiment (Q3) and tense (Q4) (Cattell and Kline, 1977).

Cattell (1973) argues that Eysenck's factors of extraversion and neuroticism are not true first-order factors but appeared as such because of Eysenck's improper use of factor analysis. Eysenck is regarded as having underfactored his data and the resulting factors of extraversion, neuroticism and psychoticisim are 'pseudosecondaries', or first-order factors which have positioned themselves roughly in line with true second-order factors. As a result, extraversion–introversion is highly similar to Cattell's second-order factor exvia–invia, and neuroticism is similar to anxiety. Psychoticism is regarded as probably a first-order approximation of Cattell's second-order general psychoticism factor, but is insufficient for describing the abnormal domain because it bears no relation to the other second-order factor of general depression (Cattell and Kline, 1977).

Thus the structures proposed by Cattell and Eysenck do not turn out to be fundamentally different. Eysenck prefers to keep things simple and work with a broad, three-dimensional picture, whereas Cattell believes that by turning the power of the microscope up and working with a larger number of traits a more accurate picture is obtained. Despite these preferences, it is recognised that their conceptualisations are essentially the same.

The structure of trait ratings

The aim of multi-trait theories of personality is to describe personality comprehensively. By examining the work of Eysenck and of Cattell in some detail we have studied two opposing views on personality structure: Eysenck favours the broad brush strokes of his three personality dimensions (extraversion, neuroticism and psychoticism), whereas Cattell advocates a more fine-grained approach (between sixteen and twenty-three factors). Now that we have seen how these two approaches can be reconciled, it is time to relate this work to other attempts to describe the structure of personality.

Personality taxonomies

It will be recalled that both Eysenck and Cattell began their investigations into personality by factor analysing rating data. Several other investigators have proposed personality structures based on analyses of trait ratings. The most influential work is the series of studies carried out by Tupes and Christal (1961) and Norman (1963) using Cattell's (1947) trait rating scales.

The subjects (servicemen in the Tupes and Christal studies, college students in the others) were split into small groups of six to sixteen, and each subject was asked to assign the other members of the group to either pole of a series of bipolar personality scales. The samples varied in length of acquaintance from three days to three years. The scales were selected from those used by Cattell (1947). The subjects' scores on each scale were calculated on the basis of the group data by subtracting the number of nominations to one pole from the number of nominations to the other pole. The rating scales were then intercorrelated using subjects' scores from all the small groups in the sample, and the resulting correlation matrix was factor analysed.

Despite the difference in subject populations, and the range of familiarity between raters and ratees across these studies, the results were remarkably similar. A five-factor structure proved over and over again to provide the best solution. These factors were labelled surgency or extraversion, agreeableness, conscientiousness, emotional stability, and culture, and have come to be known as the Big Five. They are shown, along with their scales, in Table 3.2.

Table 3.2 The five factors representing the twenty peer
nomination scales (from Norman, 1963)

Factor name	Scale labels
Extraversion	talkative–silent
	frank, open–secretive
	adventurous–cautious
	sociable–reclusive
Agreeableness	good-natured–irritable
	not jealous–jealous
	mild, gentle–headstrong
	cooperative–negativistic
Conscientiousness	fussy, tidy–careless
	responsible–undependable
	scrupulous–unscrupulous
	persevering–quitting, fickle
Emotional stability	poised–nervous, tense
	calm–anxious
	composed–excitable
	non-hypochondriacal–hypochondriacal
Culture	artistically sensitive–artistically insensitive
	intellectual–unreflective, narrow
	polished, refined–crude, boorish
	imaginative–simple, direct

Norman (1963) discussed possible explanations for why
his five-factor structure differed from the larger number
favoured by Cattell, and concluded that the additional
factors claimed by Cattell were derived from unreliable
scales and accounted for too small a percentage of the
variance to be worth considering.

The universality of the Big Five cannot be explained by
the limited nature of the samples tested to date. The Big Five
have now been identified in rating studies of children's
personalities (Digman and Inouye, 1986) and older adults
(McCrae and Costa, 1985). However, there remains some
dispute about the exact nature of at least one of the Big Five
factors. For example, McCrae and Costa (1985) claim to
have discovered a new and substantial personality factor
called openness. This factor identifies people who are open to
experience as revealed by their artistic and intellectual
interests, their creativity and imagination, their liberal,
untraditional values, independence and impracticalness. H.J.
Eysenck and M.W. Eysenck (1985) argued against this

factor, claiming that openness to experience is not a distinct factor, but instead that it is at the opposite end of the continuum to psychoticism. Openness to experience may also be interpreted as a form of the Big Five factor called culture, rather than being a new factor. It is possible that the appearance of this version of the culture factor in McCrae and Costa's data can be attributed to the substantial age difference between their mature adult subjects as compared with the more typical college-age subjects.

Most, if not all, of the personality structures based on trait ratings and advocated by the various multi-trait theorists can be accommodated by the Big Five structure (Goldberg, 1981a). For example, Eysenck's dimensions of extraversion and neuroticism, and Cattell's exvia–invia and anxiety, have their Big Five equivalents (extraversion and emotional stability), although psychoticism does not map directly onto a single Big Five dimension. These five broad areas of personality description seem to capture the essential ways in which human beings differ from one another. Goldberg (1981a) goes so far as to suggest that they may be recognised universally in language because they identify the critical questions that all human beings, regardless of cultural variations, need to know about one another: 'Will this person dominate me?' (extraversion), 'Will I like this person?' (agreeableness), 'Can I trust this person to do a good job?' (conscientiousness), 'Is this person crazy?' (emotional stability), and 'Is this person smart?' (culture).

Although the debate over the definitive structure of personality ratings is far from over (e.g. see Brand, 1984 for another view), the Big Five represents a reasonable compromise between the extreme positions offered by Eysenck and Cattell. We shall be returning to these issues in chapter 5, where the use of personality ratings to assess people's beliefs about personality will be discussed.

4 Personality and consistency

Consistency is the key concept in the definition of personality given at the beginning of this book: personality consists of the 'more or less stable internal factors *that make one person's behaviour consistent from one time to another*, and different from the behaviour other people would manifest in comparable situations' (Child, I.L., 1968, p.83, emphasis added). Trait theories set out to explain why an individual's behaviour is consistent by postulating stable, internal factors which determine behaviour. They also aim to provide assessment techniques which permit the prediction of behaviour, and these too rely on the assumption that behaviour is consistent.

Consistency refers to the similarity in a person's behaviour across occasions and across situations. These stable patterns of behaviour are used to infer personality traits, which in turn are used to explain and predict continuities and coherences in behaviour. The most damaging criticism of trait theories, if sustained, would be to undermine their basis in consistency. In this chapter, research into the consistency of behaviour will be discussed, beginning with a summary of Mischel's (1968) influential critique and finishing with the latest round of the consistency debate, also inspired by Mischel (Mischel and Peake, 1982). In the final section, modifications to the study of personality are proposed to accommodate the findings regarding the consistency and the inconsistency of behaviour.

The meaning of consistency

When personality theorists claim to have demonstrated

behavioural consistency and their critics claim to have demonstrated behavioural inconsistency, there are several kinds of consistency to which they may be referring. For example, Mischel and Peake (1982) distinguished between temporal stability (i.e. behavioural consistency in similar situations measured over several points in time) and cross-situational consistency (i.e. behavioural consistency measured over several different situations). Endler (1983) referred to longitudinal consistency (behavioural consistency across similar situations over a long time-span) versus cross-sectional consistency (behavioural consistency across dissimilar situations over a short time-span). In view of these and other different terminologies, it is helpful to have a framework which can accommodate all the various meanings of behavioural consistency.

The four types of consistency

To clarify the different meanings of consistency it is possible to represent them by means of a two-by-two table (see Figure 4.1). Demonstrating consistency always involves comparing two different time points, but either the same or different behaviours can be compared in either the same or different situations.

| | | Situation | |
		Same	Different
Behaviour	Same	Type A	Type B
	Different	Type C	Type D

FIGURE 4.1 *The four types of consistency*

The four types of consistency – A, B, C and D in Figure 4.1 – are obtained by combining the two possible cases for the situations (same or different) with the two possible cases for the behaviours (same or different). Strictly speaking, no two behaviours or situations occurring at different times may be considered identical. However, in practice, repetitions of behaviours and situations are treated as identical. Often, the investigator has to decide whether similar behaviours or situations should be treated as identical or *psychologically equivalent*. This can be controversial, as we shall see later on in this chapter.

In type A consistency, the behaviours and situations being compared across time points are the same. In test-retest reliability, where a person takes the same personality questionnaire under identical test conditions on two separate occasions, type A consistency is being investigated.

Type B consistency requires that the same behaviour be compared across different situations. For example, in an investigation into altruism, subjects' helping behaviour might be compared across two different situations where a person was in distress: one where there were several bystanders and one where the subject was alone. If altruism is a stable personality characteristic, then subjects should be consistently altruistic in both situations. If it is determined by situational factors, then the difference between several bystanders and none may result in inconsistencies in helping behaviour in the two situations. In both types A and B, consistency is demonstrated by the same behaviour occurring at each time point, either in the same or different situations.

Type C consistency requires that the behaviours be different but the situations the same. At first glance, type C consistency seems something of a contradiction. How can it be consistent for a person to behave in different ways in repetitions of the same situations? Type D consistency appears even more contradictory: if a person behaves differently in a different situation then this is being consistent. The resolution of this contradiction is achieved through the personality concept and psychological equivalence. There are far fewer personality traits than overt behaviours, hence each trait is involved in the determination of a number of different, but psychologically equivalent, behaviours.

The performance of one behaviour in a particular situation allows for the prediction of the occurrence of other psychologically equivalent behaviours, either in a repetition of the same situation (type C consistency) or even in a different situation (type D consistency). In types C and D consistency, although the overt behaviours may appear to be different, they share an underlying similarity because they are determined by the same personality trait.

Type C consistency may be illustrated by the study of group interaction, where it is commonly found that people adopt characteristic styles, the two best known being task-oriented and socio-emotional (Bales, 1951). Over a series of group discussions, or during the course of one session, it may be found that the person who asks questions also redirects the conversation back to the discussion topic (task-oriented), whereas the person who tells jokes also makes supportive comments (socio-emotional). Here the situation remains the same and, although the individuals behave differently from one time point to the next, their particular patterns of behaviours may be regarded as consistent because of the underlying psychological equivalence uniting the observed behaviour.

An example of type D consistency would be an investigation into the validity of a personality test. Thus, if a person scored highly on a questionnaire measure of extraversion it would be consistent if this person behaved in typically extraverted ways at a party later on in the day. Responding to a personality questionnaire and having a good time at a party are different behaviours in different situations but, to the extent that they are both determined by the same underlying trait (extraversion), and knowledge of the trait permits prediction of the behaviour, the occurrence of these different behaviours is evidence of type D consistency.

When consistency is discussed in the context of personality it is not usually specified which of these four types of consistency is meant. However, by examining the behaviours and situations used to assess consistency according to the classification system described above, the identification of different forms of consistency becomes straightforward. Armed with a framework for identifying the different types of consistency, it is possible to be more precise about the sorts of consistency upon which the trait theories are based, and which the critics have sought to undermine.

Mischel's attack on personality

In 1968, Mischel published a book called *Personality and Assessment*, in which he set out a powerful argument against the concept of personality, and traits in particular, backed with an impressive array of evidence. His book demonstrated that personality theorists had overstated the case for behavioural consistency. On this basis, he argued that the personality concept is invalid, and that the process of explaining and predicting behaviour would be better off without it.

Mischel did not restrict his attack to any one theory, but aimed it at two influential groups of theories: psychodynamic theories, such as that of Freud, and trait theories. The key features shared by the two types of theories he defined as follows:

> Both dynamic (state) and trait theories focus on responses as signs (indirect or direct) of pervasive underlying mental structures; both assume that these underlying inferred dispositions (whether called traits, states, processes, dynamics, motives or labeled in other ways) exert generalized and enduring causal effects on behavior; and both have been devoted to a search for signs that serve as reliable indicators of these hypothesized underlying dimensions. (Mischel, 1968, p.8).

Mischel's definition of personality is very close to the one adopted here (see the beginning of this chapter), and he also recognises that consistency is the key issue:

> Data that demonstrate strong generality in the behavior of the same person across many situations are critical for trait and state personality theories; the construct of personality itself rests on the belief that individual behavioral consistencies exist widely and account for

much of the variance in behavior. (Mischel, 1968, p.13).

Most of Mischel's book is taken up by his review of studies of behavioural consistency. Although Mischel did not distinguish between the different kinds of consistency described above, it is possible to recast his conclusions in terms of this framework.

Mischel examined the evidence for behavioural consistency from a variety of areas: not only personality, but also intelligence and cognitive style. He was justified in widening the circle of the debate in this way because the arguments for psychological constructs such as intelligence and cognitive style are similar to those for personality: they all rely on the concept of underlying factors to explain behavioural consistency.

Beginning with type A, Mischel found plenty of evidence for consistency in all three domains: intelligence, cognitive style and personality. All studies of test-retest reliability are investigations of type A consistency: subjects perform the same test-taking behaviour under the same situational conditions. Measures in all three domains are expected to achieve a high level of test-retest reliability, and many of them do.

Test-retest reliability studies compare repeated performances of highly specific and contrived behaviours. In more everyday experience type A consistency may not be so easy to demonstrate. One of the reasons for this is that it is easier to replicate situations in the laboratory than it is in real life.

The evidence for type B consistency was also satisfactory, but only so far as intelligence and cognitive styles were concerned. For example, Mischel discussed the concept of field dependence–independence which, as we saw in chapter 2, can be measured with a variety of techniques such as the RFT and EFT. These different tests may be regarded as different situations, and the required behaviour, separating figure from ground, is essentially the same in all of them. The correlations between different measures of FD-I are reasonably high, demonstrating type B consistency.

When Mischel examined the evidence for type B consistency in more personality-related behaviour the findings were disappointing. Mischel placed considerable emphasis on the classic studies of moral behaviour by Hartshorne and May (Hartshorne and May, 1928). The aim of their investigations was to test the validity of the concept of a trait of honesty, a trait considered to determine people's moral behaviour in a variety of situations. It is generally believed that someone who is basically honest will behave with honesty in all kinds of situations, regardless of situational incentives to be either honest or dishonest. However, Hartshorne and May's studies showed that honesty was influenced by situational factors. Several thousand children participated in these studies, and over a hundred different situations were devised where there was an opportunity for the children to behave dishonestly and, apparently, to avoid detection. However, all dishonest behaviour was in fact monitored. For example, while consistency was high between self-report questionnaires about moral behaviour filled out by the same children on different occasions in the classroom (type A consistency), consistency between behaviours such as cheating on a test by copying compared with cheating by adjusting the final score was low (type B consistency). Mischel agreed with Hartshorne and May's interpretation of their findings: honesty is primarily a function of situational factors and is not a consistent behaviour determined by an underlying personality characteristic.

Over the fifty years since they were carried out, Hartshorne and May's studies have been the subject of much discussion and re-analysis in an attempt to establish whether the original interpretation was correct (e.g. Burton, 1963). However, no definitive conclusions have emerged. One of the most telling comments on this work is that it used children as subjects, and evidence on the development of children's moral thinking obtained more recently (Kohlberg, 1976) suggests that a trans-situational moral code resulting in consistent moral behaviour does not develop until at least adolescence. It is therefore not surprising that Hartshorne and May's child subjects failed to demonstrate type B consistency.

On the basis of the honesty study, and several other similar investigations, Mischel concluded that the evidence for type B consistency in the personality domain was far from convincing. He argued that type B consistency is not as pervasive a phenomenon as personality theorists may have implied, but this fact alone does not constitute a major threat to the personality concept. We are not automatons, driven by inner mechanisms and unable to change our behaviour to suit the circumstances. Responsivity to situational factors is evidence of human flexibility and adaptiveness. Therefore, a certain amount of behavioural specificity is to be expected and must be accommodated by personality theories.

For evidence concerning type C consistency (different behaviour, same situation) Mischel drew on studies of the validity of personality ratings. Both Eysenck and Cattell used rating data in their early studies of personality: observers rated their subjects' behaviour on a series of scales which were then intercorrelated and factor analysed. The results of these analyses were assumed to describe the personality structure of the ratees. However, subsequent studies questioned the validity of this assumption, claiming that observers' ratings reveal the constructs used by the observer in categorising another's behaviour rather than the personality structure of the person being rated (D'Andrade, 1965; Mulaik, 1964; Passini and Norman, 1966). These studies are concerned with type C consistency in the sense that the rating scales constitute measures of different behaviours observed by the rater in the same or highly similar situations. Type C consistency is demonstrated when clusters of behaviour are found to co-occur in the same people in the same situation (e.g. talkativeness, frankness, adventurousness and sociability), and hence constitute a factor (e.g. extraversion).

The validity of personality ratings was questioned because these studies found that the same factor structure emerged in analyses of ratings made by raters with varying degrees of acquaintance with their ratees ranging from three years to fifteen minutes (Passini and Norman, 1966). In addition, when no ratees were involved and subjects simply rated the scales in terms of how similar in meaning each one was to every other, the same factor structure emerged (D'Andrade, 1965; Mulaik, 1964). These findings suggest that the trait categories used by raters for classifying behaviour exist independently of the ratees' actual behaviour. It is these conceptual categories which emerge when ratings are factor analysed, rather than the personality traits characterising the manifested personality of ratees.

On the basis of such findings, Mischel has argued that type C consistency has not been demonstrated: analysis of personality ratings tells us more about the rater than about the ratee. This is a grave indictment of personality ratings, but there is one important point Mischel has overlooked. Demonstrating a correspondence between the factor structure of ratings of actual behaviour and raters' conceptual categories could mean one of two things. If the raters' conceptual categories do not correspond with reality, Mischel's interpretation that personality ratings are invalid is correct. However, if raters' conceptual categories do correspond with reality, then similarity between these categories and the factor structure of personality ratings would suggest that raters' conceptual categories are accurate reflections of reality. The extent to which raters' conceptual categories are an accurate reflection of real-life behavioural co-occurrence is an empirical question which has been investigated since Mischel's 1968 critique. This work will be discussed in full in chapter 6.

Finally, Mischel considered the evidence for type D consistency. Personality theorists claim that behaviour in one situation can serve as a sign for how the person will behave in another situation, and the utility of the personality theorist's perspective depends on the success of this claim. Mischel reviewed the research on the correlations between personality test scores and actual behaviour (comparing the test-taking situation with other situations where other behaviours were sampled), and arrived at his now famous 'personality coefficient':

> Indeed, the phrase 'personality coefficient' might be coined to describe the correlation between .20 and .30 which is found persistently when virtually any personality dimension inferred from a questionnaire is related to almost any conceivable external criterion involving

responses sampled in a different *medium* – that is, not by another questionnaire. (Mischel, 1968, p.78, original emphasis).

The low level of consistency between scores on personality tests and actual behaviour in different situations naturally raises serious doubts as to the utility of the personality concept. Mischel proposed that more reliable prediction could be achieved by estimating future behaviour on the basis of how a person has behaved in similar situations in the past. In effect, he proposed that type A consistency, of which we can be reasonably confident, should form the basis of prediction rather than type D. In so doing, he abandoned the personality concept, in the sense that he advocated that behaviour be regarded as merely predictive of itself and not as a sign of an underlying personality factor, and hence predictive of a variety of other behaviours.

Mischel's attack on personality was aimed at its most vulnerable point – consistency – and the attack was partially successful. While type A consistency survived relatively unscathed, type B consistency was shown not to exist as generally as personality theorists have tended to assume. Although Mischel regarded type C consistency as a figment of raters' imaginations, the validity of their imaginations has yet to be disproved, and so the status of type C consistency remains unclear. Type D consistency has certainly been exaggerated by personality theorists.

Situationism

The aftermath of Mischel's critique proved to be a bleak period for the study of personality. Interest was reawakened in the long-standing debate in psychology over the relative importance for the determination of behaviour of what the person brings to bear upon the situation versus what the situation brings to bear upon the person. This debate is by no means new; the issues were articulated as long ago as 1935 by Kurt Lewin, who proposed the compromise that behaviour is a function of both the person and the environment, and it is doubtful whether the debate has progressed conceptually much further since his statement. (The history of this debate is described by Ekehammar, 1974.)

In the final section of Mischel's (1968) book, he proposed an alternative to personality theory, which he called social learning theory. It is similar to Rotter's theory in that it is based on principles of learning discovered in laboratory experiments and is applied to the full range of normal and abnormal social behaviour. It is a behaviourist position in so far as it eschews the concept of any internal personality factors. Instead, behaviour is seen as being determined primarily by environmental factors. This approach became known as 'situationism'. The weaknesses of pure situationism have been elegantly exposed by Bowers (1973).

Bowers argued that it is wrong to seek the causes of behaviour in traits or situations. The absurdity of such a search is demonstrated by the ease with which it is possible to think up experiments to 'prove' either position. For example, London's traffic provides constant proof of the superiority of situation variables over person variables: virtually everyone obeys the traffic lights. Conversely, motorway driving demonstates the role of person variables. Not everyone chooses to drive at the maximum permitted speed; drivers adopt the cruising speed which they personally prefer. In this case, the situation exerts less control over the individual, who is then free to behave more idiosyncratically. The pitting of traits against situations is an unhelpful exercise, and Bowers recommended that it be abandoned in favour of an interactionist approach which takes both into account.

Later, Mischel adopted a position more in sympathy with Bowers's arguments. One of the problems for the situationist is to account for individual differences: why do we not all respond in the same way when placed in the same situation? Social learning theory explains individual differences by arguing that everyone goes through a unique set of learning experiences which results in situational variables exerting different influences depending on the person's past experiences. Mischel has proposed that past experience affects the individual's information-processing strategies, which govern the way situational variables are perceived, and hence their effects on behaviour (Mischel, 1973, 1977a, 1977b). His theory has become a *cognitive* social learning theory. As a result of past experience, a person approaches situations with a characteristic mode of information processing which will determine the unique meaning of that situation for that person.

Interactionism

In view of the failure of either traits or situations alone to account for behaviour, many personality researchers advocated an approach in which both personality and situational factors are taken into account in the explanation of behaviour (Alker, 1972; Argyle and Little, 1972; Averill, 1973; Bem, 1972; Bowers, 1973; Endler, 1973; Endler and Edwards, 1978; Endler and Magnusson, 1976; Magnusson and Endler, 1977). This approach has been termed 'interactionism'.

Interactionism has been advocated for topics as diverse as child development, altruism, education and stress, in addition to personality (Pervin and Lewis, 1978). The task set by an interactionist approach, as described by Pervin and Lewis (p.20), is one of defining 'the critical variables internal to the organism and those external to it, and then studying the processes through which the effects of one are tied to the operations of the other'. There are various ways of translating this task into an experiment, but in the personality domain this has typically been done by using analysis of variance designs.

Bowers (1973) combined the results of eleven analysis of variance studies of person by situation interactions, and he calculated the mean percentage of variance attributable to person factors (12.71 per cent), to situational factors (10.17 per cent) and to the person by situation interactions (20.77 per cent). The numerical supremacy of the percentage of variance accounted for by interactions over both persons and situations was taken as evidence against either a pure trait position or a pure situationist position, and was considered to be a demonstration of the importance of taking both factors into account in an interactionist model.

However, the validity of using relative contributions to total variance as evidence of the superiority of interactionism over the trait position or situationism has been challenged (e.g. Olweus, 1977). First, at the empirical level the actual size of these percentage variances is essentially arbitrary, since the relative contributions to the total variance from the person factor, the situation factor, and their interaction will vary depending on the range of persons and situations sampled: the narrower the range, the lower the percentage. Averaging percentage variances from several studies sampling widely differing ranges on the person and situation factors further reduces their informativeness. Second, at the theoretical level, percentage variances do not provide an unambiguous test between interactionism, a trait position and situationism. For example, a particular trait theory may place considerable emphasis on situational factors, and hence not be invalidated by the superiority of interactions over main effects.

However, there are other more sophisticated studies to support interactionism (e.g. Endler and Edwards, 1978). For example, anxiety is generally thought of as primarily a function of the person, but the research shows that it does interact with situational variables (Endler, 1975). Anxiety is a multi-dimensional personality trait consisting of several components, such as physical-harm anxiety and ego-threat anxiety. High scorers on one of these components, say physical-harm anxiety, will become anxious only in congruent situations (i.e. where there is a threat of physical harm) and will not be anxious in an ego-threat situation. High scorers on ego-threat anxiety would show the reverse pattern.

Locus of control can be characteristic of the person or of the situation. Studies have generally found a congruence effect such as in the Karabenick and Srull (1978) study described in chapter 2. They obtained a crossover interaction: internals cheated more than externals under skill conditions, whereas externals cheated more than internals under chance conditions (see Table 2.1).

Conformity is usually regarded as determined more by the

situation (e.g. social influence) than by the person, as the classic Asch studies demonstrated (Asch, 1956). However, more recent studies have produced person by situation interactions. For example, Mausner and Graham (1970) compared the conformity of either field-dependent or -independent subjects' judgments of the flicker rate of a flashing light in relation to a confederate's judgments. Prior to the experiment, the subjects had been led to believe that they were either more or less competent than the confederate. It was found that field-independents' judgments were unaffected by this prior experience whereas field-dependents conformed more with confederates whom they had been led to believe were more competent than themselves.

All these studies demonstrate person by situation inter-actions: in each case, groups differentiated in terms of a personality dimension responded in different ways to the situational manipulation. When one variable acts on another in this manner it is sometimes called a 'moderator variable', and the results it produces 'moderator effects' (Bem, 1972; Kogan and Wallach, 1964). Thus, whenever an interaction is obtained one factor may be said to be having a moderating effect on the other, and either a person or a situation factor may be the moderator variable.

An evaluation of interactionism

When interactionism was advocated as an alternative to the pure trait or pure situationist position, it was heralded by some as a new paradigm for personality research, whereas others were critical of its basis in analysis of variance. For example, Golding (1975) demonstrated how analysis of variance can underestimate the importance of person variables when subjects' rank order on the dependent variable remains constant across situations even though the absolute magnitude of their scores changes. He advocated the use of another statistic, the coefficient of generalisability, which is sensitive to rank order effects. Another criticism of person by situation interaction studies using analysis of variance designs concerns the difficulty of specifying independently the person and the situation factors, which is a requirement for analysis of variance (Alker, 1977).

Attempts to develop taxonomies of situations reflect the inextricable links between person and situation variables (Magnusson, 1981). For example, Frederiksen (1972) proposed a taxonomy of situations based on behavioural consistency. He argued that cross-situational consistency of behaviour should not be taken as a sign of an underlying personality dimension, but as evidence that the *situations* are similar.

Price (1974) and Price and Bouffard (1974) demonstrated that there is a consensus as to which behaviours are regarded as appropriate and inappropriate for particular situations. Some situations were found to contain relatively few constraints and hence many different behaviours were regarded as permissible (e.g. in your own room or in the park), whereas other situations contained many constraints (e.g. in church or at a job interview) and only a limited range of behaviour was considered appropriate.

Van Heck (1984) conducted a comprehensive analysis of all the Dutch terms used to describe situations. A total of 248 situation-concepts were rated on 254 objective characteristics of situations, such as the objectively discernible characteristics of the persons in the situations. Factor analysis of these ratings resulted in ten factors identifying situations with common characteristics, and all of these factors were distinguished in terms of the behaviours appropriate for this category of situations. For example, the first factor identified interpersonal conflict situations whereas the second identified working-with-others situations.

Another aspect of the confounding of person and situation factors in real life, if not in the laboratory, is the tendency for people with particular personality characteristics to be drawn to particular kinds of situations. Magaro and Ashbrook (1985) found some support for the hypothesis that people will tend to gravitate to compatible situations. They tested subjects from various social or occupational groups (representing different 'situations') on measures of five personality types: hysteric, compulsive, psychopathic, manic and depressive. It was found that church members were depressives, computer programmers were compulsives, car salespersons were manics, and sorority members hysterics.

Bem and Funder (1978) capitalised on the similarity between person and situation variables by demonstrating the value of describing persons and situations with comparable terminology. They argued that a situation can be described in terms of the characteristics of a person best suited for it. It is then possible to compare a particular person with the ideal for the situation and to determine from the degree of match or mismatch how that particular person will respond to that situation. Bem and Funder give a hypothetical example of a young man considering applying to Stanford University. He might be told that successful Stanford students are intelligent, single-minded and ambitious. He would then compare his own personality with this image and predict how he would react to the Stanford environment which fostered these qualities.

Bem and Funder developed a technique for describing both persons and situations with the same items. It is a form of Q sort (Stephenson, 1953), a method for describing personality in which a set of items is sorted into categories ranging from highly characteristic of the person in question, through irrelevant, to highly uncharacteristic of the person in question. When a Q sort is applied to a *situation*, it results in a template characterising that situation, and a comparison between a particular person and the situation is easily made by assessing the similarity between the template and the person's Q sort on the same items. Bem and Funder describe a number of experiments using this technique. However, the critical test of the approach, namely determining whether prior knowledge of an individual's similarity to the template for a particular situation can reliably predict their subsequent behaviour in that situation, has yet to be conducted.

A major criticism of interactionism is that although person by situation studies demonstrate the importance of inter-actions, they do not explain them. Analysis of variance designs have been accused of being mechanistic (Overton and Reese, 1973). They merely come up with the proportions of variance accounted for by different factors, rather than exploring the processes by which one variable affects another. In order to study how interaction effects actually *operate*, Overton and Reese recommend an organismic approach to these questions, in which all the variables involved are seen as being interdependent: any change in one will affect all the others in the system. More recent interactionist approaches attempt to investigate such dynamic, as opposed to mechanistic, interactions (Endler, 1983).

By far the most telling criticisms of interactional research have come from probably the most experienced workers in this field: Cronbach and Snow (1977; Snow, 1977, 1978). Their work has mainly been confined to the study of aptitude (person) by treatment (situation) interactions in educational research; nevertheless their criticisms at a conceptual level are equally applicable to any field.

Cronbach started out with high hopes that aptitude by treatment interaction research would prove useful for psychology in general, as well as for such fields as education (Cronbach, 1957). However, over the years these hopes have receded (Cronbach, 1975). The main problem is that although it is possible to draw some, albeit rather tentative, generalisations about straight aptitude by treatment inter-actions (e.g. the effects of directed versus independent study on bright and dull students), such interactions are always open to modification by another variable (e.g. sex of subject, which yields an aptitude by treatment by sex of subject interaction). This interaction is open to moderation by yet another variable, say time of day, which yields an aptitude by treatment by sex of subject by time of day interaction, and so on *ad infinitum*. As Cronbach expressed it, 'you enter a hall of mirrors' (Cronbach, 1975, p.119).

Interactions in many areas of research, including person-ality, are notoriously hard to replicate, and this becomes understandable in view of all the different higher-order interactions which could be going on unobserved in different experiments. Many of the variables that enter into these complex higher-order interactions are of a transitory nature and specific to a particular location or stage in a culture's development. By the time their effects have been unravelled, they will have been replaced and become part of history. (Gergen (1973) makes a similar point about social psychology.) Cronbach concludes that psychology cannot be regarded as a cumulative science awaiting the organisation of the amassed facts into a grand, unifying theory. Instead, he recommends that we study local events and be satisfied with being able to achieve only short-term control. Each new generation must solve the problems posed by a fresh set of circumstances.

New approaches to personality and consistency

The evidence against behavioural consistency indicated that personality and situational variables interact together to determine behaviour. However, interactionism was a paradoxical solution to the problem of behavioural consistency, since it emphasised the importance of both personality traits and situational variables. Consequently, rather than doing away with the personality concept, the interactionist approach reaffirmed its key role. Interactionism returned personality to its former central position without resolving the fundamental consistency problem that had previously been its downfall. For this reason, the 1980s has seen another round of the consistency debate in which controversy has centred on new methodologies claiming to have demonstrated behavioural consistency. Three new approaches will be discussed here: the aggregation principle, the idiographic approach, and the levels of abstraction issue.

The aggregation principle

Epstein (1979) drew attention to a major discrepancy between questionnaire measures of personality and behavioural observations. In a questionnaire each item alone is often not a particularly reliable measure, although the test as a whole yields high levels of reliability. In contrast, behavioural indices of personality often are based on observations of single behavioural occurrences. Few investigators would be impressed by a questionnaire consisting of one item, whereas many would be willing to correlate questionnaire scores with single instances of behaviour to test the predictive power of the personality measure. Epstein (1979) presented data from his own studies in which various kinds of personality data (behavioural and test data) were obtained over several occasions. He compared the correlations obtained between a personality variable measured on two occasions with average scores obtained over several occasions. Typically, correlations obtained from single measures were low and similar to the 'personality coefficient' (i.e. around .30), whereas correlations obtained from aggregated data attained impressively high levels, often above .80. Epstein has also applied the aggregation principle to data from earlier studies, such as the classic Hartshorne and May investigations into honesty described earlier, and has obtained strong support for behavioural consistency where previous analyses had indicated none (Epstein and O'Brien, 1985).

The aggregation principle is not a novel solution to the behavioural consistency problem. Both in personality and in social psychology, the advantages of aggregating observations for increasing reliablity have been known for some time (e.g. Jaccard, 1974; McGowan and Gormly, 1976). However, Epstein's work served as a timely reminder. Now the aggregation principle has become almost routinely employed both in studies of personality consistency (e.g. Buss, 1985; Mischel and Peake, 1982) and more generally wherever behavioural consistency is at issue (Rushton, Brainerd and Pressley, 1983).

Nevertheless, aggregation is merely a method of analysis, not a theoretical advance. The investigator still has to appeal to some theoretical rationale to decide which scores to aggregate. Aggregation without due regard to determining the psychological equivalence of the items over which the aggregation is performed will only serve to confuse the picture. When aggregation is employed to enhance reliability in studes of type A consistency, there is no problem of psychological equivalence. The same behaviour is observed in the same situation over several occasions, and the mean correlation between half the occasions is correlated with the mean correlation for the other half of the occasions.

Aggregation becomes problematic in studies of type D consistency where different behaviours performed in different situations are aggregated, and the average correlation between these different behaviours for half of the occasions is correlated with the average correlation for the other half of the occasions. In this case, the psychological equivalence of the different behaviours must be established prior to aggregating them, otherwise low correlations cannot be interpreted unambiguously. It may be that the data show no evidence of type D consistency, but it could also be that the wrong behaviours have been aggregated. For example, if the combined observations of bed neatness and class punctuality do not predict subsequent observations of bed neatness and class punctuality, this may reflect the fact that bed neatness and class punctuality are not measuring the same underlying personality trait.

This point is well illustrated in Mischel and Peake's (1982) investigation. They criticised Epstein (1979) for using the aggregation principle to demonstrate what has already been established, namely the temporal consistency of behaviour. Using the present typology, most of Epstein's (1979) data measured type A and type B consistency. Mischel and Peake's critique arises from their own work (the Carleton study) on the temporal and cross-situational consistency of friendliness and conscientiousness. They conducted a large-scale study into the consistency of these two traits in which a variety of behavioural measures were recorded over several occasions and situations. In their analyses, they incorporated the aggregation principle to good effect in enhancing levels of temporal consistency, but they claimed that aggregation did not enhance levels of cross-situational consistency. They reported an average correlation for the temporal (type A) stability of all the specific behaviours of .29 before aggregation and .65 after aggregation. In contrast, the cross-situational correlations (type D consistency) averaged out at .08 before aggregation and only increased to .20 after aggregation. Consequently, Mischel and Peake concluded that the widely held assumption of cross-situational consistency is unfounded, and our faith in broad traits is misplaced. They proposed that cross-situational consistency is erroneously inferred on the basis of accurate observations of temporal consistency.

Mischel and Peake's conclusions have been challenged by

Jackson and Paunonen (1985). They were critical of Mischel and Peake's choice of behavioural measures of conscientiousness (the only data to be reported in any detail in the 1982 account). These consisted of nineteen behaviours chosen unsystematically and atheoretically, but intended to cover a variety of manifestations of conscientiousness in the context of an undergraduate's typical activities. When Jackson and Paunonen (1985) factor analysed Mischel and Peake's data to discern the actual pattern of co-occurrences between these nineteen behaviours, they found that the measures formed distinct facets of conscientiousness. The items included separate clusters measuring class participation and neatness. In addition, Jackson and Paunonen obtained data on people's beliefs about the co-occurrence of these behaviours, and factor analysis replicated the facets found in actual behaviour. Within these facets, aggregation of data across the items resulted in increases in the consistency coefficients. For example, the behaviours measured by the class participation items yielded a mean correlation of .69 when aggregated, which indicates considerable consistency in this facet of conscientiousness. This correlation is an index of cross-situational or type D consistency, because the items that were aggregated were different behaviours in different situations. However, these items had been identified as psychologically equivalent in the prior factor analyses both of actual co-occurrences of these behaviours and beliefs about co-occurrences. As Mischel and Peake themselves propounded, 'Theory-guided aggregation requires identifying psychological equivalences and the psychological similarity among situations, not just averaging everything that can be summed' (1982, p.378).

The idiographic approach

The idiographic approach to the consistency issue suggests that consistency can be found, but only for certain kinds of people, and certain kinds of behaviours, in certain kinds of situations (Bem, 1983). By emphasising that consistency will be moderated by these three classes of variables, Bem has directly confronted the question of psychological equivalence, and the problem for research to resolve has become which people, which behaviours, and which situations form equivalent kinds.

Bem and Allen (1974) investigated which kind of people may be more likely to demonstrate consistency. They hypothesised that individuals who regard themselves as consistent will actually behave more consistently than those who regard themselves as inconsistent. They studied friendliness and conscientiousness in a group of college students. Ratings on these traits were obtained from the subjects themselves, their parents and their peers, and a small number of behavioural observations were made. The idiographic measure of consistency asked the subjects to rate generally how variable they thought themselves to be on these traits across situations.

When the idiographic measure was not taken into account, the intercorrelations between the various trait measures yielded the typical pattern of low intercorrelations. However, a different pattern of results emerged when the subjects were divided into a high-variability (inconsistent) group and a low-variability (consistent) group. For friendliness, in the low-variability (i.e. consistent) group the intercorrelations among all the different measures were substantially higher than in the high-variability (i.e. inconsistent) group. The same was true for conscientiousness, except for two caveats. First, compared with the analysis for friendliness, a different way of dividing the subjects into high- and low-variability groups was used. Second, the intercorrelations were much higher for the low-variability group when the behavioural index of neatness was removed from the data. Bem and Allen used this finding to illustrate the significance of psychological equivalence for behavioural observations. They, the experimenters, had wrongly assumed that neatness was a manifestation of conscientiousness, which had resulted in the subjects appearing more inconsistent than was actually the case. When the subjects were assessed on measures that they regarded as relevant to the trait, then much higher levels of consistency were obtained.

Bem and Allen's (1974) report has been highly influential, both for the theoretical discussions it contains and for the empirical findings. As a consequence, the importance of self-assessed consistency as a moderator in the search for behavioural consistency has been widely accepted. However, Bem and Allen's work must now be re-evaluated in the light of a recently published failure to replicate their findings. Chaplin and Goldberg (1984) carried out a large-scale replication and extension of the original Bem and Allen study in which they studied eight traits using self-report measures, ratings, and behavioural observations. They used three methods for dividing the subjects into high- and low-variability groups, two that were identical to those used by Bem and Allen and one new measure derived from a questionnaire designed to measure an individual's predisposition to behave consistently. Their findings are easy to summarise: they found no substantial support for a moderating effect of self-assessed consistency on any of the three kinds of data collected for any of the traits using any of the methods of identifying the low- and high-variability groups. As a result of this dramatic failure to replicate, Bem and Allen's empirical findings must be treated sceptically, although the conceptual and theoretical contribution of their paper remains substantial.

An alternative idiographic approach has been proposed by Lamiell (1981, 1982) that is in a sense more truly idiographic than Bem and Allen's. Lamiell noted that although the consistency debate is concerned with whether or not individuals are consistent, data are typically collected for groups of individuals, and hence the original question concerning the degree of behavioural consistency remains unanswered. He proposed that the analyses of patterns of consistency or inconsistency be made at the level of the individual, comparing how a person behaves with the alternatives available to that person, and not comparing the person to how others behave. Having assessed one person's consistency in this way, this measure may then be compared with similarly derived measures for other individuals, thus permitting a combination of the nomothetic and idiographic approach, which Lamiell has named the idiothetic approach. Although well developed theoretically, Lamiell's ideas have yet to make an impact on empirical research.

The levels of abstraction issue

The last approach to the issue of behavioural consistency to be discussed takes the level of analysis of personality into account and argues that consistency can be observed at some levels but not at others. It also suggests that consistency must be viewed as a relative construct. For some purposes correlations of around .30 are ample testimony to the consistency of behaviour, whereas for others correlations of .80 or .90 are required.

The levels of abstraction issue incorporates a characteristic of personality measurement, described by Cronbach and Gleser (1957) as the bandwidth-fidelity trade-off, which refers to the differences in precision of measurement at different levels of abstraction. Where an abstract personality trait is involved, then measurement will be imprecise in the sense that the prediction of specific behaviours will be relatively poor. Nevertheless, predictions can be made for a wide range of behaviour. The measurement of extraversion provides a good example of a broadband trait. In contrast, where a less abstract trait is involved, such as punctuality, then prediction of specific punctual behaviours will be relatively good. However, this fidelity is gained at the expense of bandwidth: knowing a person's punctuality is only predictive of a relatively narrow range of behaviours. Thus predictive measurement involves a compromise or trade-off between the competing forces of broad bandwidth and high fidelity.

Level of abstraction has been operationalised as the breadth of a construct, and defined as the diversity of behaviours to which the construct refers. Reliable differences in the perceived breadth of traits have been established (Hampson, John and Goldberg, 1986). Broad traits such as extraversion and conscientiousness refer to a wide range of different kinds of behaviour (i.e. there are many different ways of being extraverted and conscientious), whereas narrow traits such as talkative and punctual refer to specific subsets of behaviours which only form part of the behavioural possibilities implied by the broader concepts. Consistency is expected to be a function of trait-breadth: measures of narrow traits will produce greater consistency than measures of broad traits. For example, measures of punctuality are expected to be more consistent than measures of conscientiousness because different instances of punctuality have more in common than different instances of conscientiousness. Punctuality refers to good time keeping, whereas conscientiousness refers to a wide variety of efficient behaviours. One punctual act is more likely to predict another punctual act than it is to predict the satisfactory completion of a work assignment. The relation between trait-breadth and consistency is mediated by psychological equivalence. Whereas any behaviours involving good time keeping are clearly psychologically equivalent, the diversity of behaviours that could be called conscientious may share fewer similarities.

The level of consistency regarded as evidence of an underlying personality construct will depend in part on the context in which personality is being studied. For example, in studies of consistency in personality over relatively long periods of time, correlations of .30 and .40 are generally regarded as impressive evidence of the continuity of personality. As we shall see in chapter 9, longitudinal studies of personality over periods as long as forty years have demonstrated correlations of this magnitude between measures of broadband traits (e.g. Block, 1981; Kelly, 1955; Conley, 1984). In contrast, there are contexts (e.g. classroom behaviour) where much narrower constructs are used and hence more precise prediction is expected.

The importance of the levels of abstraction of personality constructs has yet to be systematically investigated. However, existing studies examining the aggregation principle and idiographic factors indicate the significance of the levels issue. Indeed, Mischel and Peake stated that they plan to 'search for consistency at different levels of abstraction-generality in the data, from the most "subordinate" or molecular to increasingly broad "superordinated" molar levels' (1982, p.739).

Conclusions

The personality theorist's perspective, whether it be represented by single- or multi-trait theories, is committed to the view that personality is a major determinant of behaviour. Traits are inferred from observations of behavioural consistency. The concept of consistency is therefore central to the personality theorist's perspective.

This chapter began by proposing a typology of the different forms of behavioural consistency, and then assessed the evidence for each of the four types. The evidence suggests that whereas type A consistency is reasonably well established, types B, C and D are more problematic and certainly not as reliable as personality theorists have tended to assume. We are neither automatons driven by an internal personality programme nor slaves of circumstance. The opposite extreme to a pure trait position is situationism, and that too has proved inadequate. Common sense, backed up by psychological research, tells us that the way we behave is a function of both who we are and the situations in which we either find or place ourselves.

Interactionist models now predominate over either a pure trait or pure situationist position. However, these models do not invalidate the personality concept; on the contrary, they have given it a new lease of life. New solutions to the issue of behavioural consistency are being sought, both theoretical and methodological.

Part Two

Implicit Personality: The Lay Perspective

5 The lay perspective

Some of the most intuitively appealing insights into personality are to be found outside the realm of academic psychology. Novelists and playwrights have for centuries been astute observers of human nature, and we judge their work by their ability to portray convincing characters. Few of us are novelists or playwrights, but we are all amateur psychologists. We think we know a great deal about the workings of our own minds and the minds of others, and probably much of this knowledge is correct in so far as it serves us well in ensuring that we function effectively in our everyday lives. Most people do not need to take a psychology course to know that if information is not rehearsed while in short-term memory it is liable to be lost, or so it would seem from the number of us who mutter telephone numbers to ourselves in the brief interval between finding them in the book and dialling. Nor is it necessary to have studied Eysenck or Cattell to know that someone who has been described to you as 'sociable' is probably a good person to attach yourself to at a party, because they are likely to be talkative and friendly as well.

It is one particular aspect of our amateur psychologising, namely our ability to develop theories about our own personalities and of others, that constitutes the subject matter of this chapter. Psychologists are just as interested in studying what people think about themselves and others as they are in studying how people actually behave. Implicit personality theories may be distinguished from explicit personality theories since the latter attempt to describe what

101

personality actually is rather than people's beliefs about it. Explicit theories are developed by personality psychologists from their observations of people's behaviour. Implicit theories of personality reside in people's minds and are waiting to be discovered. However, the personality theorist cannot avoid also being a naive psychologist. The descriptive and intuitive beliefs which form the lay perspective have also served to shape the sorts of scientific questions posed about personality, and hence have partially determined the answers which have been found. More important, since personality can never be observed directly but can only be inferred, the lay perspective inevitably will influence the form these inferences take, and thus help in the construction of personality theorists' representations of personality.

In the previous chapters on explicit personality theories, a distinction was made between single-trait and multi-trait theories. The same distinction may also be made for implicit theories. People have implicit theories about particular traits, and they have implicit theories about personality as a whole. For both kinds of theorising the elements of lay theories are the words (traits) provided by the language for describing personality, and the theoretical propositions of lay theories refer to the relations believed to hold between behaviours and traits, and among the traits themselves.

Single-trait implicit personality theories

In studies of single-trait implicit personality theories, the personality psychologist investigates people's beliefs with regard to one particular trait. The kinds of questions asked typically include (a) what behaviours, activities and traits do people believe are associated with this trait, (b) how consensual are these beliefs, and (c) to what extent do these lay beliefs overlap with the scientific or explicit theories developed for the same traits? Although not always considered a personality trait, 'intelligence' has been the subject of a number of studies from the lay perspective and so it is discussed here along with the two best-known personality traits, extraversion and neuroticism.

Intelligence

The study of lay beliefs about intelligence is of interest because these appraisals often underlie such important interpersonal decisions as 'Do I want to hire this person?' or even, 'Do I want to marry this person?' Sternberg, Conway, Katron and Bernstein (1981) studied lay conceptions of 'intelligence', 'everday intelligence' and 'academic intelligence' by asking three groups of subjects (students, supermarket shoppers, and people at a railway station) to describe the behaviours associated with these concepts. These three groups differed somewhat in their implicit beliefs. The students' conceptions of intelligence and academic intelligence were similar, and different from their conceptions of everyday intelligence, whereas the supermarket shoppers and the people at the railway station believed intelligence and everyday intelligence to be similar, and different from academic intelligence. The behaviours generated in this study were rated for characteristicness of an 'ideally intelligent person' by a group of lay people (not students) and a group of experts (PhD psychologists studying intelligence). Factor analysis of the lay people's characteristicness ratings yielded three factors labelled practical problem solving, verbal ability and social competence. These factors partially overlapped, but were not identical to, the three factors that emerged from the analysis of the experts' ratings, which were labelled verbal ability, problem-solving ability and practical intelligence.

More recently, Sternberg (1985) has examined lay beliefs concerning the distinctions between intelligence, creativity and wisdom. He found that representatives of different academic disciplines (e.g. art, business, physics) had somewhat differing views about what constituted intelligence, creativity and wisdom in their fields although, overall, intelligence and wisdom were believed to be more similar to each other than either were to creativity. The implicit beliefs about intelligence found in this study were similar to those found previously by Sternberg *et al.* (1981), except for an additional emphasis on goal-oriented behaviour and the public display of intelligence. Neither of these aspects of intelligence are central to standard intelligence tests. People's conceptions of creativity emphasised unconventionality as well as aesthetic taste, imagination, inquisitiveness and intuitiveness. Implicit beliefs about wisdom included the ability to listen to others, to weigh advice, and to deal with different people. In sum, wise people were seen as conservers of worldly experience whereas creative people were seen as defiers of such experience. Many of these beliefs are not reflected in the standard measures of intelligence or creativity derived from explicit theories.

Extraversion and neuroticism

Unlike intelligence, the lay understandings of 'extraversion' and 'neuroticism' are very similar to the scientific conceptions of these traits. Semin, Rosch and Chassein (1981) studied lay beliefs about the introversion–extraversion dimension by having subjects (naive to psychology) write free descriptions of the attitudes of either a 'typical extravert' or a 'typical introvert'. Content analysis of these descriptions produced a set of traits, behaviours and activities which were then rated for their typicality for either an introvert or an extravert by another group of subjects naive to psychology. A common-sense extraversion–introversion (EI) scale was then constructed from the items rated most typical for extraversion (e.g. 'likes talking', 'impulsive', 'can't stand long periods of solitude') and most typical for introversion (e.g. 'thinks often about himself/herself', 'sensitive', 'likes playing chess and reading books'). The common-sense EI scale and the EI scale on the Eysenck Personality Inventory were found to correlate significantly (.51) in a sample of thirty-three undergraduates. Semin *et al.* (1981) concluded that the overlap between lay and scientific conceptions of extraversion was substantial.

The equivalence between personality questionnaires developed painstakingly according to psychometric principles and questionnaires written 'off the cuff' by non-experts was demonstrated in an earlier study by Ashton and Goldberg (1973). They found that the scales produced by psychology students after two hours' work predicted the criterion (peer rankings) as well as, and in some cases better than, scales from two widely used personality tests.

Furnham (1984) conducted an investigation into lay beliefs about neuroticism. Items believed to be associated with neuroticism were obtained from free descriptions written by subjects naive to personality psychology and were then rated by a second group of naive subjects for typicality. Factor analysis of these ratings yielded four factors, labelled communication problems, unstable, obsessional and phobic. Furnham did not go on to construct a common-sense neuroticism (N) scale; however, he did ask his subjects to estimate their scores on the N scale of the Eysenck Personality Questionnaire (EPQ), and these estimates correlated significantly (.40) with their actual N scores on the EPQ, indicating the similarity between the lay and scientific concepts of neuroticism.

Lay beliefs about neuroticism and extraversion appear to be more similar to the explicit conceptualisations than are lay beliefs about intelligence. They also appear to be more consensual, although a systematic comparison between different groups' lay concepts of extraversion and neuroticism has yet to be made. One obvious explanation for the convergence of implicit and explicit theories of extraversion and neuroticism is that lay beliefs are derived from the dissemination of the scientific conceptions of these traits. Intelligence, on the other hand, exists as a lay concept independent of its various scientific conceptualisations.

Multi-trait implicit personality theories

The aim of research into multi-trait implicit personality theories is to discover the widely shared beliefs people hold about personality in its entirety, as opposed to beliefs about particular traits. Studies focus on the personality-descriptive terms found in language since a language is assumed to encode all the important individual differences distinguished by its users (Goldberg, 1982).

The specialised trait language, and the beliefs we hold about which traits are likely to co-occur in the same individual and which are not, are collectively referred to as implicit personality theory (Bruner and Tagiuri, 1954; Schneider, 1973). The term 'implicit' is used to indicate that lay people are not necessarily capable of fully articulating their understanding of personality. Imagine how difficult it would be to answer a question such as 'What are your beliefs about which personality traits co-occur?' On the other hand, if you are confronted with a particular individual and asked to make a personality judgment such as whether the person is kind or cruel on the basis of other information about the individual's personality, you may well be able to do so.

Two approaches to the study of the structure of multi-trait implicit personality theories will be described. First, conceptual studies of how the implicit personality theory of a culture is embodied in the language of personality description will be examined. Second, empirical studies of the implicit personality theories of language users, which examine how personality-descriptive terms are employed in trait descriptions and inferences, will be discussed.

Trait taxonomies

There are approximately 30,000 words (about 5 per cent of the English language) which can be used to describe personality, although most of them (like most words in general) are not commonly used. The purpose of trait taxonomies has been to bring some form of principled organisation to the corpus of traits which reflects users' beliefs about the relations among these words. Not all trait taxonomers would regard themselves as studying implicit personality theory. For example, as we saw in chapter 3, Cattell used trait lists as the starting point for his investigation of explicit personality theory. However, taxonomers share the belief that the language of personality description defines the field of personality for scientific investigation or, as Wiggins expressed it, 'The universe of content of human tendencies is contained within the covers of an unabridged dictionary of the English language' (Wiggins, 1979, p.396). In effect, taxonomers are studying implicit personality theory at its most generalised (as opposed to individualised) level. The language is assumed to embody the normative implicit personality theory of its users. This discussion is limited to examples of non-empirically derived taxonomies in which personality experts study trait lists and arrive at a consensus about the optimal form of organisation. These conceptual taxonomies may be tested empirically later, but their initial derivation is from experts' judgments.

Taxonomers typically view trait terms as referring to the constituents of personality. For example, Norman (1963) stated, 'The construction of more effective theories of the development, structure, and functioning of personality will be facilitated by having available an extensive and well-organized vocabulary by means of which to denote the . . . attributes of persons' (p. 574). Goldberg (1981a) likened trait taxonomies to the periodic table in chemistry in which trait terms correspond to chemical compounds: 'In our most grandiose moments, my colleagues and I see our scientific task as one of discovering the basic elements that underlie the personality compounds found in the various natural languages' (p. 44). Different ways of organising traits serve different purposes, but probably one of the most creative of

Descriptive contrast

		Positive	Thrifty	Generous
Evaluative contrast				
		Negative	Stingy	Extravagant

FIGURE 5.1 *Peabody's evaluation-explicit taxonomic principle applied to generosity*

organising principles was that introduced by Peabody (1967, 1968, 1970). Peabody (1967) observed that the meaning of trait terms is a combination of evaluative and descriptive components. All traits imply either something good or bad to varying degrees (the evaluative component) in addition to referring to a particular aspect of personality (the descriptive component). Consequently, it is possible to refer to an aspect of personality in either an evaluatively positive or an evaluatively negative way. Figure 5.1 sets out the four ways of referring to 'generosity' which represent the possible combinations of the evaluative and descriptive components.

'Thrifty' and 'stingy' are roughly synonymous on the descriptive component (they both describe the opposite of generosity), but contrast on the evaluative component ('thrifty' is positive or good whereas 'stingy' is negative or bad). Correspondingly, 'generous' and 'extravagant' are descriptively similar but contrast evaluatively since generous is more positive than extravagant (which implies an excess of generosity). Peabody's principle can be extended to a larger cluster of traits referring to generosity (and its opposite) at different levels of extremity or intensity. The more extreme the positive words, the more 'good' or desirable they become,

	Desirable	
Thrifty		Generous
Frugal		Charitable
Miserly		Extravagant
Stingy		Wasteful
	Undesirable	

FIGURE 5.2 *The extended evaluation-explicit organisation of generosity*

whereas the more extreme the negative words, the more 'bad' or undesirable they become. Goldberg used the evaluation–explicit principle to construct a trait taxonomy which has by now undergone nine major revisions (Goldberg, 1981a, 1981b, 1982). He used social desirability ratings (Norman, 1967) to determine the evaluative component of the traits and he used the dictionary to assist in the selection of descriptively similar traits. In the ninth version of this taxonomy, 893 traits were grouped into forty-two categories referring to different aspects of personality. An abbreviated and much simplified version of the 'generosity' category is shown in Figure 5.2.

Horizontally, the terms are dichotomised on the descriptive dimension according to whether they refer to generosity or its opposite. The trait terms are arranged vertically along the desirability dimension. 'Generous' and 'thrifty' are typically rated as more desirable than 'charitable' or 'frugal', whereas 'extravagant' and 'miserly' are typically rated as less undesirable than 'wasteful' or 'stingy'. The procedure by which the organisations such as that exemplified in Figure 5.2 were achieved is illustrated in Figure 5.3.

The procedure begins by identifying the root term

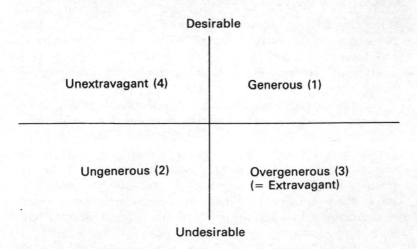

FIGURE 5.3 *The derivation of evaluation-explicit organisation of traits*

referring to the general category in question ('generous') and its negation ('ungenerous'), which is usually both descriptively and evaluatively opposite to the root term. The amplification of the root term is typically undesirable (e.g. overgenerous). The negation of the amplification would be placed in the diagonally opposing quadrant (i.e. 'un-overgenerous') but since such terms do not exist in English, a root term synonymous with the amplification is found (e.g. 'extravagant') and then its negation is used instead (e.g. 'unextravagant').

One of the intriguing revelations of this taxonomic work was the discovery that in only around 50 per cent of the categories could traits be found for all four quadrants. For example, categories referring to skills typically do not have any candidates for the lower right-hand quadrant (e.g. 'musical' cannot be meaningfully amplified – 'overmusical'?).

Peabody and Goldberg have been working on taxonomic principles applicable, in theory, to all personality traits whereas Wiggins has worked on a subset of traits referring to one aspect of personality. He began with around 4,000 words identified by Norman (1967) as relatively familiar and non-obscure terms for describing personality. Wiggins proposed that traits may be subdivided into six different kinds: interpersonal (e.g. aggressive), material (e.g. miserly), temperament (e.g. lively), social roles (e.g. ceremonious), character (e.g. dishonest), and qualities of mind (e.g. analytical). He has focused in particular on interpersonal traits.

Extending Foa and Foa's (1974) work, Wiggins (1979) identified eight features of social meaning derived from all possible combinations of three dichotomous facets of interpersonal behaviour: social events (accept vs. reject), the social object (self vs. other), and the resource (love vs. status). Interpersonal traits may be classified according to their values on these eight features. For example 'extraverted' is characterised by acceptance for both self and other of both love and status, whereas its antonym 'introverted' is characterised by rejection for both self and other of both love and status. 'Dominance' shares all but one of the features of 'extraversion' (acceptance for self of love and status, acceptance for other of love but rejection for other of status). The antonym 'submissiveness' is characterised by acceptance of status for other, rejection of both love and status for self, and rejection of love for other. Using this schema, inter-personal traits may be classified and arranged such that adjacent traits only differ from one another on one feature. If traits can be found for every feature–combination, then the relations between those traits can be represented in the form of a perfect circle (or circumplex; Guttman, 1954). An idealised circumplex for interpersonal traits constructed from the above schema is shown in Figure 5.4.

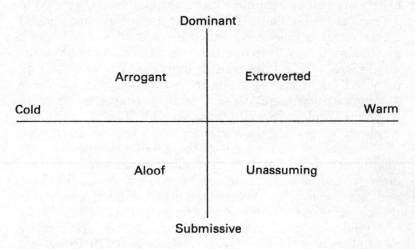

FIGURE 5.4 *An idealised circumplex of interpersonal traits (after Wiggins, 1979)*

The taxonomies described above give some indication of the variety of possible schemes. The availability of alternative structures should not be taken to imply that there is no consensual implicit personality theory embodied in language. Conceptual trait taxonomies provide a starting point for subsequent research, and are therefore constructed with particular substantive research issues in mind. For example, the evaluation–explicit taxonomy provides an alternative rationale to Cattell's personality sphere for the selection of a representative sample of traits (Peabody, 1984). Trait taxonomies provide an initial approach to the study of implicit personality theory, which is then complemented by empirical investigations into implicit personality theories of the kind described in the next section.

Trait description and trait inference

In everyday life we make use of implicit personality theory in two ways. When we compose a spoken or written description of ourselves or others, a part of that description will probably consist of personality traits: we are able to convert our direct experience of a person into a more abstract form expressed in a series of traits. These descriptions are usually meaningful to others, as is demonstrated by the second use of implicit personality theory: inferring the presence of additional traits on the basis of a brief trait description. For example, an employer might sum up his or her impression of an employee as 'conscientious' and write this in a character reference when the employee applied for a new job. The potential new employer, on reading the reference, would form an impression of the applicant on the basis of this limited description, and might well infer that the candidate was also 'reliable', 'orderly' and 'hard-working' rather than 'careless', 'slapdash' and 'lazy'. These two manifestations of implicit personality theory in everyday life have formed the basis of two techniques used in laboratory investigations: personality description and trait inference (Hampson, 1983; Rosenberg and Sedlak, 1972a).

In studies of naturalistic personality descriptions, subjects are free to say or write anything they wish in order to describe the target's personality. The investigator is particularly interested in the use of trait words and in whether certain groups of traits repeatedly co-occur in different subjects' descriptions. For example, in Rosenberg and Sedlak's study of college students' personality descriptions, 'intelligent', 'friendly', 'self-centred', 'ambitious' and 'lazy' were frequently used, but they were not all used to describe the same person. If a person had been described as 'intelligent', then 'friendly' would be likely to also occur in the description, whereas 'self-centred' would not (Rosenberg and Sedlak, 1972b). The advantage of naturalistic personality descriptions is that they provide a close approximation to real life and the experimenter's influence is minimal because the choice of traits is left to the subject. For these reasons, they are particularly popular in the study of children's implicit personality theories (e.g. Livesley and Bromley, 1973), where the experimenter is interested in the extent of the child's trait vocabulary as well as in the patterns of trait co-occurrence. The major disadvantage of naturalistic descriptions is the problem posed by the scoring of the protocols. Individual researchers have tended to develop their own scoring schemes, which often makes it difficult to compare the results of different studies.

The way subjects describe other people's personalities can also be studied, rather more artificially, by the experimenter supplying a range of personality traits from which the subject selects those that best fit the person being described. This is known as the trait sorting method, and its main advantage is that it presents fewer scoring problems in comparison with free descriptions. On the other hand, the results are circumscribed by the experimenter's choice of traits. A trait-sorting task was used by Rosenberg, Nelson and Vivekananthan (1968). They asked subjects to think of up to ten people they knew who were as different from one another as possible, and then to distribute sixty-four personality traits (supplied by the experimenter) amongst those ten people. An alternative to trait sorting is trait rating. Here, each trait on a list provided by the experimenter is assessed in terms of how well it characterises the person in question (e.g. Passini and Norman, 1966).

Naturalistic descriptions, trait sortings and trait ratings all provide the experimenter with information about how subjects use traits to describe other people. The second aspect of implicit personality theory, its use in inferring the presence of additional traits on the basis of limited information, is studied under even more artificial conditions. Typically, subjects are presented with brief trait descriptions of hypothetical individuals (these are sometimes as brief as one word) and asked to decide whether or not such a person would possess a series of other traits listed by the experimenter. An example of an early study which used the trait inference technique is Hays's (1958) investigation into the co-occurrence likelihoods of all the possible pairs of the following traits: 'warm', 'cold', 'dominant', 'submissive', 'intelligent', 'stupid', 'generous' and 'stingy'.

Investigations into implicit personality theory, whatever method they use, are rather like shining a torch on a very dark night. The potential number of judgments we are capable of making about patterns of trait co-occurrence is enormous. No wonder the bulk of these judgments is never made explicit. The aim of research is to illuminate a carefully selected proportion of these judgments with the hope of discovering the principles by which these beliefs are organised.

The structural representation of implicit personality theory

From all the methods described above, scores may be derived which indicate the believed co-occurrence likelihood of trait pairs. Having obtained estimates of the co-occurrence likelihood of all the possible trait pairs studied in a particular investigation, the researcher is faced with a similar problem to that confronted by the multi-trait personality theorists described in chapter 3: how to discover the organisational principles underlying this mass of data. The problem requires some form of multivariate analysis, and the popular techniques are factor analysis, cluster analysis and multi-dimensional scaling. All these techniques are designed to represent the interrelations within a set of items (in this case personality traits) in such a way as to reveal their underlying dimensions (Powell and Juhnke, 1983).

Similar kinds of investigations into people's beliefs about non-personality concepts have established three dimensions of word meaning: evaluation, potency and activity (Osgood, 1962). Hence these three dimensions appeared to be likely candidates for the dimensions underlying implicit personality theory. However, Osgood and Ware's investigation of personality concepts yielded a large evaluation factor and little else (Osgood, 1962). In a recent review, Brown (1986) concluded that evaluation is the predominant organisational principle underlying implicit personality theory. Is it the case that our beliefs about people are built around evaluation alone? We have already seen how Peabody (1967) was able to develop an organisational principle for trait taxonomies based on distinctions in terms of the descriptive component of personality terms, which suggests that it is useful to think of personality language as indicating more than whether a person is 'good' or 'bad'.

Rosenberg and his colleagues have worked extensively on the adequacy of Osgood's three dimensions for the structural representation of implicit personality theory (Rosenberg and Sedlak, 1972a). They have found considerable support for the Osgood structure. Traits such as 'popular' and 'sociable' are contrasted with 'unhappy' and 'vain' on the evaluative

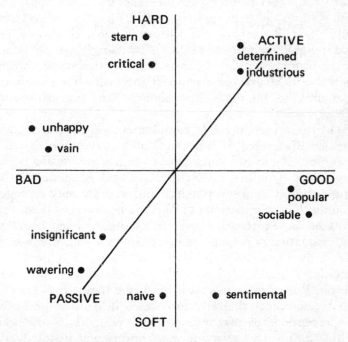

FIGURE 5.5 *The two-dimensional configuration of twelve traits showing the position of the three axes good-bad, active-passive and hard-soft (freely adapted from Rosenberg et al., 1968)*

dimension (good–bad), 'industrious' and 'determined' contrast with 'wavering' and 'insignificant' on the activity dimension (active–passive), and 'stern' and 'critical' contrast with 'sentimental' and 'naive' on the potency dimension (hard–soft). This organisation is shown in Figure 5.5. These studies usually explore the structure of between sixty and eighty traits, not merely twelve as shown in the figure for the sake of clarity.

Where more than three dimensions are found to underlie the data, these additional factors may be variants of one of the Osgood factors. For example, Rosenberg argues that the evaluative dimension often breaks down into separate dimensions for social good–bad and intellectual good–bad. The three Osgood factors emerge most clearly in studies where the experimenter provides the traits. In both trait-sorting studies (e.g. Rosenberg *et al.* 1968) and trait inference studies (e.g. Rosenberg and Olshan, 1970), all three factors have reliably been found. Not surprisingly, there is least consensus among naturalistic personality-description studies, where the unstructured nature of the task allows individual differences to be more prominent (Kim and Rosenberg, 1980).

When less than the full complement of Osgood's dimensions are discovered, it is potency and activity which are the casualties. These two dimensions often combine for personality terms (Goldberg, 1981b). Kim and Rosenberg (1980) argued that evaluation, potency and activity only emerge as the underlying dimensions of implicit personality theory as a result of the aggregation over individuals. They concluded that evaluation is present in everyone's implicit theories, but that individuals differ in their emphasis on potency and activity.

From Rosenberg's work we might be tempted to conclude that evaluation is the only important dimension underlying lay perceptions of personality. However, this conclusion is neither intuitively satisfying nor empirically justified. Why would the English language contain thousands of different ways of distinguishing between 'good' and 'bad' people? More important, how can the evaluation model account for the long-established body of work on the language of personality description which suggests that there may be as many as five distinct content areas covered by the descriptive components of trait words? It is to this work that we shall now turn.

One of the techniques for studying implicit personality theory referred to above is the use of trait ratings. The experimenter supplies the list of traits on which the rater judges the target's personality. Where the rater is well acquainted with the target, such ratings are regarded as measures of the target's personality (e.g. Cattell's L data). Where the rater and target are strangers, these ratings cannot reflect the target's personality, but presumably reflect the rater's implicit personality theory (Passini and Norman, 1966). However, the intriguing finding has emerged that the same five dimensions are found to underlie trait ratings irrespective of the degree of acquaintance between the rater and the ratee (Norman, 1963; Passini and Norman, 1966; Tupes and Christal, 1961).

In chapter 3, trait rating studies of explicit personality were reviewed. All these studies used a similar procedure. The subjects were divided into small groups of six to sixteen people, and each subject was asked to judge all the other members of the group on each of twenty to thirty-five bipolar personality scales. These scales were derived from Cattell's work and were intended to provide a comprehensive yet economical coverage of the personality sphere. Each subject's score on each scale was derived by combining the judgments made by the other members of the group. Tupes and Christal (1961) studied eight samples of servicemen; Norman (1963) studied four samples of college students. Across these samples, length of acquaintance between raters and ratees ranged from three days to three years. However, similar factor structures were found. The five broad personality factors and some high-loading scales were shown in Table 3.2 (page 70). The Big Five factors are surgency or extraversion, agreeableness, conscientiousness, emotional stability and culture.

In addition to these studies, where the raters had at least some prior acquaintance with the ratees, there are two trait-rating studies in which the raters had minimal or zero knowledge of the ratees. Passini and Norman (1966) used a sample of college students who were unacquainted prior to the study and whose 'acquaintance' was limited to fifteen minutes together, during which time they were not allowed to speak to one another. Norman and Goldberg (1966) used a simulation technique in which 'raters' had absolutely no contact at all with 'ratees'. Despite the raters' ignorance of the ratees, the same five-factor solutions emerged from the trait ratings as had been found in the other studies.

The correspondence between the factor structures, irrespective of how well the raters knew the ratees, raises the question of what, exactly, personality ratings are measuring. Is it the personality of the ratees or the implicit personality theories of the raters that is reflected in the five-factor structure underlying trait ratings? We shall postpone a detailed consideration of this question for the next chapter. For the present, it should be noted that despite the overall similarity of the findings across various samples, there were some small differences associated with the relationship between rater and ratee. For example, Norman (1963) reported that the factor structure obtained from his sample that had known each other longest was the cleanest in the sense of being the most orthogonal. Norman and Goldberg (1966) and Passini and Norman (1969) proposed various ways in which the two sources of influence on ratings (raters vs. ratees) could be distinguished.

The trait-rating studies have demonstrated that there is more to implicit personality theory than evaluation alone. Trait language not only evaluates whether a person is 'good' or 'bad' but it also describes in what ways the person is 'good' or 'bad'. Five content areas of personality have been identified: surgency or extraversion, agreeableness, conscientiousness, emotional stability and culture. The disparity between Rosenberg's simple evaluation model and the more complex five-dimensional model favoured by Norman and his colleagues is comparable to the dispute between Eysenck and Cattell over the structure of explicit personality theories. In implicit personality theory, as with explicit personality theory, the number and nature of the underlying dimensions is dependent upon the level of detail favoured by the theorist. To return to the metaphor used in chapter 3, when the microscope is low-powered, then evaluation stands out as the most salient dimension. However, when the power is turned up, then a more complex structure is revealed. Neither view is more correct; it all depends on the purpose for which implicit personality theory is being investigated. In most cases, however, the five-factor structure is likely to be more useful than the simple evaluation model. One purpose of investigating the organisation of implicit personality theory is to understand the way people form impressions of personality, which is the subject of the next section.

Using implicit personality theory to form impressions

The Asch and Wishner studies of central traits

The question that has puzzled psychologists, from Asch (1946) to the present day (e.g. Brown, 1986), is how we combine the pieces of information contained in a brief description of a person to produce an overall impression, and then use the resulting impression to make additional inferences about that person.

Consider the task which Asch (1946) set his subjects. Two groups heard a brief description of an imaginary person who was either:

(a) intelligent, skilful, industrious, *warm*, determined, practical, cautious; or
(b) intelligent, skillful, industrious, *cold*, determined, practical, cautious.

The subjects were then required to write down their impressions, in the form of a short essay, of the person they had just heard described. In addition, they also completed a checklist task in which they had to select the one trait from each of eighteen pairs of opposites (e.g. generous–ungenerous, strong–weak) which was the more compatible with the impression they had formed.

From their essays and their choices on the checklist, it was clear that groups A and B had formed strikingly different impressions, even though there was only a difference of one word between the two descriptions. Group A, whose description contained 'warm', formed far more positive impressions than Group B, whose description contained 'cold'. Asch (1946, p. 263) gave examples of these contrasting pictures as revealed in the essays:

> (a) (warm): 'A person who believes certain things to be right, wants others to see his point, would be sincere in an argument and would like to see his point won.'
> (b) (cold): 'A rather snobbish person who feels that his success and intelligence set him apart from the run-of-the-mill individual. Calculating and unsympathetic.'

The same picture emerged from the checklist choices: Group A selected the positive traits such as 'generous', 'good-natured' and 'strong' more frequently than did Group B.

Asch's task presented no difficulty for his subjects. The problem for Asch, and for subsequent psychologists, was to explain how the subjects had arrived so easily at uniform impressions on the basis of discrete bits of information and why it was that a difference of just one of these bits of information had such an effect.

Asch proposed two contrasting models of impression formation: the 'elementaristic' model and a gestalt view. In the elementaristic model, the uniform impression is seen as the result of the summation of all the separate bits of information. According to this model, the impressions formed by groups A and B were the result of adding intelligent + skilful + industrious + warm or cold + determined + practical + cautious. Asch rejected the elementaristic model since it failed to explain the disproportionate effect of changing the single element 'warm' or 'cold'. The gestalt model was more promising: the separate pieces of information were seen as being capable of influencing one another in an interactive rather than an additive way. Thus the inclusion of 'warm' or 'cold' in the list influenced each of the other traits, which explains how they had a disproportionate effect. The interactive effects of one element upon another were seen as changing the nature of those elements, and hence resulting in an impression, or gestalt, which was greater than the simple sum of the parts.

To test the gestalt model, Asch (1946) carried out several experiments in which the content of the description was varied. He discovered that not all traits were capable of exerting as profound an influence on the final impression as 'warm' and 'cold' had done. For example, when identical descriptions to those in the 'warm' or 'cold' experiment were used with the replacement of 'warm' or 'cold' by 'polite' or 'blunt', there was no marked difference between the impressions formed by groups A and B. Asch concluded that some traits were more influential or 'central', while others were more 'peripheral'. Central traits changed the gestalt more dramatically than peripheral ones by exerting a stronger influence on each of the other elements.

In a re-analysis of some of Asch's experiments, Wishner (1960) came up with a different explanation for the central versus peripheral trait effects. Wishner's first step was to discover people's beliefs about the co-occurrence likelihoods of the traits that Asch had used in his descriptions and in his checklists. In effect, he charted the structure of the particular subsection of implicit personality theory which Asch had studied. This was done by selecting fifty-three of Asch's traits and asking college students to rate their instructors on these traits. From these ratings, he was able to estimate the co-occurrence likelihood of each trait combination and express it in the form of a correlation. A high positive correlation indicates co-occurrence is likely; a high negative correlation indicates co-occurrence is very unlikely; correlations around zero indicate no consensus on co-occurrence likelihood. Some of the correlations between the traits in Asch's descriptions and those in the checklist are shown in Table 5.1.

Wishner argued that it should be possible to predict which traits would have a central effect in a description from prior knowledge of their correlations with the traits in the checklist. Where a checklist contains a large proportion of traits with strong correlations with only one of the traits in the description, then this trait will behave like a central trait. Take Asch's 'warm' or 'cold' experiment. The traits forming the rows of Table 5.1 are each one member of the pairs in Asch's checklist. They are shown in order of magnitude of

Table 5.1 Estimates of the correlations among some of the
traits used by Asch (1946) (from Wishner, 1960, p. 101)

| | Description Traits | | | | | | |
Check-list traits	Warm	Unintelligent	Clumsy	Indus-trious	Determined	Practical	Cautious
Ungenerous	−33	04	−07	−12	−10	−09	−15
Irritable	−57	01	18	−18	−20	−24	07
Humorous	24	−16	−12	−04	38	01	−24
Sociable	70	00	−07	26	30	16	−11
Popular	50	−33	−26	24	35	35	01
Self-centred	−30	14	−03	−13	−01	−20	−08
Unhappy	−54	21	07	−36	−35	−22	08
Humane	34	−06	00	28	−12	27	29
Imaginative	48	−17	−17	24	43	18	−31
Restrained	−13	15	03	04	−14	08	35
Unattractive	−10	36	−04	−23	−08	−05	−15
Unreliable	−28	31	34	−41	−15	−44	−15
Strong	07	−28	−10	14	39	31	01
Dishonest	−43	28	06	−30	−14	−28	−08
Important	17	−50	−28	30	35	23	−18
Serious	02	−09	−34	27	18	25	24
Persistent	18	−30	−28	20	60	12	16

their difference in choice by Asch's 'warm' and 'cold' groups
(e.g. 'ungenerous' was chosen by 9 per cent of the 'warm'
group and 92 per cent of the 'cold' group, 'sociable' was
chosen by 91 per cent of the 'warm' group and 38 per cent
of the 'cold' group). It will be seen that the correlations in
the 'warm' column for the first nine traits include the largest
in the whole table. In other words, 'warm' correlated more
strongly with those traits in the checklist that showed the
greatest difference between the 'warm' and 'cold' groups.

Since this was something of an *ad hoc* analysis, Wishner
went on to test his hypothesis using a new list of traits in the
description and a new checklist. The traits in the description,

which were uncorrelated with one another, were 'scrupulous', 'cautious', 'good-looking', 'humane' and 'ruthless', 'flexible', 'serious' and 'fearless', with one group hearing 'humane' and the other hearing 'ruthless'. The checklist contained six traits highly correlated with 'humane' and 'ruthless' and six with low correlations with these traits. The checklist traits were uncorrelated with the other traits in the description. The correlations had been estimated from an earlier rating study. Wishner repeated the Asch experiment using these traits. He predicted, and found, that the difference between the 'humane' and 'ruthless' groups in their checklist choices was largest on those checklist traits which had correlations with 'humane' and 'ruthless'.

Wishner's experiments demonstrated that so-called central effects depend on the relations between the traits in the description and the traits in the checklist. Where a large proportion of the checklist consists of traits correlating highly with one of the traits in the description, this trait will operate as a central trait. The more recent work on the structural representation of implicit personality theory reviewed in the previous section allows us to follow Wishner's line of reasoning a little further. We have seen how the beliefs about trait co-occurrence (expressed as correlations in Wishner's study) may be represented in terms of five dimensions. The studies of implicit personality theory indicate that the most likely candidates for central traits will be those most strongly related to one of the five dimensions, since it is these traits which will have high correlations with other traits associated with the same dimension and low correlations with traits associated with the other dimensions. Thus, by setting a trait representing one dimension in a context of traits representing other dimensions in the description, and by having a substantial number of checklist traits representing the central trait's dimension, central trait effects will be found.

Although Wishner advanced our understanding of what is meant by a central trait, he did not attempt to develop Asch's gestalt model of trait combination. His continued support for Asch's view that people form unified impressions out of a series of elements is rather surprising given that his experiments had shown how the effects of different descriptions were due to the relations between only one of the elements in the descriptions and the checklist traits. Since in Wishner's experiments central effects were explained without proposing any form of combination between the elements in the description, a more parsimonious conclusion is that subjects did not integrate the elements in the description. Instead, they made their checklist choices on the basis of the trait in the description which was most relevant.

Wishner's (1960) study explained Asch's findings with regard to the checklist trait choices, but did not address the free description data. The essays Asch's subjects wrote suggested that they had formed unified impressions of the persons described with the stimulus traits. This evidence of unity contradicts the trait-choice data which implied the absence of an integrated impression. Recently, Asch has returned to the question of unity in impression formation (Asch and Zukier, 1984). Subjects were given brief person descriptions consisting of pairs of discordant traits (e.g. sociable–lonely, brilliant–foolish) and were asked to describe these people and how their qualities related. The descriptions were then examined for modes of resolution between the discordant properties. Not surprisingly, in view of the explicit instructions, subjects were able to resolve most of the discrepancies using various strategies. For example, introducing the distinction between inner and outer qualities resolved 'sociable–lonely': 'Someone appears very sociable but inwardly he is lonely'. The brilliant–foolish combination is resolved with the segregation strategy: 'A person may be brilliant intellectually but foolish in practical, common-sense matters'. Asch and Zukier (1984) conclude that unified impressions are not necessarily simplistic, but are formed through complex beliefs about the causal and inferential relations between traits. Their study confirms our intuitions that, when asked, we can resolve contradictory qualities within a single impression. However, it does not establish that we routinely engage in a unification process.

Quantitative models of trait integration

The use of implicit personality theory to make trait

inferences is studied by providing subjects with a description of an imaginary person (the target) in terms of a set of traits (which we will refer to as given traits) and asking for judgments about the likelihood that other traits (which we will refer to as probe traits) would also characterise that imaginary person. For example, the target might be described by the given trait 'bold' and subjects might be asked to judge whether such a person would be likely to possess a series of probe traits, such as 'fearless', 'timid', etc.

The first study to investigate quantitatively how traits in a given description are combined to produce a unified impression which is then used as the basis for subsequent inferences about probe traits was performed by Bruner, Shapiro and Tagiuri (1958). They developed a technique which has been adopted in most subsequent studies in this area. It involved obtaining ratings on the probe traits in relation to the givens presented singly as well as in combination. It was then possible to see how responses on the same probe trait differed depending on the number and the nature of the given traits. Bruner *et al.* used four traits in all: 'considerate', 'independent', 'intelligent' and 'inconsiderate'. These were presented singly, in twos, and in threes (all four were not presented in combination because of the incompatibility of 'considerate' and 'inconsiderate').

Each given trait combination was rated by a separate group of subjects. Thus, in a single given trait group, the subject might be asked, for example, to rate the likelihood that an 'intelligent person' (given trait) would also be 'aggressive' (probe trait). A subject in a three given trait group might be asked to rate the likelihood that a person who is 'considerate', 'independent' and 'intelligent' would also be 'aggressive'.

For the purpose of analysis, the ratings were simplified to a yes or no (+ or −) decision. The single given trait decisions were then compared with the multi-trait decisions on the same probes. For example, the single given trait 'intelligent' was regarded by most subjects as likely to co-occur with 'aggressive':

intelligent → aggressive? = +

and the single given trait 'inconsiderate' was also regarded as co-occurring with 'aggressive':

inconsiderate → aggressive? = +

When 'intelligent' and 'inconsiderate' were presented together as two given traits then an 'intelligent and inconsiderate' person was also seen as being 'aggressive':

intelligent + inconsiderate → aggressive? = +

The addition of another given trait with the same relation to 'aggressive' (e.g. 'independent') in the three given traits condition resulted in a positive decision.

Where the single inferences led to different decisions, then decisions in the two given conditions were roughly half positive and half negative. Where there were three given traits, with two having single inferences to the probe of the same sign and one different, the combined judgments tended to be the same as the two decisions of like sign.

More recent quantitative studies of impression formation by Anderson (1974, 1978) and Warr (1974) are designed along the same principles as the Bruner *et al.* study. Although both Asch and Wishner favoured a gestalt model of trait combination, Anderson has followed the lead set by Bruner *et al.*, and worked on elementaristic models. Anderson's models have been developed to account for how information is combined (integrated) in a variety of social decisions, in addition to trait inferences. For example, in the attribution of blame, the amount of blame attributed to a person involved in an unpleasant event is given by the following equation (Anderson, 1976):

Blame = Intent + Consequence − Extenuation
− Personal Goodness.

Although in the above equation the model is an additive one, much of Anderson's work has been concerned with demonstrating where an averaging rather than an additive model provides a better account of how information is integrated (e.g. Anderson, 1962, 1965, 1974, 1978). The critical experiment to distinguish between the averaging and additive models of impression formation involves four given traits, two of which produce extreme ratings on the probe trait when represented as a pair, and two of which produce less extreme ratings on the same probe when presented as a pair. For example, the given traits 'sneaky and deceptive' might produce a more extreme rating on the probe 'dishonest' than the given traits 'cowardly and boastful'. When all four traits are presented in combination, an additive model predicts a more extreme rating on the probe trait than the more extreme of the two paired conditions. Thus a 'sneaky, deceptive, cowardly and boastful' person would be rated as more dishonest than a 'sneaky and deceptive' person. An averaging model predicts that the four given traits condition will result in a less extreme rating than the more extreme of the two paired conditions. Thus a 'sneaky, deceptive, cowardly and boastful' person would not be rated as extremely on the probe 'dishonest' as a 'sneaky and deceptive' person would be, but would be rated as being more dishonest than a 'cowardly and boastful' person. This example is summarised in Table 5.2 with imaginary ratings to illustrate how the effects of the averaging model are quantifiable. Generally, Anderson has found support for an averaging model rather than an additive model in studies of impression formation.

Table 5.2 An illustration of averaging effects in trait combination

Given traits	Ratings on the probe trait 'dishonest' ranging from −5 (definitely not) to +5 (definitely)
Sneaky and deceptive	+4
Cowardly and boastful	+2
Sneaky, deceptive, cowardly and boastful	+3

Warr and his colleagues have also studied trait combination in impression formation. In particular, they have been concerned with the effect on the probe trait ratings of varying the relation between the givens and the probes, and they have found certain conditions in which the averaging model does not apply. Warr (1974) used a Bruner *et al.* design in which the given traits were presented either singly or in pairs, in relation to the same probes. He found that the effects of increasing the given information from one to two traits sometimes led subjects to make more extreme ratings on the probe traits than they had to either of the two givens presented singly, and sometimes resulted in less extreme ratings than the more extreme of the two givens presented singly. He called these, respectively, push-over and pull-back effects.

Push-overs and pull-backs were found to occur according to the magnitude of the discrepancy between the probe trait ratings for the givens presented singly. Where the discrepancy was large (i.e. one of the givens produced a very extreme rating on the probe trait and the other given produced a more neutral rating), then pull-backs would occur. For example, the given traits 'attractive' and 'orderly' might result in a pull-back when presented together in relation to the probe 'likeable' because 'attractive' would be rated as extremely likely to co-occur with 'likeable', whereas 'orderly' would be much less likely to do so. Pull-backs support Anderson's averaging model: the addition of the second, less strongly related, element results in a less extreme combined inference.

Push-overs occurred where there was only a small discrepancy between the probe trait ratings when the givens were presented singly. For example, the givens 'attractive' and 'humorous' would probably result in similarly extreme ratings on the probe 'likeable' and, when presented together, the combined inference would be even more extreme. Push-over effects are not predicted by Anderson's averaging model.

When the discrepancy between the two givens was large and they were evaluatively dissimilar, then a phenomenon called discounting occurred. Consider the given trait combination 'hostile and sociable' in relation to the probe trait 'rude'. When presented singly, the given trait 'hostile' would probably yield a far more extreme rating in relation to 'rude' than the given trait 'sociable'. Subjects would be more confident to say that 'hostile' and 'rude' co-occur than to say that 'sociable' and 'rude' do not co-occur. Given such a large discrepancy between the two single given inferences, instead of 'sociable' producing pull-back effects in the combined condition, it may actually be ignored. If this occurs, the rating for the probe trait 'rude' will be the same in the combined condition as it is when 'hostile' is presented as a single given. This example is summarised in quantitative terms in Table 5.3.

Table 5.3 An illustration of discounting effects in trait combination

Given trait or traits	Ratings on the probe trait 'rude' ranging from −5 (definitely not) to +5 (definitely)
Hostile	+5
Sociable	−2
Hostile and sociable	+5

It seems that when trait combinations involve a large discrepancy, credulity is stretched to breaking point and the less likely trait is discounted. Discounting represents a second instance where the averaging model does not apply, and it has been observed not only by Warr (1974), but also in other studies (e.g. Wyer, 1970).

The quantitative studies of impression formation, illustrated here by the work of Bruner *et al.*, Anderson, and Warr, have investigated how the elements of given information are combined by looking at the output derived from the combined versus single given information. The effects of varying the input (given traits) are observed on the output (probe trait ratings) and intervening combinatorial principles are inferred. Although Anderson described his averaging and additive models of trait combination as 'cognitive algebra' (Anderson, 1974), he did not attempt to describe the cognitions involved in trait integration. He developed mathematical models capable of predicting the size of probe trait ratings in relation to particular givens, but these models do not refer to the mental operations required to achieve the observed behaviours.

Cognitive models of trait integration and inference

The Bruner *et al.* design readily lends itself to translation into cognitive processing terminology. Harris and Hampson (1980) tested various competing models of the processes involved in trait integration. The basic model was derived from a network account of semantic memory (Collins and Loftus, 1975). It was proposed that traits form nodes in a mental network connected by paths whose length is an inverse function of the correlation (positive or negative) between the traits: correlations near zero correspond to long paths, whilst large (positive or negative) correlations correspond to short paths. The sign of the correlation between two traits was assumed to be an inherent property of the path connecting them. For example, 'warm' and 'sociable', which are highly positively related, would be connected by a shorter path than 'warm' and 'tidy', which are less strongly related. 'Warm' and 'rude' would also be connected by a short path, since they are highly negatively related.

When a person is asked to decide whether someone of a given trait description would be likely to also possess the probe trait, activation spreads out in every direction from the given trait node until the probe trait node is reached. The subject's decision is based on the speed with which the path is completed and the sign of the path. It was postulated that the longer the path (i.e. the weaker the correlation between the traits) the less confident the decision. Either confidence ratings or reaction times can be used to assess the subject's confidence that a person of the given trait description also possesses the probe trait. The model makes two predictions about reaction times: first, that decision times will follow the same pattern as probe trait ratings, the more confident the rating the faster the reaction; second, the direction of the response (yes or no) will make no difference to its speed. Both these predictions were supported in an experiment in which only single givens were used.

Harris and Hampson (1980) went on to test between integrative and non-integrative models of the inference process required to decide about a probe trait on the basis of two given traits. They used the Bruner *et al.* design,

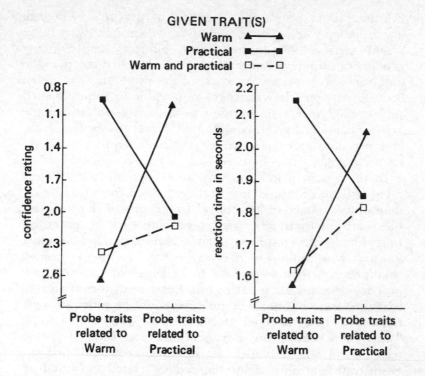

FIGURE 5.6a *Mean confidence ratings for probe traits related to 'warm' and probe traits related to 'practical' in each of the given trait conditions (adapted from Harris and Hampson, 1980)*

FIGURE 5.6b *Mean reaction times for probe traits related to 'warm' and probe traits related to 'practical' in each of the given trait conditions (adapted from Harris and Hampson, 1980)*

comparing responses to single versus combined given traits on the same probes. Integrative models predict that decisions based on two given traits will be at least as slow as the slower of the two decisions made separately when the two givens are presented singly. A non-integrative model predicts that decisions will be as fast in the combined condition as the faster of the two single given condition decisions.

The given traits were 'warm', 'practical' and 'warm and practical'. Half the twelve probe traits were strongly related to 'warm' and half were strongly related to 'practical'. The task was to judge whether a person of the given trait description would possess the probe traits. Subjects either made confidence ratings or timed decisions, and all subjects made judgments with respect to each of the three kinds of given trait descriptions. It was therefore possible to compare each subject's judgments on the same probes across the two single and the combined given conditions. The results for the rating and reaction time data were strikingly similar, and are shown graphically in Figures 5.6a and 5.6b.

In the 'warm' condition, probes related to 'warm' were rated with more confidence and responded to more quickly than probes related to 'practical'. In the 'practical' condition, the reverse pattern emerged: probes related to 'practical' were rated with more confidence and responded to more quickly than probes related to 'warm'. In the combined condition, where subjects had to judge about a 'warm and practical' person, their ratings and reaction times indicated that they were basing their judgments on the more strongly related of the two given traits. For the probes related to 'warm' they were as confident and fast when the given traits were 'warm and practical' as they had been with just the given trait 'warm', and for the probes related to 'practical' they were as confident and fast when the given traits were 'warm and practical' as they had been with only the single given trait 'practical'. These findings showed that subjects were just as confident in the combined condition as they were in the more confident of the two single given conditions. Thus a non-integrative model of trait inference received strong support, whereas models assuming trait integration were rejected.

These findings accord nicely with the earlier studies of the central-trait effect (Wishner, 1960). Although Wishner used a much larger list of given traits, he observed that central-trait effects occurred for the given trait, which, unlike any of the other given traits, correlated highly with the checklist (probe) traits. In the Harris and Hampson (1980) study, the same central-trait effect was observed. In addition, by testing the various cognitive processing models, it was possible to demonstrate that integration of the given traits was not necessary in order to make the probe trait decisions.

The investigation of trait integration and trait inference was inspired originally by Asch's elegant studies. It is a little ironic that, as this particular line of research has evolved under the successive influences of the dominant models in psychology (gestalt, behaviourist, and cognitive), the plausibility of Asch's original gestalt view of impression formation has been steadily eroded. However, it is a tribute to Asch's genius that the topic of impression formation has returned to the centre stage in social psychology with the advent of the application of cognitive approaches to social questions. In the relatively new discipline now called social cognition the representation and processing of information about persons forms a core topic (Wyer and Srull, 1984). The questions asked and problems raised have expanded the horizons of impression formation research beyond the present discussion of central traits and related issues, and beyond the scope of this book.

Conclusions

The psychological investigation of the lay perspective on personality has revealed the theories about personality which people use for descriptive and inference purposes. Implicit personality theories, along with other kinds of social beliefs such as stereotypes, allow us to categorise people and their behaviour. The advantages of the categorising ability inherent in implicit personality theories are the same for the lay person as the advantages derived from explicit personality theories: both implicit and explicit theories facilitate the discrimination between individuals and the prediction of subsequent behaviour. The aim of the present chapter has been to show that we have now reached a considerable degree of understanding of the lay perspective with respect to the contents of implicit personality theories and the manner in which they are used. The next chapter is concerned with the relation between the lay perspective and reality: to what extent are implicit beliefs about personality accurate reflections of reality?

6 Implicit versus explicit personality theories

In the previous chapter we examined various approaches to the study of implicit personality theories – the beliefs people hold about personality. In earlier chapters we examined several explicit personality theories – psychologists' attempts to infer the structure of personality from observations of behaviour. For the most part, these two lines of research have proceeded independently with little or no evidence of integration. It seems odd that social psychologists and personality theorists should have so studiously ignored each other, but what is even more surprising is that there are some studies in which virtually identical data are collected and then subjected to entirely different interpretations from these two perspectives.

Imagine a study where the members of a discussion group which had been meeting regularly for a year were asked, when they met for the last time, to rate one another on a series of personality traits. Each group member's profile of trait ratings was calculated by averaging the scores awarded by all the other group members. The traits were intercorrelated and factor analysed to discover the underlying structure of the ratings. Would such a study tell us about the structure of the ratees' personalities, or would it tell us about the structure of the raters' implicit personality theories? In other words, do personality ratings tell us about the personality of the ratee, or the way the rater perceives personality?

Trait ratings are one of the three kinds of personality data used in the study of explicit personality theory (e.g. Eysenck and Cattell both used trait rating data in their early studies). Trait ratings are also used as a way of examining people's implicit personality theories (e.g. Passini and Norman, 1966). In the relatively few cases where this anomaly has been recognised, typically it is seen as constituting a threat to the validity of trait ratings either as measures of personality or as measures of perceptions of personality. The aim of this chapter is to examine the issues raised by the various interpretations of what is being measured by trait ratings, and to attempt to integrate the social psychological studies of the perception of personality with personality theorists' work.

The three interpretations of personality ratings

Trait ratings from the personality theorist's perspective

In the development of explicit personality theories, trait ratings are viewed as one of the prime forms of personality data. Of all the personality theorists, Cattell has probably been the strongest advocate of rating data, which he called L (for Life) data. All forms of personality data are subject to error introduced by the measurement technique. Cattell (1957) recommended various precautions to minimise the distortions introduced by the rating process. For example, several raters should observe the same ratee and their ratings should be averaged; the raters should observe their ratees in a wide variety of situations for at least three months, and preferably for a year, before making their ratings; the rating scales should be defined in non-ambiguous terms with clear indications of the behaviours to which they refer.

In Cattell's own analyses of rating data he found twelve to sixteen underlying personality factors. However, when other investigators have re-analysed Cattell's rating data, and when they have examined their own rating data, typically they have found that five factors provide an adequate representation of the structure underlying trait ratings: surgency or extraversion, agreeableness, conscientiousness, emotional stability, and culture (see chapter 3).

Explicit personality theorists are aware that trait ratings

are vulnerable to subjective error resulting from raters' idiosyncrasies, but they do not seriously question the validity of regarding rating data as a measure of ratees' personalities. However, Passini and Norman's (1966) findings challenged such faith in the interpretation of rating data. They found virtually the same five factors in ratings from samples of strangers as other investigators had found in samples varying in acquaintance from three days to three years (Tupes and Christal, 1961). Since Passini and Norman's raters could not have based their ratings on their perceptions of the actual trait co-occurrences in the ratees, their ratings must have been based on their beliefs about trait co-occurrence. The fact that beliefs about trait co-occurrence produce identical factor structures as are found in data purporting to be based on observations of actual trait co-occurrences suggests an alternative interpretation of what trait ratings measure. It has been proposed that personality factors derived from rating data are more parsimoniously interpreted as reflections of the raters' implicit personality theories than of the ratees' personalities (e.g. Mischel, 1968; Shweder, 1982).

Trait ratings from the lay perspective

Investigations into implicit personality theory have used trait ratings as a means of obtaining people's beliefs about trait co-occurrence. For example, Wishner (1960) derived corre- lations between traits from students' ratings of their instructors and Rosenberg studied the structures underlying the patterns of trait co-occurrence in descriptions of real people (see chapter 5). In none of these investigations were the targets' personalities the focus of interest; the targets served as probes for revealing the subjects' implicit person- ality theories. The juxtaposition of these two interpretations of trait ratings (reflections of the structure of observed trait co-occurrence versus reflections of the structure of beliefs about trait co-occurrence) reveals a confound that is usually ignored in studies of implicit personality theories. Where real people are used as entry points into the subjects' implicit personality theories, the actual trait co-occurrence patterns for these targets will interact with the subjects' implicit theories and correspondingly affect the trait ratings. If the use of trait ratings in studies of explicit personality theories can be criticised because they may reflect nothing more than the raters' implicit beliefs, the converse criticism is also possible: the trait ratings of real targets used in studies of implicit personality theory may reflect nothing more than the ratees' personalities.

A linguistic account of trait ratings

It has been suggested (D'Andrade, 1965; Mulaik, 1964) that trait ratings measure neither the observed nor the believed co-occurrence likelihood of traits, but instead are measures of the overlap in meaning or semantic similarity among trait terms. D'Andrade obtained ratings of the similarity in meaning between each of the twenty bipolar scales typically used in trait rating studies (see Table 3.2, page 70) by selecting one of the poles for each of the scales and presenting all possible pairs of these traits to a group of students who were asked to rate the pairs for similarity in meaning. The group data were then averaged so that a mean similarity rating between each and every other trait was obtained. Using this matrix of similarity ratings, D'Andrade obtained the correlations between each of the traits and factor analysed them. The results of the analysis were similar to those obtained by Tupes and Christal (1961), Norman (1963), and Passini and Norman (1966). The same five factors emerged. D'Andrade had shown that the pattern of trait relations, so reliably obtained when using these twenty bipolar scales to rate other people, may also be obtained when no other people are involved and subjects are simply required to rate the similarity in meaning among trait terms. His findings could be interpreted as suggesting that the five-factor structure of these scales is due to the overlap in meaning between them, and not to either beliefs or observations of their actual co-occurrence.

Mulaik (1964) obtained ratings of twenty real people, twenty stereotypes and twenty personality traits on seventy-six bipolar rating scales. The ratings of real people were regarded as measuring observed trait co-occurrences, the ratings of stereotypes were regarded as measuring believed trait co-occurrences, and the ratings of traits were regarded as measuring linguistic knowledge. Similar factor structures were found in all three sets of rating data. Mulaik argued that the most parsimonious, but not necessarily correct, explanation for these findings was that people possess a pre-existing set of beliefs about the conceptual similarity between traits (i.e. linguistic knowledge), and that these beliefs distort our view of both real people and stereotypes. However, he also stated that if it could be shown that 'raters of the meaning of trait words make such ratings according to their knowledge of how traits go together in persons and not according to their knowledge of meanings as such' (Mulaik, 1964, p.510), then he would be prepared to accept the explanation that the similarity between all three sets of data is due to observations of trait occurrence resulting in corresponding beliefs about trait co-occurrence that are encoded into the meaning of trait words.

What do trait ratings measure?

The previous discussion reviewed three interpretations of what trait ratings measure, which may be summarised as follows:

(1) the observed co-occurrence likelihood of traits (ratees' personalities);
(2) beliefs about the co-occurrence likelihood of traits (raters' implicit personality theories);
(3) Overlap in meaning among traits (raters' linguistic knowledge).

D'Andrade (1965) was aware that the similarity between the factor structures obtained from (1) ratings based on observations, (2) ratings based on beliefs, and (3) ratings based on linguistic knowledge, did not in itself invalidate any of the three interpretations of these data as measuring (1) ratees' personalities, (2) raters' beliefs about personality, and (3) raters' linguistic knowledge.

. . . it is possible that the so-called psychological traits dealt with in this paper exist both as components in the terms used to describe the external world and in the external world as well. Such an isomorphism, if it exists, might be the result of the external world affecting first the discriminations made by speakers of a language, who then eventually develop a sememic structure within the language to encode these discriminations. (D'Andrade, 1965, pp. 227–8)

The studies described so far have suggested three possible interpretations of what personality ratings are measuring, but they have been unable to demonstrate the superiority of any one interpretation because they have lacked an objective criterion measure of trait co-occurrence. If it could be shown that the factor structure of trait ratings does not correspond to the pattern of trait co-occurrence identified by some means other than via human raters, then the validity of trait ratings as measures of observed trait co-occurrence would be seriously in doubt. In that case the alternative interpretation, that ratings reflect implicit beliefs which are based on linguistic knowledge, would be supported. The alarming implications of this line of reasoning is that trait ratings are mere projections of raters' pre-existing beliefs, which distort rather than reflect reality. If trait ratings were to be invalidated in this way, then the argument could be extended to any personality measure involving human judgments. The next section reviews studies which address these issues.

Investigations into the epistemological status of implicit personality theory

The distinguishing feature of studies testing the epistemological status of implicit personality theory is that they all claim to compare people's beliefs about the relations between traits with supposedly actual trait relations. Individual studies differ in the procedures used, but despite the variety of ingenious methodologies it is highly doubtful whether any have in fact succeeded in fulfilling this intention. A selection of these studies, chosen because they represent the different methodologies and are frequently cited, are briefly

Table 6.1 Investigations into the epistemological status of implicit personality theory

Studies using immediate behaviour ratings	Measures of personality and implicit beliefs	Statistical method of comparison	Results and conclusions
D'Andrade (1974) (reanalysis of Borgatta, Cottrell and Mann, 1958, and Mann, 1959)	Bales's social-interaction categories: 1 Immediate behaviour ratings 2 Ratings from memory 3 Conceptual similarity ratings	Correlations between the inter-category correlation matrices obtained in each measure	1 had a low correlation with 2 and 3 which were highly correlated. Pre-existing beliefs about item similarity distort ratings from memory.
Shweder (1975, part 1) (reanalysis of Newcomb, 1929)	Behavioural items: 1 Immediate behaviour ratings 2 Ratings from memory 3 Conceptual similarity ratings	Correlations between the inter-item correlation matrices obtained in each measure	1 had low correlations with 2 and 3 which were highly correlated. Pre-existing beliefs about item similarity distort ratings from memory.
Studies using self-report questionnaires *Lay and Jackson (1969)*	Personality Research Form items: 1 Actual responses 2 Co-occurrence likelihood estimates	Multi-dimensional scaling of co-occurrence likelihoods, factor analysis of actual responses	Dimensions similar across 1 and 2 People's beliefs are accurate representations of reality
Stricker, Jacobs and Kogan (1974)	MMPI Pd scale items: 1 Actual responses 2 Conceptual similarity sortings of items	Factor analysis of the actual responses, each subject's response pattern compared with the factor structure	Subjects' response patterns similar to the factor structure. People's beliefs are accurate representations of reality

Studies using self-report questionnaires	Measures of personality and implicit beliefs	Statistical method of comparison	Results and conclusions
Mirels (1976)	Personality Research Form items: 1 Actual responses 2 Co-endorsement likelihood estimates	Item by item comparison between 1 and 2, no dimensional analysis	21 out of 26 item pairs had significantly different co-endorsement estimates as compared with actual patterns of co-endorsement. People's beliefs are inaccurate
Jackson, Chan & Stricker (1979)	Personality Research Form items: 1 Actual responses 2 Mirels's data on co-endorsement likelihood estimates	Co-endorsement likelihoods for item pairs were correlated with measures of actual item co-occurrence	1 and 2 highly similar, Mirels's results attributed to his method of analysis of 1 which used a conditional probability index. People's beliefs are accurate representations of reality
Shweder (1975, part 2)	Questionnaires by Bales (1970); Sears, Maccoby and Levin (1957): items from the MMPI: 1 Actual responses 2 Ratings of conceptual similarity 3 Measures of personality	Comparison of multi-dimensional scaling solutions of the Bales items, factor analyses of the Sears, Maccoby and Levin items and correlations for the MMPI items between 1 and 2	1 and 2 highly similar in all three studies. People's beliefs distort their judgments of actual behaviour

summarised in Table 6.1 and are discussed in more detail below. The studies in Table 6.1 are divided into two groups according to which measure of supposed actual trait relations was used: immediate behaviour ratings or self-report questionnaires.

Studies using immediate behaviour ratings

The first two studies listed in Table 6.1 exemplify the approach developed by D'Andrade and Shweder (e.g. D'Andrade, 1965, 1974; Shweder, 1975, 1977, 1982; Shweder and D'Andrade, 1980). Their studies were designed to determine to what extent trait ratings are affected by pre-existing beliefs about trait co-occurrence which, Shweder and D'Andrade argue, are reflections of semantic or conceptual similarity between trait terms, and not faithful reflections of actual trait co-occurrence. For Shweder and D'Andrade the issue is whether trait ratings are accurate reflections of real trait co-occurrence or systematic distortions of reality to conform to pre-existing (erroneous) beliefs about trait co-occurrence. In terms of the three interpretations of trait ratings summarised above, the accurate-reflection hypothesis proposed that trait ratings measure ratees' personalities (1) whereas the systematic-distortion hypothesis proposes that trait ratings measure raters' implicit personality theories (2) which are derived from their linguistic knowledge (3) and not from observations of reality (1).

In order to test between the accurate-reflection versus systematic-distortion hypotheses, Shweder and D'Andrade have identified three sets of data among which the critical comparisons can be made: actual trait co-occurrence, rated trait co-occurrence made after a delay, and the rated conceptual similarity between the traits. The data corresponding to actual trait co-occurrence are based on immediate behaviour ratings. The Shweder-D'Andrade systematic-distortion hypothesis states that trait ratings made from memory will be more subject to the distorting influence of conceptual (i.e. semantic) similarity than on-line recordings of behaviour. Therefore, a relatively pure measure of actual trait co-occurrence may be obtained by having raters record ratees' behaviour as it happens using a simple coding scheme involving the minimum of inference. Typically, Shweder and D'Andrade used a rating procedure called identity coding, in which the rater uses a small number of trait categories and encodes a behavioural observation by checking the one category that best describes the observation. Table 6.2 (i) shows the set of six categories used by D'Andrade (1974). The pattern of co-occurrence of trait categories in immediate ratings is presented in the form of a correlation matrix in which each category is correlated with every other (see Figure 6.1 [i]).

Rated trait co-occurrence made from memory was assessed by collecting trait ratings for the same ratees on the same trait categories as those used in the immediate behaviour ratings, but after a delay instead of on-line. The intercorrelations among the categories based on these memory ratings are then computed (see Figure 6.1 [ii]). Finally, the semantic or conceptual overlap between the same set of categories was obtained by having subjects rate all the possible pairs of categories in terms of their similarity in meaning. The intercorrelations among the categories based on semantic-similarity ratings may then be compared (see Figure 6.1 [iii]).

The three sets of data generate three correlation matrices representing the relations among the trait categories as they emerge in each form of data. By comparing each of these matrices with the other two, using inter-matrix correlations, Shweder and D'Andrade were able to examine the degree to which the matrices were similar, and hence to test their competing hypotheses about what memory-based trait ratings measure. Shweder and D'Andrade conducted seven different studies in which these comparisons were made and they claimed substantial support for the systematic-distortion hypothesis. It is typically the case that the memory ratings matrix and the semantic-similarity ratings matrix correlate highly (on average .75), whereas the immediate ratings matrix has a low correlation both with the memory ratings matrix (on average .25) and with the semantic-similarity ratings matrix (on average .26) (Shweder, 1982). In other words, Shweder and D'Andrade argued that trait ratings cannot be based primarily on the accurate recall of actual trait co-occurrence since memory-based trait ratings are only somewhat similar to immediate ratings of the same persons on the same categories. Trait ratings are more likely to reflect the systematic distortions of the raters' pre-existing beliefs, since memory-based ratings correlate highly with semantic similarity ratings. Two of their studies, cited in Table 6.1, will serve to illustrate their arguments.

D'Andrade (1974) presented data from two studies he had found in the literature in which ratings of behaviour recorded on the spot were compared with ratings of the same behaviour made from memory (Borgatta, Cottrell and Mann, 1958; Mann, 1959). In both studies the behaviour under investigation was small-group interaction, and the forty categories used to rate it included six Bales interaction-process analysis categories (Bales, 1970). D'Andrade limited his attention to these six categories. Both studies provided immediate ratings of the group members' interaction on the Bales categories (see Table 6.2 [i]).

Table 6.2 The three sets of interactional-analysis categories (from D'Andrade, 1974)

(i) Immediate rating categories	(ii) Memory rating categories	(iii) Semantic similarity categories
1 Shows solidarity, raises others' status, jokes, gives help, reward	1 Shows solidarity and friendliness	1 Shows solidarity
2 Shows tension release, shows satisfaction, laughs	2 Is responsive to laughter	2 Jokes, laughs
3 Gives suggestions, direction, implying autonomy for other	3 Makes the most suggestions	3 Suggests, gives direction
4 Disagrees, shows passive rejection, formality, withholds help	4 Disagrees most	4 Disagrees
5 Shows tension increase, asks for help, withdraws 'out of field'	5 Tends to be nervous	5 Shows tension, nervous
6 Shows antagonism, deflates others' status	6 Tends to be antagonistic	6 Shows antagonism

Both studies also provided ratings, on a similar but not identical set of categories (see Table 6.2 [ii]), made by the group members of one another after meeting nine times. To these two sets of ratings D'Andrade added a third, which consisted of ratings of the semantic similarity between another set of similar, but not identical, categories (see Table 6.2 [iii]). Thus he was able to compare immediate ratings with ratings from memory and semantic-similarity ratings on what he regarded as equivalent categories. This was done by correlating each category with every other within each set of

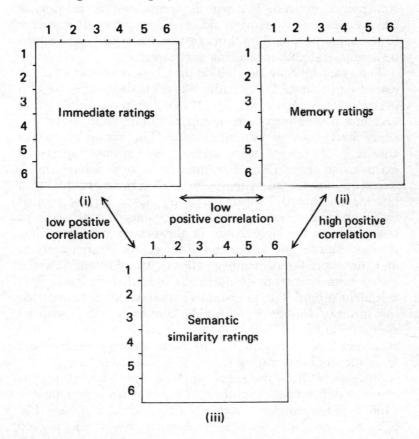

FIGURE 6.1 *Diagrammatic representation of D'Andrade's (1974) results*

data and then comparing the three correlation matrices (see Figure 6.1).

In both studies it was found that the immediate ratings matrix (i) did not correspond to either the memory ratings matrix (ii) or the semantic-similarity ratings matrix (iii). The greatest correspondence was obtained between the semantic-similarity ratings matrix and the memory ratings matrix. D'Andrade concluded from these findings that ratings of behaviour made from memory are subject to systematic distortion which is produced by the rater confusing the similarity in meaning between the terms with the memory of whether the two categories did or did not actually co-occur in the same people. The 'human behaviorscope', as he puts it, is not a reliable measuring instrument.

The study by Shweder (1975, part 1) was similar in many respects to that of D'Andrade. Shweder also made use of a previous study (Newcomb, 1929) in which immediate ratings and memory ratings were compared. The subjects in this study were boys at summer camp. The rating categories consisted of thirty items measuring various aspects of extraversion (e.g. 'Takes the initiative in organising games', 'Gets up before the rising hour', 'Gets into trouble of a mischievous or adventurous nature'). Each boy was rated twice on these items, first by his counsellor as soon as possible after the occurrence of the behaviour (immediate ratings), and second at the end of the camp, by six observers and the counsellors (memory ratings). In addition, Shweder also obtained semantic-similarity ratings of these items from a student group. The inter-matrix correlations revealed that the memory ratings were highly similar to the semantic-similarity ratings, whereas the immediate ratings had relatively low correlations with both memory ratings and semantic-similarity ratings.

Shweder (1982) used the evidence in support of the systematic-distortion hypothesis to mount an attack on the validity of both implicit and explicit personality theory. His primary target was implicit personality theory. He argued that it is derived from the semantic or conceptual similarity between trait terms, which does not bear a direct correspondence to reality. Shweder (1982, p. 94) explicitly stated his belief that language does not correspond to reality. Shweder (1982, p. 75) proposed that semantic similarity is judged on the basis of 'the relative number of predications common to the two terms', but no extensive elaboration on the nature of these 'predications' followed. Apparently, the conceptual similarity between two trait terms (e.g. 'dominant' and 'aggressive') is the result of many factors to which the covariation of 'dominant' and 'aggressive' behaviours across individuals makes only a minor contribution.

The secondary target of Shweder's critique was explicit personality theory based on trait ratings. He argued that explicit theories based on rating data cannot generate useful models of the structure of personality because rating data are systematic distortions of reality. Raters tend to contaminate their observations of trait co-occurrence with their beliefs about trait co-occurrence (i.e. implicit personality theories). These beliefs, as Shweder and D'Andrade have already claimed, are based on semantics which may not correspond to reality. Shweder's critique of explicit personality theory amounts to a proposition about the process of making trait ratings. However, no detailed account of the rating process and its susceptibility to distortion is given.

Not surprisingly in view of its seriousness, the Shweder–D'Andrade critique has been the focus of extensive debate in the personality literature. As a result, several conceptual and empirical flaws in the Shweder–D'Andrade position have been revealed. Block, Weiss and Thorne (1979) made several criticisms of the methodology adopted in Shweder and D'Andrade's studies comparing immediate behaviour ratings, memory ratings, and semantic ratings. An essential feature of the design of these studies is that the same categories are used in each of the three sets of ratings, but Block *et al.* (1979) pointed out that significant changes in the category descriptions were not uncommon. In Table 6.2 the categories used in each of the three rating procedures in D'Andrade's (1974) studies are shown and it can be seen that not only do all three sets of categories contain ambiguities allowing for idiosyncratic interpretations (e.g. (ii) 2: 'Is responsive to laughter'), but there is also considerable variation across the three versions of the same category (e.g. Category 1).

Therefore, variation in the category definitions could account for the differences between the correlational structures discovered in the three sets of ratings.

In Shweder's (1975) re-analysis of Newcomb's data, the categories were identical across the three sets of ratings, but many were ambiguous and non-specific. For example, 'Engages in group misdemeanor' or 'Actively moves about most of the day' are open to idiosyncratic interpretations depending upon raters' personal definitions of 'misdemeanour', 'actively' and 'most'. In addition, it is difficult to see how the counsellors making supposedly immediate ratings could have carried out the instructions to rate the item as soon as possible after it had occurred, since their ratings required a general impression of the day's activity. These categories, then, cannot be claimed to be measuring clearly defined behaviours as they occur, which is the essential requirement for ratings of actual behaviour. Block *et al.* (1979, p. 1062) point out that a measure of actual behaviour should ensure that 'No pertinent behaviors are omitted and no inference is required of the recording observer.' Neither the interactional-analysis categories nor the Newcomb categories satisfy these requirements.

In addition to criticising the procedural aspects of the Shweder and D'Andrade studies, Block *et al.* (1979) viewed the statistical analyses as dubious. They noted several factors affecting the relative size of the correlations within each data set which make comparisons of inter-matrix correlations hard to interpret. In two recent investigations (Romer and Revelle, 1984; Weiss and Mendelsohn, 1986), the conceptual and empirical problems associated with comparing the three matrices of intercorrelated immediate, memory and semantic ratings have been examined in detail to expose the inadequacy of the Shweder–D'Andrade critique.

Both Romer and Revelle (1984) and Weiss and Mendelsohn (1986) identify Shweder and D'Andrade's failure to provide an account of the process by which raters arrive at their judgments as the source of the major weaknesses of the systematic-distortion hypothesis. It will be recalled that the immediate behaviour ratings in Shweder and D'Andrade's studies were typically in the form of identity codings:

frequency counts of simple behaviour identifications. The reason for using these data was to keep the immediate behaviour ratings as objective and non-inferential as possible. However, Romer and Revelle (1984) demonstrated that identity coding attenuates the magnitude of the correlations among the categories, which therefore enhances the discrepancy between the immediate ratings matrix and other matrices based on scaled (as opposed to 'present vs. absent') ratings.

To make this distinction clear, consider the rating categories in Table 6.2. In the immediate, on-the-spot behaviour ratings (i) the rater coded a given observation with one of the six categories. In the memory ratings (ii) the rater considered the ratee in terms of all six categories and rated each category using a scale. These are two different procedures, and it is not surprising that they produce different inter-category correlational structures. Romer and Revelle (1984) demonstrated empirically that identity codings prevent the semantic similarity between the categories from being reflected in the encoding of on-line behaviour. When scaled ratings across all categories are used to construct the immediate behaviour ratings, then the systematic-distortion effect is not found; immediate, memory-based, and semantic-similarity ratings are all highly related. However, the 'on-line behaviours' used in their study were in fact sentences describing fictitious targets in relatively abstract terms such as 'Rich was self-confident at the meeting'. So the empirical side of this study was somewhat weaker than the theoretical argument.

In defence of the systematic-distortion hypothesis, Romer and Revelle's (1984) demonstration could be viewed as inappropriate, in that it carefully puts back into the immediate ratings all the potential for observational bias that Shweder and D'Andrade took pains to remove. With further consideration this defence loses its force because of the absence of a model of the rating process in the Shweder–D'Andrade position. The rater must draw upon pre-existing beliefs in order to make a rating; 'Behaviour takes its meaning only by virtue of its encoding' (Romer and Revelle, 1984, p. 1041). The coding of immediately observed behaviour requires the same semantic knowledge as is used when ratings are made from memory. Romer and Revelle do not dispute that observations are liable to some distortion, but they explain a substantial amount of the systematic distortion claimed by Shweder and D'Andrade in terms of the inadequacies of identity coding as a true estimate of the role of semantics in immediate behaviour ratings.

Borkenau (1986) conducted an investigation somewhat similar to Romer and Revelle's (1984), with the added methodological refinement of using the self-reported behaviour of real persons instead of fictitious target descriptions. Subjects reported the frequency with which they had recently performed each of 500 acts whose perceived prototypicality (i.e. goodness as examples) for five traits had been established previously. Like Romer and Revelle, Borkenau argued that the same act is indicative of more than just one trait, and he demonstrated that semantic similarity reflects the degree of act overlap. Moreover, contrary to Shweder and D'Andrade but similar to Romer and Revelle, Borkenau found high levels of correspondence between the structure of self-reported act frequencies and the semantic-similarity structure of the trait terms.

Weiss and Mendelsohn (1986) take up another weakness resulting from Shweder and D'Andrade's failure to provide an explicit model of the rating process. Shweder (e.g. 1977) has repeatedly claimed that raters tend to substitute their pre-existing beliefs regarding 'what is like what' for actual behavioural co-occurrence. Weiss and Mendelsohn (1986) attempted to derive a model of this process. Presumably Shweder was proposing that although the ratee provided the initial information to enter into the rater's pre-existing conceptual network, subsequent ratings were more strongly influenced by the associations within this network than by the associations to be observed in the ratee. A powerful test of this model proved relatively straightforward. By having raters make only one rating for each ratee, it would be impossible for the ratings to be generated from pre-existing beliefs. Weiss and Mendelsohn (1986) compared the inter-category correlation matrix derived from multiple ratings obtained in the normal way (i.e. raters rating ratees on all scales) with the matrix derived from single ratings (i.e. each rater rating each ratee on only one category). The systematic-distortion hypothesis predicts that the single ratings will differ substantially from the multiple ratings. However, the two matrices proved to be highly similar, and Weiss and Mendelsohn concluded that Shweder and D'Andrade had overstated their case for systematic distortion.

Despite the conceptual and empirical weaknesses uncovered by the various responses to Shweder and D'Andrade's views on trait ratings, all the investigators have acknowledged that human observers are liable to some error and bias in encoding behaviour. The dispute is over the size of the distortion and the best way to measure it. If trait ratings are merely a reflection of the semantic similarity of the rating categories, then raters should be insensitive to characteristics of the ratees that contradict the semantic similarity between the items.

Berman and Kenny (1976) examined the effects of pre-existing beliefs on processing personality information in a laboratory study. First they discovered people's beliefs about the co-occurrence of a variety of trait pairs and located pairs believed to correlate positively, negatively or not at all. They then presented subjects with descriptive statements about fictitious targets of the form, 'John was rated high on the trait sociable' and 'John was rated high on the trait friendly'. In these descriptions the co-occurrence of the trait pairs within each target was varied such that it sometimes corresponded to the believed positive, negative or zero correlation and it sometimes did not. Thus, whereas John might be described as highly friendly and sociable (corresponding to the believed correlation), Dave might be described as high on friendly but low on sociable (which goes against beliefs). After viewing the descriptive statements, subjects performed a delayed recall task in which they tried to remember how the targets had been described. The findings demonstrated that recall of manipulated trait correlations was strongly influenced by the pre-existing beliefs about the actual correlations between traits. For example, both John and Dave would be recalled as high on sociable and friendly (consistent with pre-existing beliefs) even though only John had been presented in that way. More recently, these findings have been replicated and extended (Berman, Read and Kenny, 1983).

Berman and Kenny (1976) used this demonstration to support the systematic-distortion hypothesis. However, this study has been criticised by Block (1977), who dismissed it as irrelevant for the personality rating issue. He regarded it as essentially an experiment about memory, and not an experiment about the accuracy of observations of behaviour.

A more realistic investigation of the same issue was conducted by Lamiell, Foss and Cavenee (1980). Teachers rated the frequency of their students' participation in various activities from their general impression (i.e. memory, not immediate ratings), and the same teachers also rated the activities for conceptual (semantic) similarity. Lamiell *et al.* (1980) were then in a position to see if, for a given rater, behavioural observations were similar to semantic-similarity beliefs. When the data were analysed for the raters as a group, then the typical Shweder–D'Andrade effect was found: the memory ratings were highly similar to the semantic-similarity ratings. However, when the data were analysed on a teacher-by-teacher basis, a much weaker relation was found between the memory ratings and the semantic-similarity ratings. Contrary to the systematic-distortion hypothesis, the teachers were able to retain impressions of their students in which conceptually dissimilar activities co-occurred.

In sum, the Shweder–D'Andrade systematic-distortion hypothesis has not withstood the rigorous examination to which it has been subjected. Although trait ratings are vulnerable to distortion, the extreme position put forward by Shweder and D'Andrade that trait ratings are projections of raters' pre-existing beliefs which bear no relation to reality is no longer tenable in the light of the arguments and findings summarised above. The systematic-distortion hypothesis fails for two main reasons: the failure to discover a criterion measure of personality with which to unconfound the systematic-distortion versus the accurate-reflection interpretation of the correspondence between memory ratings and semantic-similarity ratings, and the failure to develop an account of how systematic-distortion operates in the rating process. The next section reviews studies in which a different personality criterion is adopted, and we shall see if the use of self-report questionnaires can shed more light on the issue of what is measured by trait ratings.

Studies using self-report questionnaires

The next group of studies shown in Table 6.1 used a different measure of actual trait co-occurrence against which to assess people's beliefs. The measures of personality in the external world were self-report questionnaires, and these measures were compared either with semantic similarity ratings or co-occurrence estimates of the questionnaire items. The aim was to see how far people's beliefs about the overlap in meaning among the items (semantic similarity) and the beliefs people hold about which items co-occur (co-endorsement estimates) correspond to the actual patterns of co-occurrence as revealed by the respondents' questionnaire responses.

Lay and Jackson (1969) found a strong correspondence between co-endorsement estimates and actual co-endorsement of the questionnaire items. Stricker, Jacobs and Kogan (1974) found a strong correspondence between semantic similarity estimates and the actual co-endorsement of the items. In both these studies, the correspondence was interpreted as supporting the validity of people's beliefs: responses to questionnaires were regarded as accurate measures of actual behaviour and, since people's beliefs corresponded to this measure, then the beliefs were also regarded as accurate. Mirels's (1976) study failed to find any correspondence between co-endorsement estimates and actual co-endorsement, but Jackson, Chan and Stricker (1979) demonstrated that this failure was due to the type of statistical analysis Mirels used; when the data were analysed along the lines favoured by Jackson *et al.* a strong correspondence was found. However, Mirels (1982) subsequently disputed Jackson *et al.*'s (1979) approach and reaffirmed his conclusion that implicit personality theory is invalid. The dispute became three-cornered with the appearance of Tzeng and Tzeng's (1982) paper, in which they criticised both Mirels's and Jackson *et al.*'s approach to the study of implicit personality theory.

In contrast, Shweder (1975, part 2) interpreted his finding of correspondence between semantic-similarity estimates and actual co-endorsement to mean that when people respond to a questionnaire they base their responses on their beliefs about the semantic similarity between the items rather than on their knowledge of their own behaviour. He regarded this as the more parsimonious explanation, which would only be refuted were it to be demonstrated that semantic similarity and co-endorsement correspond to actual behaviour.

Shweder is correct to regard self-report questionnaire data as liable to contamination by implicit beliefs, and Lay and Jackson are wrong to regard them as accurate representations of reality. Asking someone to fill in a questionnaire provides the investigator with a specific behaviour sample (the respondent's self-perceptions), and these cannot be assumed to be unbiased and isomorphic to actual behavioural occurrence. Again, these studies have failed to find a satisfactory measure of actual behaviour. However, it is not, as Shweder argues, more parsimonious to regard question-naire responses as illusions because they correspond to semantic-similarity ratings. Such a view begs the question of where these illusory beliefs came from. It is more parsimoni-ous to regard the correspondence between the way people fill out questionnaires, co-endorsement estimates and seman-tic similarity among the items as due to all three being descriptions of the same data – perceived behaviour patterns. Such an interpretation is more parsimonious than Shweder's because it avoids having to develop a theory for the origins of the so-called 'illusory' beliefs people hold about semantic similarity and co-endorsement. However, a choice between the two interpretations cannot be made until a satisfactory measure of actual behaviour uncontaminated by pre-existing beliefs is obtained.

Conclusions

None of the studies summarised in Table 6.1 have succeeded in comparing people's beliefs about personality with the true co-occurrence likelihoods of personality traits, because the measures were all liable to contamination by observers' pre-existing beliefs. Whether these beliefs should properly be regarded as contaminating cannot be established until they have been compared with the reality they claim to represent. Until then we cannot assume that they are either accurate or inaccurate. The studies in Table 6.1 have not advanced our understanding in this debate. The failure of investigators to arrive at a convincing measure of the external reality we call personality must raise doubts about the wisdom of such an enterprise. Will it ever be possible to construct rating scales non-ambiguously describing behaviour which raters can use to observe and record reality accurately?

Some personality psychologists believe that it will. For example, Fiske (1974) has argued that we should strive to increase the objectivity of our measurements and attempt to narrow the gap between molecular behavioural observations and abstract, global personality constructs. While procedures to enhance the reliability of measurement techniques are always welcome, even the most well-defined molecular behaviour must entail a 'theoretical and constructive assertion about the world' (Block *et al.*, 1979, p. 1062). Why that particular behaviour? How do these concrete behaviours map onto an inferred, abstract personality construct? In order to retain the concept of personality, these questions have to be answered.

The issues examined in the studies summarised in Table 6.1 cannot be resolved. We will never be able to unravel completely people's beliefs about the semantic similarity between trait terms (linguistic knowledge), their beliefs about relations among traits (implicit personality theories) and their observations of trait relations, without losing the object of our studies, namely personality itself. Pre-existing categories, distilled from previous experience, influence ongoing perception; this is an inescapable feature of human cognition. The attempts to distinguish between systematic distortion and accurate reflection were misconceived and bound to generate controversies rather than conclusions.

However, the debate has not been in vain. It is reminiscent of the behavioural consistency debate (see chapter 4) in that a potentially devastating critique of personality has resulted in a reappraisal of the field and, eventually, generated some exciting new developments. The solution to the issues raised by the question of what is measured by trait ratings is to restate the problem and, in so doing, to discover that it goes away. The particular question posed by trait ratings is part of the wider question of the relation between implicit and explicit personality theories. The traditional way the question was posed asked whether explicit personality theories were merely projections of implicit personality theories. We can now see that this question is unanswerable because of the logical impossibility of separating personality constructs from observations of personality. However, perhaps we should never have asked this question in the first place. Implicit and explicit personality theories are confounded because that is the nature of personality. Behaviour in itself does not amount to personality. It has to be imbued with social meaning in order that it may be used to construct personality (Hampson, 1984). The reliable observation of a molecular act such as a muscle twitch is not an observation of personality. When that twitch is construed as a friendly smile, or an aggressive gesture, then we have constructed something relevant to personality by taking the raw behaviour and enriching it with social significance. Once the inherent confounding of implicit and explicit personality theories is accepted, then the question of whether the former systematically distorts or accurately reflects the latter becomes meaningless.

Reconciling implicit and explicit personality structures

Viewing implicit and explicit personality theories as inherently confounded implies that the structure of implicit and explicit personality theory should be fairly similar. They do not have to be identical, but it should be possible to predict where and when differences will occur. The generally agreed structures for explicit and implicit personality theory were presented in chapters 3 and 5 respectively. It is now time to compare these structures.

It will be recalled from chapter 3 that despite a certain amount of disagreement between theorists, studies of trait ratings as measures of personality have yielded essentially the same structures. Although Cattell prefers to extract around sixteen factors, when other investigators re-analyse his data they typically find that a five-factor solution is adequate (Norman, 1963). In chapter 5, rational trait taxonomies were described which clustered traits according to their semantic relations. Personality structures derived from trait ratings viewed as measures of people's implicit personality theories were examined. The Osgood dimensions of evaluation, potency, and activity were found to structure implicit personality theory in some studies, although potency and activity tended to merge. However, the structure of implicit personality theory is inadequately described by evaluation alone, since this ignores all the variation in the descriptive content of trait language. When the structure of the descriptive content is explored, the same five-factor structure as that found for explicit personality theory is commonly found (e.g. Passini and Norman, 1966).

Implicit and explicit personality theories are describing the same subject matter (personality), and the arguments in this chapter have led to the conclusion that implicit and explicit personality theories should not be segregated. Is it possible to put the various structures obtained in studies of implicit and explicit personality theory together? This is a massive task. Despite the fact that the studies described in the first two sections of this book are all investigations into personality constructs, they have used widely different variables and modes of analysis. With all these different voices clamouring to describe personality in their own terms, we must 'decode the babel' of structures (Goldberg, 1981b) to discover the underlying similarities. Efforts in this direction are under way but are far from complete (Goldberg, 1981a, 1981b, 1982; Peabody, 1984, 1987).

Most of the attempts to compare and investigate different personality structures have used studies in which trait ratings have been factor analysed. The search for a common personality structure will eventually be extended to other kinds of personality data (e.g. questionnaires). Comparisons

	0	I	II	III	IV	V
Norman		Surgency	Agreeableness	Conscientiousness	Emotional stability	Culture
Cattell		Exvia	Cortertia	Superego	Anxiety	Intelligence
Eysenck		Extraversion (Psychoticism)		(Psychoticism)	Neuroticism	
Osgood	Evaluation	Potency/ Activity				
Rosenberg	Evaluation	Activity Potency				
Wiggins		Dominance	Affiliation			

FIGURE 6.2 Structures of personality (after Goldberg, 1981b)

of personality structures obtained from different data sets show that the five factors identified by Norman (1963) remain the most useful framework (Goldberg, 1981b) (see Figure 6.2).

The Big Five (Factor I – surgency, Factor II – agreeableness, Factor III – conscientiousness, Factor IV – emotional stability, and Factor V – culture) are the typical number of factors, not all of which are found in every data set. The Osgood factors of potency and activity combine to form Factor I – surgency. Factors I, II and III are by far the largest and most robust of the Big Five, whereas Factors IV and V are more controversial. Although attempting to organise the various structures in terms of the Big Five has probably resulted in some measure of misrepresentation for all the structures summarised in Figure 6.2, it is Eysenck's three-dimensional structure that is the most difficult to place. His preference for three extremely broad factors means that all three contain elements of two or more of the Big Five. The placement of psychoticism is particularly problematic.

At this point, we know some of the determinants of the differences among personality structures found across studies, although clearly we have much yet to explain. Peabody and Goldberg (1986) observed that structures resulting from analyses of ratings of real people tend to result in a larger number of more specific factors accounting for less of the variance than structures resulting from analyses of the similarity in meaning among trait words. They examined the operation of three determinants to account for these differences: selection of variables, the selection of targets, and the raters' categorisation style. Peabody (1984, 1987) has demonstrated the effects of the selection of variables on personality structures. We have already discussed the significance of the initial selection of items in the study of both implicit and explicit personality theories. The aim has always been to achieve a fair representation of the many thousands of possible traits that could be examined. The significance of item selection is illustrated with respect to Factor IV – emotional stability. Peabody (1984) demonstrated that emotional stability has assumed greater significance than it otherwise would because psychologists have a professional interest in this area of personality and have tended to add more scales to measure it than the natural language of personality description would warrant. The initial item selection can result in the over- or under-emphasis of particular aspects of personality. Obviously, if the initial item selection leaves out an aspect of personality (e.g. intelligence), then that area will not be represented in the resulting structure. Therefore, in comparing personality structures, some of the variation can be accounted for in terms of the original item selection. For example, Wiggins only includes what he defines as interpersonal traits, hence his emphasis on Factors I and II (Wiggins and Broughton, 1985).

A second determinant is the selection of the targets for personality description. This determinant affects structures derived from studies of either implicit or explicit personality theory where the data consist of judgments about real people, including self-assessments. Peabody has noted that if only the self and liked targets are used, then the resulting factors tend to be smaller (i.e. account for less variance) and Factor II – agreeableness is most affected. Factor II refers to the descriptive content most directly related to likeability (e.g. warm-cold, pleasant-irritating), and consequently emerges more strongly when a range of liked and disliked targets is used. The third determinant of personality structure is the effect of raters' categorisation style. Peabody and Goldberg (1986) demonstrated that some raters, the broad categorisers, tended to rate traits as either semantically similar or dissimilar without considering the finer nuances of word meaning. Their ratings yielded a few broad factors typical of those found in semantic-similarity studies. Other raters, the narrow categorisers, were more discriminating, and their ratings produced the complex structures characteristic of the rating studies of real people.

The attempts to decode personality babel indicate that no one absolute, definitive personality structure will emerge and be shown to be the best way to describe both implicit and explicit personality theory. However, the picture is far less confused than might have been suspected. The Big Five provide a useful framework against which to map overlaps and deviations, and these variations in structure are beginning to be understood.

Part Three

The Self Perspective and Personality Construction

7 The self perspective

The self has been a burgeoning research topic over the last decade in both personality and social psychology. The aim of this chapter is to consider those aspects of self research that bear upon the construction of personality. Explicit and implicit theories need to be complemented by a third kind of personality theory, self theories. The subjects of explicit and implicit personality theories are able to construct their own theory about their personalities. What are the consequences of this capacity to develop theories about ourselves? In the first part of this chapter we shall look at the origins of self-knowledge: what it means to know ourselves, what self-knowledge consists of, and how it is obtained. In the second part we shall look at the consequences of self-knowledge.

Sources of information about the self

We possess the ability to stand back and observe ourselves, even though we may not always be truthful about what we see. This reflexive quality of human nature has long been a source of fascination for both philosophers and psychologists. For some, it is this capacity to be aware of ourselves and to regard ourselves as 'objects' that distinguishes humans from other animals.

Our self-observations can take several forms: we may try to perceive ourselves as we think others see us; we may try to observe our private thoughts and feelings and thus discover things about ourselves that would not be available to others unless we chose to tell them; and we may simply observe our own behaviour in the same way that we observe another person's behaviour and make inferences about the sort of person we are from these self-observations. The first form of self-observation – perceiving ourselves as we think others see us – assumes that other people constitute a major source of information about the self. In order to obtain self-knowledge, we find out how we appear to others. Such is the view of a school of thought known as symbolic interactionism.

Other people

Symbolic interactionism is primarily associated with the names of Charles H. Cooley and George H. Mead. The 'symbolic' part of the term refers to the assumption that the environment consists of objects whose significance lies in their social meanings. We are surrounded by a world of symbols, not a world of objects. 'Interactionism' refers to the fact that, via symbols, we are able to communicate with one another. To do this requires the ability to regard the world from another's perspective. The unit of analysis for symbolic interactionism is not an isolated individual, but the interaction between two people: the self and the other. One of the results of interacting with another and taking the other's perspective is that the self is confronted with itself. It is in this way, the symbolic interactionists argue, that we are made aware of ourselves.

It was Cooley (1902) who aptly described the self-awareness derived from taking the other's perspective as the 'looking-glass' self. However, Mead is probably the best known exponent of this tradition. Although he was a philosopher, he taught a course in social psychology, and it was in these lectures that he developed his ideas on the self.

Mead believed that the essential quality of the self is that it is reflexive: the self can be an object to itself (Mead, 1934). We experience ourselves in the same way that we experience other people and objects in our environment. However, Mead argued, this experience can only come about through interacting with other people via the medium of language. It is by this process that we acquire a picture of ourselves referred to by Mead as the 'generalised other', or the 'me' that 'I' am aware of. The generalised other is composed of other people's attitudes towards us; it is the product of socialisation. Without interacting with others we would have no looking-glass in which to see ourselves. The self is therefore both social and socialised. By being made aware of ourselves through the attitudes of others, we are aware of the effect our behaviour has on other people.

The self is composed of two parts, or phases as Mead called them: the 'me' (the generalised other) and the 'I' (which reacts to the 'me'). The 'I' is the part of the self that decides how the 'me' will behave next. Once we begin to carry out the actions decided by the 'I', they immediately become part of our history, part of the 'me'. So the 'I' can never be captured, it has always become part of the 'me' by the time we are aware of it.

The major contribution of Mead's theory of the self is his insistence on its social origins. Interaction with other people is essential for the development of the self: 'Selves can only exist in definite relationships with other selves' (Mead, 1934, p. 164). This means that if a baby was abandoned on a desert island, and miraculously survived to adulthood in the absence of humans, this person would have no self and would not be aware of itself. The sense of self, which feels so fundamental, is regarded by Mead not as an inherent property of human nature, but as the product of experience. Of course we cannot test Mead's theory by depositing a baby on a desert island, but we may be able to draw some conclusions from those rare cases of children who appear to have been reared in the absence of human beings.

This strange occurrence has occasionally been documented. One of the most detailed reports comes from India, and concerns two girls who were believed to have been reared by wolves (Maclean, 1979). They were aged 3 and 6 years when they were first discovered. They were described as behaving in every way like their foster-parents, the wolves. They ran on all fours, ate raw meat and howled. During the day they slept curled up together in a dark corner and at nightfall they would become restless and alert. They were fearful of human beings and ignored other children. The Indian minister who found them tried to teach them language. Unfortunately, the younger girl died not long after they had been found and taken into his care, but the older girl did acquire a few words and learned to walk upright. Perhaps, as she began to interact with her new caretakers and learned to perceive her surroundings as possessing symbolic meaning, she began for the first time to experience the dawning of a sense of human selfhood. Tragically, she too fell ill and died before she had acquired enough language to test this theory.

Mead's insistence that the self depends on language suggests another intriguing possibility. In the past ten years, advances have been made in teaching sign languages to chimpanzees. The Gardners, for example, brought up a chimp called Washoe as if she was a human infant, and taught her the rudiments of a sign language (Gardner and Gardner, 1969). She became proficient at signing her material needs and preferences for toys and play companions. In making these signs she referred to herself (e.g. 'Washoe eat'). The claim made by the Gardners, and other researchers, that they have succeeded in teaching their chimpanzees a language equivalent to a human language has been challenged (e.g. Fodor, Bever and Garrett, 1974; Seidenberg and Petitto, 1979). Nevertheless, this work does raise the possibility that in teaching language to a chimpanzee we may also be giving it a sense of self.

Symbolic interactionism regards the self as the product of language, an assumption which is impossible to refute since we cannot interrogate an organism which does not have a language to find out whether it has a self. It also assumes that the self is an all-or-none concept; an animal is either linguistically sophisticated and self-aware or it is not self-aware. This restricted view does not permit the possibility that an animal could be self-aware in so far as it is capable of distinguishing between its physical self and its environment, even though it may not be fully self-aware in the sense that it is capable of thinking about itself.

Evidence for partial self-awareness is available for chimpanzees (e.g. Gallup, 1970) and preverbal human infants (e.g. Lewis and Brooks, 1975). In these studies, the subject is shown its reflection in a mirror (it is confronted with its looking-glass self in the literal sense). There are two sorts of responses to mirror reflections. One is to treat the reflection as though it were another animal, which is usually indicated by the subject attempting some form of social behaviour with the reflection. The other is for the subject to recognise the correspondence between the reflection and the self. Physical self-recognition is shown by self-directed behaviour, such as touching parts of the body which would otherwise be invisible (e.g. the eyebrows for the chimpanzee or the tip of the nose for babies). Both chimpanzees and human infants over 15 months old demonstrated self-recognition in their responses to the mirror.

These findings argue against the symbolic interactionist position by demonstrating that a partial form of self-awareness is possible without language. However, Gallup was unable to observe any evidence of self-recognition in the lower species of primates (stump-tailed macaques and rhesus monkeys). Consequently, if it is established conclusively that chimpanzees are capable of acquiring language, the symbolic interactionist position would be supported, since it could be argued that physical self-recognition only occurs in animals with the potential for the more complete self-awareness involving language. Harré (1983) offered an alternative evaluation of the relevance of animal self-awareness to understanding the nature of the human sense of self. He agreed with Mead that the self owes its form to the social context, but he argued that the self and self-awareness are different: 'to be a person is to entertain a special kind of theory, not to have a special kind of experience' (p. 99), and 'to be conscious is not to have a special kind of perception, denied to chimpanzees, but to utilize a theory of a kind that chimpanzees have not' (p. 137).

Symbolic interactionism proposes that other people are a major source of information about the self, and this proposition is open to empirical investigation. If it is the case that our self-perceptions are based on the way we perceive others to perceive us, then a number of predictions follow. First, there should be a substantial correspondence between people's self-perceptions and their perceptions of the way others see them. Second, there should be a substantial correspondence between people's self-perceptions and others' actual perceptions of them. Third, there should be a substantial correspondence between people's perceptions of how other people perceive them and how other people actually perceive them.

Studies investigating these three predictions have been reviewed by Shrauger and Schoeneman (1979). These studies indicated that the highest levels of correspondence were to be found between people's self-perceptions and their perceptions of how others see them. However, only a weak correspondence has been demonstrated between people's self-perceptions and the way people actually see them. The studies relating people's predictions of the way others see them and the way others actually see them have yielded a mixed pattern of results. Shrauger and Schoeneman point out that even if all three perceptions had been supported, it still would not constitute conclusive support for the symbolic interactionist position, because the direction of causal relations would remain unknown. Is it the way others see us, and the way we think that others see us, that causes us to hold certain self-perceptions? Or conversely, does holding certain self-perceptions cause the way we are perceived by others and our perceptions of the way we are perceived by others?

The only way to determine the direction of causality is to study *changes* in self-perceptions, perceptions of others' perceptions, and others' actual perceptions over time, taking repeated measures of each of these viewpoints. Unfortunately, this type of study has not been carried out. An approximation to it is to study the effects on self-perceptions of feedback about the self from others. Studies in the laboratory have been able to manipulate the content of feedback and observe its effects on self-perceptions. The general finding is that self-perceptions are changed by feedback but, as Shrauger and Schoeneman caution, the significance of these findings is in doubt because subjects may feel obliged to report changes in self-perceptions which may not have actually occurred.

Shrauger and Shoeneman's (1979) review was damaging for symbolic interactionism but recent evidence and reconceptualising of the issues has been more favourable. Marsh, Barnes and Hocevar (1985) noted that an important relation was missing from Shrauger and Schoeneman's analyses – people's self-perceptions and others' perceptions of these people's self-perceptions. For this comparison, the observers must be instructed to infer how the target perceives him or herself, not how they perceive the target. Marsh *et al.* arranged for their subjects to complete a self-concept measure and to have the person who knew them best complete the same questionnaire as if they were the targets. They found high correlations between self-perceptions and others' perceptions of self-perceptions, supporting symbolic interactionism.

The comparison of various perceptions of the same person with that person's self-perception raises the issue of which of these perceptions is the most 'accurate'. Snyder (1984) has reconceptualised the notion of accuracy in person perception to take the construction of personality into account. He claimed that person perception must be more accurate than previous research has indicated because, to some extent, the target's personality characteristics are attributed on the basis of the mutually dependent behaviours of the target and the perceiver. The target's personality is constructed or negotiated by the target and perceiver because perceivers behave according to their expectancies about the target and, if these expectancies are congruent with the target's desired impression, the target will behave so as to confirm the expectancy. More naturalistic studies of person perception, which allow such negotiation processes to occur, would produce higher levels of correspondence between self and other perceptions.

Part of the discrepancy between self and other perceptions may be due to the privileged access to past and present experiences granted to the self-perceiver. This additional information may affect the self-perceiver's perceptions of the self and also of others' perceptions of the self, resulting in the disparity between the self-perspective and the perspective of others.

Privileged information

When we think about ourselves, one of the questions we

frequently end up asking is 'Why did we do so and so?', 'Why did we choose that job?', 'Why did we quarrel with that friend?', 'Why did we like this book and not another?'. These the sorts of questions other people ask us in daily conversation. We may sometimes have difficulty in answering, but usually we are able to explain our preferences and behaviours in a way that is satisfactory to ourselves and others. It is generally assumed that we arrive at these explanations by thinking about the factors that we believe affected our decision.

The assumption that we have access to the cognitive processes which determine our thoughts and actions was seriously challenged by Nisbett and Wilson (1977). They reviewed evidence from cognitive and social psychology that suggested that we do not have access to higher cognitive processes. According to Nisbett and Wilson, we explain our behaviour by reporting our beliefs or theories about it, rather than by analysing what actually occurs. Their evidence against introspective awareness was drawn from a range of previous literature as well as some experiments of their own. Much of the evidence came from experimental social psychology, where the findings suggest that people are often unaware of the cognitive processes the experimenter has demonstrated to be responsible for behaviour change. For example, in reattribution studies attempts are made to change behaviour by causing subjects to change their attributions with respect to that behaviour (Storms and Nisbett, 1970; Valins and Ray, 1967; Zimbardo, Cohen, Weisenberg, Dworkin and Firestone, 1969). However, while the experimenters assume that the behaviour change is accompanied by a conscious appraisal of the reattribution process, post-experimental questioning of the subjects typically reveals that they are unaware of the stimuli controlling their behaviour and that they regard the experimenters' explanations as interesting theories but inaccurate for them.

However, people are capable of producing explanations for their behaviour and descriptions of their thought processes, even though these explanations and descriptions may often, though not always, be inaccurate. Nisbett and Wilson suggested that the origin of such explanations and descriptions lies in *a priori* causal theories. These are theories about stimulus-responses relations which are widely shared within a culture, and may be derived from explicit rules (e.g. 'I was driving slowly because it was a built-up area') or beliefs about our own and other people's behaviours (e.g. 'I am feeling happy today because the sun is shining').

In some instances there may be no *a priori* theory in existence to provide an account of a particular situation, in which case a person will cast around for the most plausible account. This search process will be open to the biases of human thinking uncovered by Tversky and Kahneman (1973, 1974; Kahneman and Tversky, 1973). For example, the representativeness heuristic results in people assuming that the similarity between a stimulus and a response implies that the two are causally related. *A priori* causal theories will not necessarily be wrong, but when they are right it cannot be concluded that introspection has been accurate, but rather that by a lucky accident the *a priori* theory coincided with the actual state of affairs.

Nisbett and Wilson's argument is disturbing; it suggests that we have areas of apparent self-knowledge about which we feel confident and others find reasonable, but which are not the product of self-examination and may not be accurate. This anti-introspectionist view is extreme; it challenges the validity of such uses of introspection in cognitive studies as reports on problem-solving processes (e.g. Newell and Simon, 1972) or mental rotation (e.g. Shepard, 1975). In addition, it challenges the current trends in social psychology, where more attention is being paid to people's own explanations of their behaviour (Harré and Secord, 1972), and current theorising in therapeutic behaviour change, where changes in abnormal behaviour are seen as the product of change in the patient's cognitions (e.g. Bandura, 1977).

In presenting such an extreme view, Nisbett and Wilson have provoked strong reactions (e.g. Smith and Miller, 1978; Rich, 1979; White, 1980; Quattrone, 1985). Perhaps their most cogent critics have been Smith and Miller who, in addition to making methodological comments on Nisbett and Wilson's own studies, have put forward three major criticisms of their position. First, it is not open to refutation: Nisbett and Wilson argued that people's reports on their mental processes are not usually correct and that even when they are, this is due to a lucky coincidence. Instead of claiming that people's introspections are never correct, the question should be under what conditions, if any, people's introspections are valid. Second, Nisbett and Wilson have not paid attention to the distinction between what subjects may regard as the cause of their behaviour, given their ignorance of experimental manipulations, and what the experimenter, who is fully cognisant of all the variables, regards as causing the subjects' behaviour. This is particularly important where a between-subjects design has been used, as in the re-attribution studies. Third, Nisbett and Wilson drew an inadequate distinction between mental processes and mental content. They argued that while we have access to mental content, we do not have access to mental processes. However, it is hard to maintain such a distinction. Take, for example, Shepard's work on mental rotation, where subjects are asked to imagine rotating a shape presented visually through, say, 180 degrees (Shepard, 1975). Subjects can be stopped in mid-rotation and asked to describe the appearance of the shape at that point. Will their introspections be concerned with content or process?

Despite the doubts about the viability of their extreme position, Nisbett and Wilson have demonstrated that subjects in certain social and cognitive experiments were unaware of their unawareness, although this ignorance seems less remarkable in the light of Smith and Miller's comments. However, Nisbett and Wilson never denied that we do have access to mental contents such as memories of our past experiences, and there must be situations in which our rich self-knowledge results in a better understanding of ourselves than is possible for an outside observer. For example, our idiosyncratic emotional reactions to places or people of special significance for us can sometimes seem inexplicable to others.

Nisbett and Wilson are not the only psychologists to have adopted an extreme position about the limitations of self-perception. Bem (1972) has claimed that, regardless of whether we have access to our mental processes or not, we do not necessarily use them as a basis for our self-knowledge. Instead, we often make use of the same information which is available to an observer in understanding ourselves.

Self-observations of behaviour

Bem's theory of self-perception was strongly influenced by Skinnerian behaviourism, from which it derived an underlying assumption that at first seemed to stand the world on its head. Skinner argued that we do not know about our internal states until we have learned to discriminate among them and label them. Statements such as 'I have a headache' or 'I feel depressed' appear, on the face of it, to refer to internal stimuli available exclusively to the speaker; the speaker knows that he or she feels depressed or in pain, and makes a statement to that effect. But how do we know that what we are feeling, which is a private event, corresponds to what other people call depression or a headache? Skinner argued that statements referring to private events are learned in the same way that names for objects in the environment are learned, by pointing and naming. The child falls over and bumps her head and the mother comforts her, saying, 'There, there, you've got a headache now from bumping your head.' To Skinner, the problem for psychologists to explain is not why we are unaware of some internal states, but how it is that we are ever aware of any internal states at all.

Bem developed Skinner's ideas about the acquisition of language for describing internal states to self-perceptions. He argues that we use the same external information that is available to everyone when we make inferences about ourselves. For example, in deciding whether we are enjoying a comedy show on television, we observe how much we are laughing and how much our attention is wandering from the programme. Similarly, if a market researcher stops us in the street and asks us whether we prefer tea bags or loose tea, we remember we always buy tea bags and conclude that we must prefer them. In both these instances an observer would have been able to assess our internal state as accurately as we could, because the inferences were based on overt behaviours. Bem does not deny that the self-perceiver has access to private information, nor that this information plays a role in self-perception, but he argues that it is used far less than we have assumed.

When it first appeared, self-perception theory was regarded as an alternative to cognitive dissonance theory, and there were several studies attempting to compare the explanatory powers of these two accounts (e.g. Bem, 1967). (For a full discussion, see Mower White, 1982.) The aspect of self-perception that concerns us here is the account of the self-perception of personality dispositions. According to Bem's theory, we decide what sort of person we are in the same way as an observer decides, that is, by observing our behaviour and making inferences from it. For example, ask yourself, 'Am I a generous person?' If you have any hesitations in saying 'yes' or 'no', then you may find yourself remembering how you behaved in previous situations where you could have exhibited generosity: did you buy a round of drinks at the pub the other day, or give some money to the person collecting for a charity? On the basis of your past behaviour, you assess whether or not you deserve the label of 'generous'.

It is a common reaction to feel uneasy about Bem's theory. After all, it is undeniable that from the standpoint of the self we have a different perspective from that of the observer; we are in possession of information of which the observer is ignorant. Since this is the case, how can Bem assert that we come to know ourselves in the same way that another person knows us – through behavioural observation? Bem's position becomes more acceptable if it is stressed that it was always intended as an explanation for self-perception under conditions of uncertainty; it is a theory about how we come to know ourselves when the 'internal cues are weak, ambiguous or uninterpretable' (Bem, 1972, p. 2). In other words, when the information about ourselves to which we have privileged access fails us, it is then that we, like other people, can only understand ourselves by examining how we behave. There is a sense in which Bem's position is similar to that of the symbolic interactionists, who argue that our self-concept is the result of our perceptions of how other people see us. When we refer to our behaviour to decide what we are like, we make the same inferences from that behaviour as would another person (e.g. giving to the charity is generous), and hence arrive at an opinion of ourselves that would presumably match the opinion of us that we would expect another to hold. The findings, on the correspondence between self-perceptions and our perceptions of how others see us, reviewed by Shrauger and Schoeneman (1979), lend indirect support to Bem's theory.

Having considered the three sources of information about the self that have received considerable theoretical and empirical attention, it is reasonable to conclude that self-perceptions make use of them all. In part, we perceive ourselves as we think others see us, even though this view may not always correspond to how others actually see us. We augment this knowledge with the private information about ourselves to which only we have access, although there are times when this information is either unavailable or misleading. When these two sources are inadequate, we turn to self-observations of our behaviour to arrive at self-understanding.

The most striking point to emerge from this discussion is the disparity between self-perceptions and others' actual perceptions of us. Perhaps in this disparity lies an explanation for our fascination with obtaining other people's perceptions of ourselves, be they our friends, psychologists, psycho-analysts or astrologists. Since we can never truly be objects to ourselves and see ourselves as others see us, our perceptions of ourselves and others are inescapably seen through our own eyes. Occasionally our attention is drawn to the disparity between our self-perceptions and another's perceptions of us, giving us a tantalising glimpse of how we really appear from another perspective. No wonder we are fascinated and desire the impossible – to step outside ourselves and take a longer look.

The consequences of self-perception

As a consequence of self-awareness and linguistic sophisti-cation, human beings construct selves for themselves. In the second half of this chapter, we consider some of the research into various aspects of these selves. One consequence of the capacity to represent ourselves as an object to ourselves is that we can formulate a concept of ourselves in much the same way as we formulate concepts for other people and things. We shall look at various approaches to the study of self-concepts. Once we have a concept of ourselves, we can decide whether or not we like it. How people feel about themselves – their general self-evaluation – is investigated in studies of self-esteem. The final aspect of the self to be considered is the measurement of individual differences in the style or way in which people think about themselves. We shall review two of these measures and their correlates.

Self-concepts

The investigation of concepts for the self has proceeded in essentially the same way as the investigation of concepts for others (see chapter 5). Indeed, the same tasks used to study people's implicit personality theories about others, free descriptions and trait ratings, have been applied to the study of people's theories about themselves.

Free descriptions have a particular appeal in the study of self-concepts, because an unstructured task is seen as more likely to expose material of importance to the person (Bromley, 1977). In free description tasks, the subjects may be asked to describe themselves, in writing or orally, by including any material they wish (e.g. Livesley and Bromley, 1973). A slightly different, but equally unstructured, approach is to ask subjects to respond to questions such as 'Who are you?' or 'Tell me about yourself' (McGuire and McGuire, 1982). As with free descriptions of others, self-descriptions generated in this way present scoring problems.

A rather more structured method, which still gives the subjects scope to express important elements of their self-concepts, has been developed by Rosenberg and his colleagues (e.g. Rosenberg and Gara, 1985). They have extended their techniques developed for the study of person perception (e.g. Kim and Rosenberg, 1980) by having the subject list twenty to fifty different personal identities (e.g.

mother, spouse, homeowner), list features associated with these identities (such as feelings and traits), and then to judge each of the identities in terms of each of these features. A similar but yet further structured task was developed by Hoelter (1985), in which he supplied the dimensions on which identities, restricted to those arising from group memberships (e.g. health club, consciousness-raising group), were assessed. Both Hoelter's (1985) and Rosenberg and Gara's (1985) techniques assumed that the self-concept is composed of a multiplicity of selves, and encouraged subjects to think of themselves in this way. By introducing some structure, a view of the self-concept (as multiple, not unitary) has been imposed which may not be equally applicable across all subjects.

Structured tasks for describing the self-concept are rare in studies of multiple, context-specific selves, but are common in studies of the global self-concept. Carl Rogers (1951) applied the Q-sort technique to the assessment of clients' self-concepts, and it is now used both clinically and for research. The subject is given a set of cards on each of which is written a descriptive statement that can be applied to the self (e.g. 'I express my emotions freely', 'I often feel humiliated'). The nature of the statements can be varied to suit the aims of the investigation. The task is to sort the cards into piles ranging from those statements 'least like me' to those 'most like me'. Instead of sorting the items, subjects can be asked to provide ratings directly. For example, Rogers (1977) obtained ratings of self-descriptiveness for a set of trait adjectives.

However, self-descriptiveness ratings do not distinguish between personally relevant and irrelevant traits. When asked, subjects can usually rate the self-descriptiveness of most traits even if they have never before thought about themselves in those terms. When the investigator is using self-ratings to assess personality, the perceived self-relevance of the trait may not be of any significance. However, the self-concept is generally regarded as a subset of personality characteristics (and other attributes) perceived to be particularly relevant or important to the person (Kihlstrom and Cantor, 1984). For this reason, Markus (1977) advocated the use of 'importance to self-concept' ratings in addition to ratings of self-descriptiveness. Traits that were extremely descriptive (or non-descriptive) and important were identified with the self-concept. Subsequently, Burke, Kraut and Dworkin (1984) questioned this procedure by demonstrating that importance ratings relate so highly with self-descriptiveness that they are only an alternative way of measuring the overall level of the trait. Kihlstrom and Cantor (1984) suggested that reaction-time procedures may provide a way of indexing centrality to the self. As we saw in chapter 5, reaction-time measures of trait co-occurrence corresponded closely to confidence ratings (Harris and Hampson, 1980). Similarly, items that are either extremely self-descriptive or non-descriptive are responded to more rapidly than less extreme items (e.g. Kuiper and Derry, 1981).

Both structured and unstructured tasks have been used to access the contents of self-concepts, but these procedures do not reveal the way in which self-concept information is mentally represented or how it is used in processing other information about the self and others. Two models for representing the self-concept will be described here to illustrate the kinds of solutions currently favoured: Kihlstrom and Cantor's (1984) associative network model and Markus's (1977) schema model.

Kihlstrom and Cantor (1984) proposed that the self-concept is embedded in a hierarchical system of social concepts and is represented much like other systems of knowledge about the social and non-social world. They regard self-concepts as prototypes abstracted from self-observations across various situations. The 'Self' could be represented along with concepts for all the other people one knows as a highly specific, subordinate concept at the bottom of a hierarchy of person-types headed by the broadest concept 'Person'. Alternatively, it could be represented much nearer the top of the hierarchy. 'Person' may branch into 'Self' versus 'Other', thus introducing a major high-level distinction between the self and other concepts. The 'Self' branch of the hierarchy may then subdivide into as many branches as are necessary to represent the multiplicity of selves. Either model may be represented in an associative network composed of nodes, of which the 'Self' is one, connected by paths. The nodes represent two forms of self-knowledge: declarative knowledge, such as autobiographical memories and factual information about the self; and procedural knowledge, such as interaction skills, trait inference rules and self-presentational strategies. The network operates by spreading activation, which is triggered when an incoming stimulus activates a node.

Schema models of self-concepts, first introduced by Markus (1977), have so far been more popular than network accounts (e.g. S.L. Bem, 1981; Markus, Crane, Bernstein and Siladi, 1982; Markus, Smith and Moreland, 1985). In a schema model, information about the self is organised as cognitive structures referred to as self-schemata. A self-schema is a generalisation that develops as a result of past experience, and is used in subsequent processing of self-relevant information. For example, a person's knowledge about how independent she has been in a variety of situations in the past may become summarised in an independence schema. Schematics will either perceive themselves as independent or dependent, whereas aschematics will not perceive independence as self-relevant. For schematics, schemata have consequences for the way subsequent information related to independence is processed.

Markus (1977) tested the hypothesis that self-schemata have consequences for the processing of self-relevant information by comparing female students with and without self-schemata with respect to dependence-independence. The presence or absence of this self-schema was estimated from three converging sources: self-ratings on this dimension, ratings of the importance of this dimension for the subjects, and checking 'dependent' or 'independent' on an adjective checklist. On the basis of these data, Markus identified subjects with dependent self-schemata, independent self-schemata, and those who were aschematic. In a range of experiments, she then demonstrated that these groups processed information related to dependence-independence in different ways. For example, in a reaction-time experiment dependent subjects were faster to decide whether dependent traits were self-relevant than independent traits. For independent subjects the reverse pattern of reaction times was obtained, and for aschematics there was no difference in reaction times for the two types of traits. Subsequently, Markus *et al.* (1982) obtained similar findings for masculinity and femininity schemata.

Models of the self-concept developed in social cognition borrow heavily from cognitive psychology and computer metaphors of the mind. Gergen (1984) has criticised these models for being too passive and structural, whereas the self is active and agentic. Along with Harré (1983), Gergen (1984) emphasises the socially constructed nature of the self and prefers metaphors such as the dialogue, dance, or drama to the machine metaphor. The social cognitive models leave little room for the emotional aspects of the self, which have been given prominent roles in earlier theories, Freud's being the prime example. Indeed, cognitive approaches such as schema theory would seem at odds with the Freudian model of id, ego and superego and the emphasis on instinctual energy and unconscious processes. However, with impressive integrative ingenuity, Epstein (1982) proposed a cognitive self-theory which embraces both psychoanalytic and learning theory principles. With this theory, Epstein explains how individuals create self-theories which provide the motivation for behaviour. Whereas Epstein (1982), Gergen (1984) and Harré (1983) offer a more complete and intuitively satisfying account of the nature of the self, none of these approaches are as amenable to empirical investigation as are the social-cognition models.

Self-esteem

The measurement of self-esteem has been comprehensively reviewed by Wylie (1974, 1979). A person's level of self-esteem is believed to be predictive of a wide variety of behaviour, and therefore self-esteem has been regarded by some as a stable, trait-like disposition. However, to the extent that the self is composed of a number of self-concepts or multiple identities, it is theoretically possible to have a different evaluation for each of these selves. Also, to the extent that self-concepts change, then self-esteem levels may also change. These considerations indicate that the measurement of self-esteem will not be straightforward, as the record of low correlations among the various measures suggests (Demo, 1985).

Global measures of self-esteem (e.g. Coopersmith, 1967; Rosenberg, 1965) assess general self-evaluation whereas specific measures of self-esteem (e.g. Helmreich and Stapp, 1974) assess self-evaluation in particular contexts, such as social or academic ones. On both kinds of measures respondents report their self-evaluations directly, rating questionnaire items such as, 'In general, I am satisfied with my life' or 'I would describe myself as self-confident'. Obviously there is a tendency to respond in a socially desirable fashion to such items. More subtle measures have been developed, particularly for clinical work, which are based on the discrepancy between actual versus ideal self-perceptions (e.g. Kelly, 1955; Rogers, 1961; Sullivan, 1953). The greater the discrepancy between actual and ideal selves, the lower the client's self-esteem.

It is generally the case that people like feeling good about themselves. Consequently, it has been assumed that people are motivated to achieve and maintain high levels of self-esteem. Exactly why high self-esteem should be so important to us is not clear. What purpose could feeling good about ourselves serve? One possibility is that it served an evolutionary purpose: only self-aware animals that feel good about themselves will make the effort to look after themselves properly, thus ensuring that they survive to propagate the species.

The motivation to achieve self-esteem forms the basis for a number of theories about the self, including the theory of objective self-awareness proposed originally by Duval and Wicklund (1972) and subsequently modified by Wicklund (1975, 1978). The key propositions may be summarised as follows: attention at any one moment is assumed to be directed either towards the self or towards external events. When attention is self-directed, discrepancies between the ideal self and the actual self are bound to emerge. These discrepancies will give rise to feelings of negative affect, which will motivate the person to overcome the discrepancy in one of two ways: either by behaving so as to narrow the gap between the actual self and the ideal self or by disregarding the discrepancy through avoidance of the state of objective self-awareness.

As originally stated, Duval and Wicklund's theory proposes that there is always a negative discrepancy between our aspirations and our actual performance; on close self-examination we will always regard ourselves as failures. Even those rare moments of positive evaluation, where for once our actual achievements have outstripped our ideals and aspirations, will only give us brief satisfaction. Almost at once we will adjust our aspiration level to exceed our recent success, thus returning us to the normal state of negative evaluation (Wicklund, 1975).

The same somewhat jaundiced view is to be found in attribution theory, where a phenomenon variously termed ego-defensive, ego-protective or ego-biased attribution has been extensively investigated since first being noted by the early theorists (Heider, 1958; Jones and Davis, 1965; Kelley, 1967). The research has been primarily concerned with situations involving positive and negative outcomes, such as achievement tasks. The typical finding is that subjects are more likely to attribute successful performance to characteristics within themselves (e.g. persistence, intelligence, etc.), whereas failure is attributed to external factors beyond their control, such as luck or some feature of the situation (e.g. Johnson, Feigenbaum and Weiby, 1964).

These and other findings indicate that we have a tendency to distort our world view in order to maintain or enhance our self-esteem. Both objective self-awareness and ego-defensive attribution theories assume that the need for self-esteem results in behaviour designed to support our fragile self-images. The implication is that such self-serving behaviour will prevent a person from obtaining veridical feedback, one consequence of which may be the perpetuation of a distorted or biased self-perception (Ross, 1977).

Individual differences

Everyday experience suggests that some people are more self-knowledgeable than others, and that this has consequences for their interpersonal behaviour. Their self-knowledge may take the form of being more sensitive about the impact they have on other people, or of being more insightful about their own strengths and weaknesses. Less self-knowledgeable individuals should have more discrepant self-perceptions.

Over the last decade, there has been a growing interest in trying to measure the various forms and styles of self-knowledge that differentiate among people. One of the motivations driving this research has been the hope that a variable might be found which would account for individual differences in behavioural consistency. Stimulated by the idea that consistency will be found in some, but not all, people, investigators (e.g. Bem and Allen, 1974) have aimed to discover an aspect of the self that moderates the consistency with which personality traits are behaviourally expressed. Another reason for the recent enthusiasm for such measures is the resurgence of interest in Goffman's (1959) dramaturgical view of social behaviour (e.g. Harré, 1979; Schlenker, 1980). According to this view, personality is constructed from a person's consciously manipulated self-presentation. A person who is deficient in self-presentation skills, or is unaware of the importance of self-presentation, is expected to behave differently from the skilled, aware person and will also be perceived differently by others. Two measures that have each generated a considerable amount of interesting research with regard to both behavioural consistency and self-presentation are the Self-Consciousness scale (Fenigstein, Scheier and Buss, 1975) and the Self-Monitoring scale (Snyder, 1974).

The Self-Consciousness scale is concerned with two aspects of the self: the public self, which is the observed self and therefore important in the determination of self-presentation, and the private self, which is the repository of all the private information concerning attitudes, feelings and thoughts. The scale aims to measure the extent to which a person has an enduring tendency to focus on either the public or the private aspects of the self. In terms of the three sources of information about the self described earlier in this chapter, the person who is publicly self-conscious relies more on other people and self-observations of behaviour, whereas the person who is privately self-conscious relies on privileged information. The public self-conscious subscale contains items such as, 'One of the last things I do before I leave my house is to look in the mirror' and 'I am concerned about my style of doing things'. The private self-conscious subscale contains items such as, 'I reflect about myself a lot' and 'I am alert to changes in my mood'. People high on the public dimension are expected to be particularly attentive to their public selves, whereas people high on the private dimension are expected to be particularly attentive to their private selves.

The scale as a whole has proved to be acceptably reliable and the two subscales are factorially distinct, correlating around .25 (for reviews see Buss, 1980 and Scheier and Carver, 1981). Therefore, public versus private self-consciousness should not be seen as a bipolar contrast but as two distinct dimensions: being high on one does not necessarily imply being low on the other.

In several studies, public and/or private self-consciousness has been shown to moderate the relationship between self-reported attitudes and traits and actual behaviour (Scheier and Carver, 1983). According to self-consciousness theory, people who are high on private self-consciousness are expected to behave consistently because their behaviour is regulated more by an awareness of inner feelings, needs and goals, and they are less aware of situational factors such as the impressions they make on others. In contrast, people high on public self-consciousness are expected to behave inconsistently because they are aware of situational cues and adapt their behaviour to conform to these situational pressures.

Scheier, Buss and Buss (1978) provided a demonstration of greater consistency for high-private self-conscious subjects. Subjects completed the Self-Consciousness scale, a self-rating of aggression, and later participated in an experiment involving aggressive behaviour (administering variable intensity levels of electric shock to a confederate in a learning experiment). For high-private self-conscious subjects, the correlation between self-rated aggression and shock intensity was substantial and highly significant (.66), whereas for low-private self-consciousness subjects this correlation was virtually zero. In contrast, public self-consciousness did not predict consistency. For both high-public and low-public self-conscious subjects, the correlations between their self-rated aggression and actual aggression were around .3. Similar findings of greater consistency between self-report and behavioural measures for high-private self-conscious subjects have been reported for dominance (Turner, 1978) and for attitudes towards physical punishment (Scheier, 1980).

The Self-Consciousness scale has also been used to predict individual differences in various self-presentation behaviours (Scheier and Carver, 1983). In these studies, the emphasis is on the public self-consciousness subscale. The theory predicts that high-public self-conscious subjects will be more likely to alter their behaviour to suit their perceptions of the situation than will low public self conscious subjects. This prediction was confirmed in a study of conformity (Froming and Carver, 1981). Subjects participated in a study described as an investigation into auditory perception. Their task was to report the number of clicks that they heard over headphones. They also heard several other 'subjects' (actually confederates) give their estimates of the number of clicks. The confederates reported an inaccurate number, and the measure of conformity was derived from the subjects' degree of error. High-public self-consciousness was significantly correlated with conformity. In other words, high-public self-conscious subjects were more likely to report an erroneous number of clicks when they heard other 'subjects' do the same.

The Self-Consciousness constructs have been shown to moderate behavioural consistency and self-presentation in a number of laboratory experiments of the kind described, but a more convincing demonstration would involve naturalistic studies, in particular studies where an unobtrusive measure of actual behaviour is used. In addition, more studies of the processes by which self-consciousness influences behaviour are needed. For example, Nasby (1985) provided an interesting combination of concepts from social cognition and personality by proposing that high-private self-conscious persons have more extensively articulated self-schema than do low-private self-conscious persons.

A different theoretical approach to self-knowledge and styles of thinking about the self has been proposed by Snyder (1974). The Self-Monitoring scale (Snyder, 1974) was devised to measure the extent to which individuals monitor their self-presentation, expressive behaviours, and non-verbal displays of affect. Snyder proposed that high self-monitors are sensitive to other people's self-presentations and are able to tailor their own accordingly, whereas low self-monitors' self-presentations are primarily determined by internal aspects, such as attitudes and feelings. The Self-Monitoring scale contains items such as, 'I would probably make a good actor' and 'I am not always the person I appear to be'. In many ways, the self-monitoring and the self-consciousness constructs appear to be similar: high self-monitoring corresponds to public self-consciousness, whereas low self-monitoring corresponds to private self-consciousness. However, this apparent similarity should immediately raise some suspicions. Factor analytic studies of the Self-Consciousness scale have confirmed the theoretical wisdom of regarding the public and private aspects of self-consciousness as separate dimensions, whereas the self-monitoring construct is bipolar both in its theoretical conceptualisation and in its operationalisation.

Initially, enthusiasm for the self-monitoring construct was considerable, and the early research supported some of the behavioural predictions derived from the theory (see Snyder, 1979, for a review). In the area of behavioural consistency it was predicted that high self-monitors would show behavioural variability across situations because of their sensitivity to situational cues but low self-monitors would show cross-situationally consistent behaviour because their behaviour is determined by their inner states. Snyder and Monson (1975) claimed support for this prediction in their study of self-predicted behaviours. High and low self-monitors estimated the probability that they would perform certain behaviours across a range of situations. High self-monitors predicted greater cross-situational variability than did low self-monitors. In the area of self-presentation, high self-monitors are expected to be superior to low self-monitors both in their own expressive skills and in their ability to decode the expressive displays of others. These predictions were supported by Snyder (1974), who demonstrated that high self-monitors simulated more easily decodable emotions than did low self-monitors, and by Geizer, Rarick and Soldow (1977), who found that high self-monitors were more accurate in detecting deceptive self-presentation displays.

Despite the early promise, subsequent research which attempted to replicate the original findings and to test further predictions derived from the theory has not generated unambiguous support for the self-monitoring construct. These contradictory findings indicate that some parts of the theory require substantial revision, and also that the Self-Monitoring scale has certain deficiencies. John and Block (1986) reviewed studies concerned with the major propositions of self-monitoring theory. With regard to behavioural consistency, self-monitoring no longer appears to be a likely candidate as a key moderator variable. Several studies have failed to find the predicted relation between self-monitoring and self-reported (past) behavioural variability (e.g. Penner and Wymer, 1983). The pattern of research is similarly negative with regard to the relation between self-monitoring and self-presentation; high self-monitors have not been found to display superior expressive skills (Snyder's original finding has not been replicated), nor have they been found to possess superior sensitivity to other people's expressive behaviour (e.g. Riggio and Friedman, 1982).

The Self-Monitoring scale is flawed in several respects. For example, the scale does not reflect all aspects of the theory; there are no items covering the interpersonal sensitivity component, which may account for the failure to find a relation between self-monitoring and expressive skills. Despite the original conceptualisation of self-monitoring as a single dimension, subsequent factor analyses of the items have shown that it is composed of at least two independent factors: acting and extraversion, and other-directedness (e.g. Briggs, Cheek and Buss, 1980).

In sum, revisions are required to take account of the contradictory findings that have emerged since Snyder's

(1974) initial, stimulating report. Meanwhile, the scale probably can be a useful research tool so long as its factorial nature is taken into consideration. Given the popularity of the self-monitoring construct, it seems likely that the necessary theoretical and methodological refinements will soon be made, and indeed some initial steps in this direction have already been taken (Gangestad and Snyder, 1985).

Of the two measures reviewed here, the Self-Consciousness scale appears at this point to be the more reliable and valid and to spring from a more coherent theory. However, the belief that different styles of self-knowledge would explain differences in behavioural consistency has not received unequivocal empirical support (see Chaplin and Goldberg, 1984; Wymer and Penner, 1985). Individual differences in the nature and style of self-knowledge remain relatively poorly understood and are a potentially rich subject for future research.

Conclusions

This chapter has examined the sources and consequences of the human capacity for self-awareness and self-knowledge. In exploring sources of self-knowledge we examined the symbolic interactionist ideas about the importance of our perceptions about the ways that other people see us, and the behaviourist view that self-knowledge is no different from any other kind of knowledge. We also discussed the limitations of introspection to yield accurate access to privileged self-information. The consequences of self-perception were examined with regard to the content and structure of self-concepts, the measurement of self-esteem, and the measurement of individual differences in styles of self-perceptions. The self has proved an immensely popular research topic over the past thirty years, and potentially fruitful developments are emerging as a result of the combination of social cognition and personality.

However, the fascination with the self and hence with individual differences is a phenomenon peculiar to Western cultures. Evidence from other cultures suggests that the self-concept receives far less emphasis. Data of an anthropological nature collected by Luria during the 1930s, but not reported until recently, suggest that illiterate Russian peasants living in remote villages did not appear to possess self-concepts of a psychological nature (Luria, 1976). In reply to a question such as 'Are you satisfied with yourself or would you like to be different?' the peasants would respond in terms of their material achievements and material aspirations by saying, for example, 'It would be good if I had a little more land and could sow more wheat.' For these people, their sense of self was confined to an evaluation of their material, rather than psychological, well-being. Perhaps this is not surprising in a preliterate society where the daily struggle for physical survival was the foremost consideration.

The emphasis on more material, concrete aspects of people as opposed to more psychological, abstract aspects has also been observed among well-educated non-Western people. Shweder and Bourne (1984) compared Americans' personality descriptions with those generated by equivalently educated people from Orissa, India. The Oriyans were typically more concrete in their descriptions, even though their language is rich in trait terms. For example, instead of saying, 'She is friendly,' they might say, 'She brings cakes to my family on festival days.'

Cross-cultural differences in concepts for the self and others reflect the local theory about personhood and the relation between persons and society (Harré, 1983; Shweder and Bourne, 1984). The possibility of enormous cultural variation in self-theories is suggested by contrasting Western views of the self with those of present-day China. We in the West believe that each individual has a private self which is not necessarily available to change by outside intervention. We recognise that people sometimes behave in ways contrary to their private thoughts and feelings, and we respect this privacy. In contrast, the Chinese concept of individuality has no room for a private self (Munro, 1977). Since all thoughts are regarded as being promptings to act, thoughts are inevitably made public through behaviour. Since behaviour has social consequences, the state is responsible for both behaviour and thought, and hence an individual's sense of self is public and available for change. It is difficult for someone socialised in a Western culture, for whom the sense of a private, inaccessible sense of self seems an inevitable consequence of being human, to appreciate that this sense is absent for the modern-day Chinese. For Chinese students this whole chapter, which has emphasised the importance of a private self, is presumably a baffling misconception!

Over the present and preceding chapters three perspectives on personality have been presented – that of the personality theorist, the lay person and the self. It has been argued that none of these perspectives may be regarded as more accurate or more adequate than the others, and therefore that the most complete representation of personality is likely to be obtained by combining all three views. The description obtained by the personality theorist from a personality test may be modified by a person's own assessment of his or her personality (self-perspective) and the opinions of others (lay perspective). In the next chapter, the three perspectives will be brought together in a discussion of the construction of personality.

8 The construction of personality

Now that the three perspectives on personality have been presented in some detail, it is time to discuss how they may be fitted together, and the advantages of the constructivist approach that they jointly imply. It will be argued that although each perspective constitutes a valuable area of study in its own right, nevertheless a more complete understanding of personality is obtained by a consideration of all three perspectives. The implications of the constructivist view will be considered for developments both in personality theory and in assessment.

An overview of the three perspectives

The personality theorist's perspective

In the first part of the book, several theories developed by personality psychologists from their studies of explicit personality were presented. Although different views on the structure of personality are proposed in these theories, nonetheless they all share some important features.

The personality theorist regards personality as being a characteristic residing within the individual which is a major determinant of the individual's behaviour. Consequently, the study of personality from this perspective involves deriving the structure of personality from observations of overt behaviour (explicit personality). Personality theories arising from the personality theorist's perspective are of two kinds:

191

single-trait theories, which concentrate on one aspect of personality (e.g. locus of control), and multi-trait theories, which are concerned with describing the entire personality structure (e.g. Eysenck's personality theory). Personality assessment is central to the personality theorist's perspective. Since personality theorists believe that personality is a major determinant of behaviour, one of the contributions of this perspective has been the development of methods of personality measurement which are intended for the prediction of behaviour.

The personality theorist's perspective has been seriously challenged. The concept of personality utilised by this perspective relies on the demonstration of behavioural consistency. Personality is inferred from some forms of behavioural consistency and is used to predict other forms of behavioural consistency. Chapter 4 discussed the evidence for and against behavioural consistency.

Mischel, in his earlier work (Mischel, 1968), claimed that the evidence for behavioural consistency was inadequate, and advocated *situationism* in place of personality theory. Mischel's social learning theory assumes that behaviour is primarily determined by situational factors, not by personality, and hence the same person could be expected to behave inconsistently as a result of changes in situational contingencies. However, the weaknesses of a pure situationist position soon became apparent (see Bowers, 1973), and *interactionism* became the most influential alternative to either personality theory or situationism. Interactionism regards behaviour as the product of both personality traits and situational variables: personality and situation *interact* to produce behaviour. Taking both personality and situation into account has resulted in better explanation and prediction of behaviour than was achieved by relying on either personality or situation alone.

Ostensibly, personality theorists are not particularly interested in lay views about personality (the lay perspective), or indeed in the beliefs the subjects of personality studies hold about themselves (the self perspective). The investigation of explicit personality is intended to be the objective measurement of inferred, underlying psychological properties of individuals. However, the claimed independence of the study of explicit personality from the lay and self perspectives does not stand up to close examination. Lay beliefs influence the choice of constructs to be studied and the way they are measured.

How do personality theorists decide which personality constructs to study? Although some constructs were discovered in the context of non-personality research (e.g. field-dependence–independence), it is quite often the case that personality researchers use lay beliefs as their starting point. For example, both Eysenck and Cattell used existing beliefs about personality (enshrined in the writings of earlier psychologists and philosophers, or in the language of personality description, respectively) as the basis for their subsequent systematic investigations. Having selected the construct for investigation, many researchers (particularly those studying traits) proceed by designing a questionnaire measure. The rationale behind questionnaire measurement is that the underlying trait determines a pattern of psychologically equivalent, relatively stable behaviours. The questionnaire items are written with the intention of capturing these behaviours.

One might expect that writing questionnaire items is an objective and systematic exercise following strict guidelines about how to assess their psychological equivalence for the trait in question. However, it turns out that this is not the case (Angleitner, John and Löhr, 1986). Instead, the process by which items are written remains largely mysterious. Apparently the test designer relies upon his or her knowledge and beliefs about behaviour-trait relations in composing many questionnaire items. (In addition, grave robbing is not unknown: Goldberg (1971) has traced the origins of some of the items in present-day tests through a chain of predecessors going back to the turn of the century.) Therefore, the lay perspective is implicated in the measurement process. Personality theorists resort to their lay beliefs when devising personality measures as well as when deciding what to measure.

However, personality theorists tend not to resort to the lay beliefs of the subjects of their investigations. Questionnaire respondents are not asked to comment on the wisdom of the items they encounter. Nor are respondents' self perspectives taken into account. Personality questionnaires rarely ask the respondents to judge themselves directly on the trait being measured. Instead, they are asked to report on a mixed bag of past behaviours, attitudes and interests from which the investigator arrives at the trait assessment.

The over-reliance on personality researchers' own intuitions has been responsible for at least some of the failure to find satisfactory levels of behavioural consistency. For example, Bem and Allen (1974) erroneously assumed that personal neatness was relevant to the trait of conscientiousness. More recently, Mischel and Peake (1982) put together a collection of nineteen behavioural measures of conscientiousness, largely on an intuitive basis, which subsequently were shown by Jackson and Paunonen (1985) to be a heterogeneous collection of miscellaneous variables. By selecting five of the measures which intercorrelated, Jackson and Paunonen constructed a reasonably reliable measure of studiousness, but many of the variables (e.g. class participation) could not form facets of conscientiousness in this way. Assessment of the psychological equivalence of behaviours should be conducted prior to the empirical investigation of behavioural consistency and should take account of the lay and self perspectives.

The lay perspective

Chapters 5 and 6 presented the second perspective from which personality can be studied – the lay perspective. Here, the subject matter for investigation by psychologists is the theories people as lay persons hold about other people's personalities. Both single-trait and multi-trait implicit theories were discussed. The research suggests that there is considerable consensus for both types of implicit theory: people share a common understanding of the behaviours they believe to be associated with traits, and also of the co-occurrence relations between traits. In chapter 6, the structure of personality discovered through the study of explicit personality, and the structure of personality underlying implicit personality theory, were compared and found to have much in common.

Part of chapter 6 was also concerned with the difficulties

associated with attempting to demonstrate the accuracy of implicit beliefs. As a result of this discussion, it was concluded that personality does not have an objective existence independent of the human observer. Trait ratings are always made with the connivance of human perceptual and categorising processes which convert a behavioural observation from a raw sensory experience into a socially meaningful action. The lay perspective and the personality theorist's perspectives are therefore intertwined. Rather than forcing them apart, the constructivist view accepts their interdependence.

The self perspective

In chapter 7, the third and final perspective on personality was presented: the self perspective. In addition to having lay theories about the personalities of others, we also have theories about our own personalities. We are capable of describing ourselves, and we use our self-knowledge to understand, predict and guide our own behaviour. The self perspective accounts for those aspects of personality which are under conscious control. Although individuals probably vary in this regard, part of personality is subject to impression management; people can use their knowledge about personality to manipulate their behaviour with the intention of conveying a desired impression.

From the personality theorist's perspective, impression management is typically regarded as a source of error and something to be prevented. Efforts to eliminate social desirability from questionnaire measures, and the inclusion of lie scales, are examples of the personality theorist's techniques to combat impression management. In contrast, from the dramaturgical view of personality (e.g. Goffman, 1959; Harré, 1979, 1983), the consciously manipulated public display of different selves constitutes personality. This is an extreme position which ignores the enduring characteristics that people bring to social situations (Buss and Briggs, 1984). From the constructivist view the self perspective is seen as one of three components of equal weight, which together constitute personality.

Constructing personality from the three perspectives

The constructivist view of personality involves the combination of all three perspectives presented in this book. From the constructivist view, personality is seen as the combination of three equally important components: the *actor*, the *observer* and the *self-observer* (Hampson, 1984). These three components map onto the three perspectives (personality theorist, lay and self, respectively).

The *actor* component refers to the characteristics the person brings to the social situation in which personality is constructed. These include all the genetic factors that may influence the kinds of behaviours of which the person is capable or predisposed to perform, as well as the person's past history and present goals. The personality theorist's perspective is primarily concerned with the study of the actor. For example, Rotter's locus of control measure is a generalised expectancy with which the actor is believed to approach most situations. Eysenck's dimensions of extraversion and neuroticism are believed to be determined biologically and hence are cross-situational.

However, the personality theorist's perspective has neglected the contributions of the observer and self-observer. By adopting the same approach to personality traits as psychologists have used for studying other psychological properties (such as intelligence), personality theorists have failed to take account of the essentially social nature of personality. It is misguided to assume that a socially constructed form of personality description, such as a trait, can be fully understood by examining the actor alone.

The *observer* component refers to the way the actor is perceived by other people. The actor's behaviour (using this term broadly) is used by observers to construct an impression of the actor's personality. This is done by adding social significance and meaning to the raw behaviour. As a result of a shared language of personality description we possess categories for behaviour and for people (e.g. 'friendly', 'a jerk'). When used, these categories do more than tell us about directly observable information: they also add inferred meaning.

The *self-observer* component is the direct consequence of the human capacity for self-awareness. We can observe ourselves in the same way that we can observe other people, and we can see ourselves as we think other people see us. Consequently, we can infer the social significance of our actions and appreciate the personality impression we are making upon others. We build theories about ourselves in the same way that we build theories about other people.

The dynamic nature of personality construction

The reason why the three components are difficult to separate is that they have reciprocal influences. The actor's behaviour is interpreted in a certain way by the observer, who then responds accordingly. The actor's subsequent behaviour is influenced by the observer's response. The actor's ability to be a self-observer will allow the actor to form an impression of the impression forming in the observer's mind, and the actor may wish to adjust his or her behaviour in order to manipulate this impression. All this sounds complicated and calculating. However, these processes are essential for any kind of effective communication and, in a sense, the process of personality construction is a form of communication. The participants together are arriving at a mutually acceptable construction of a part of reality (Swann, 1984). The process is further complicated by the fact that all participants are involved in the construction of both their own personalities and the personalities of the other participants.

Snyder and his colleagues have studied many aspects of these reciprocal processes (e.g. Snyder, 1984). In one set of studies they investigated the link between the observer's impression of the actor and the effects this has upon the actor's self-impression. For example, they demonstrated that men who were led to believe that they were having a telephone conversation with an attractive woman elicited friendly, likeable and sociable behaviour from the woman, whereas men led to believe the person on the phone was unattractive elicited cool, aloof and distant behaviour (Snyder, Tanke and Berscheid, 1977). Skrypnek and Snyder

(1982) demonstrated that when observers were informed of the sex of the target person with whom they were communicating blindly, the target behaved in ways consistent with the corresponding gender stereotype, even if it did not match their actual sex. For example, male targets misidentified as female would find themselves volunteering for stereotypically female tasks. These behavioural confirmations of a prior personality impression can become internalised and persist. 'These people literally become the people they are thought to be' (Snyder, 1984, p.257).

Other studies have shown that beliefs create reality the other way around as well. For example, when subjects were told that they were about to interact with someone who perceived them in a stigmatised way (e.g. believed that they were psychiatric patients), then the subjects behaved in ways which confirmed the stigma and produced the feared rejection (Farina, Allen and Saul, 1968).

Beliefs about other people create reality, but what about beliefs about ourselves? Do the beliefs we hold about ourselves affect our behaviour and the behaviour of those around us in a self-confirming manner? There is evidence that people who see themselves in certain ways (e.g. as sensation seekers) actively seek out situations which are consistent with these self-perceptions (e.g. go parachute jumping), thus giving them the opportunity to behave in self-confirming ways (Zuckerman, 1974). A problem with these findings is the direction of causality: did the beliefs cause the person to seek out the situation, or did the behaviour in the situation cause the beliefs about the self? Fong and Markus (1982) demonstrated that beliefs about the self can affect the behaviour of other people. People who were themselves schematic for extraversion asked others questions about extraverted behaviour, and consequently elicited extraverted responses from them.

However, beliefs do not always give rise to confirming behaviours. There are some cases where beliefs have resulted in disconfirmation. For example, Ickes, Patterson, Rajecki and Tanford (1982) found that when people were friendly towards others previously labelled as hostile, this resulted in behavioural disconfirmation of the original negative label.

Although there is more evidence of behavioural confirmation than disconfirmation, Snyder (1984) proposed that both effects could be accommodated by the theory that people behave towards others according to their pre-existing beliefs or theories, which in turn determine the way these others will behave. Behavioural confirmation or disconfirmation can be predicted from the nature of the theory with which the person is operating.

The work of Snyder and his colleagues exemplifies one area of the broader topic of impression management. The study of how people create and maintain a (usually) positive view of themselves embraces a wide range of topics and styles of investigation (Schlenker, 1985). Whereas Snyder's work is typically carried out in the laboratory using ingenious simulations of real-life phenomena, many investigations into impression management are conducted in more naturalistic ways. Some investigators adopt the dramaturgical view of personality, in which public behaviour is regarded as a performance and social life is likened to theatre. For example, Harré (1979) believes that the public aspects of life are essential for the creation of the 'social being' of the person: 'It is from the *ex*pression of oneself in public performances and the qualities of such performances that other people form an *im*pression or series of impressions through their interpretations of the action' (Harré, 1979, p. 5, his emphasis). A special opportunity for studying impression management arises in those instances where something happens to disrupt or even invalidate a person's projected impression. What remedial strategies does the person employ in these circumstances?

Goffman (1955) called these actions 'facework'. One form of facework with which we are all familiar is associated with dealing with embarrassment. The research reviewed by Edelmann (1987) suggests that the best way to save face after an embarrassing incident is to acknowledge the event but to treat it humorously rather than to appear distressed. Other forms of face saving (e.g. apologies, excuses, justifications) have been discussed by Semin and Manstead (1983), who regard them as essential for the maintenance of the 'flawless progress of social interaction' (p.1).

The construction of personality is a social process involving the active participation of the actor, observer and self-observer. Removing social support (as in long periods of solitary confinement) or radically changing it (as in moving to a foreign country) is likely to result in the adjustment problems associated with the deconstruction of personality (i.e. breakdown). However, on the positive side, the constructivist view allows for more possibility of personality change than do many of the traditional personality theories. Instead of being at the mercy of genetics or conditioning, we can play an active role in the construction of our own personalities.

The implications of the constructivist approach

The recognition of the joint contributions of the three perspectives to the construction of personality has several consequences for the psychology of personality. To conclude this chapter, some examples of the constructivist influences on personality theory and personality assessment will be discussed.

Personality theory

Theorising in personality has typically focused on the actor, by defining personality as an inferred property of the individual, and has ignored the observer and the self-observer. However, it has been argued here that the failure to take account of implicit personality theory has resulted in many of the shortcomings of these traditional theories.

Over the past decade, there has been a growing interest in the possibility of developing theories which take both explicit and implicit notions of personality into account. These new approaches all adopt the lay perspective as their point of origin by beginning with the investigation of the lay use of personality concepts.

Personality-descriptive nouns and adjectives are the vehicles for the construction of personality. Personality concepts are used to categorise people and their behaviours, and they function like any other category to enrich the observations with additional meaning.

The common source of inspiration for these theories has been Rosch's model of semantic categories for objects in the world such as furniture, fruit and vegetables (Rosch, Mervis, Gray, Johnson and Boyes-Braem, 1976), which encompasses both the patterns of co-occurrence that exist in the world and the cognitive constructions we put upon them. Rosch's model has a particular appeal for the personality domain because it was developed for real-world knowledge as opposed to experimenter-contrived categories. Natural categories are characterised by imprecise membership criteria based on family resemblance (Rosch and Mervis, 1975), which provides a more reasonable basis for category membership in the personality domain than the all-or-none criteria of the classical view (Medin and Smith, 1984; Smith and Medin, 1981).

According to Rosch, semantic categories are summary mental representations of similar objects. Many of these categories can be organised hierarchically, such that some categories (e.g. clothing, furniture) are more superordinate, inclusive or broad than others (e.g. shirt, chair). Members of a category at any level are referred to as instances, and instances are composed of attributes. Category membership is based on prototypicality. Instances may be more or less prototypical members of the category, depending on their proportions of shared attributes. Rosch *et al.* (1976) demonstrated that for many categories of natural objects there is a preference for a basic level of categorisation which falls between the superordinate and the subordinate levels. For example, when describing the object upon which you sit at your desk, you will probably call it a *chair* (basic level), rather than an item of furniture (superordinate level) or an office chair (subordinate level).

Rosch's model has been applied to the personality domain in somewhat different ways by different investigators. Since most research on categorisation has focused on natural objects, which are encoded in English as nouns or noun-phrases, it was logical for Cantor and Mischel (1979) to extend Rosch's work to the study of personality nouns and noun-phrases that specify personality types (e.g. gourmet, comic joker, patron of the arts). Cantor and Mischel equated object categories with person concepts, and instances of these categories with individuals.

To test their model, Cantor and Mischel (1979) constructed taxonomies of person concepts around four superordinate concepts: the extraverted person, the cultured person, the person committed to a belief or a cause, and the emotionally unstable person. Subjects sorted person concepts under these four headings and were encouraged to make as many subdivisions within each superordinate category as they wished. In the main, the subjects reproduced the three-level hierarchical taxonomy Cantor and Mischel had built intuitively into the materials. For example, under the superordinate category of extraverted person, the public relations type was placed at the basic (middle) level, and the door-to-door salesman was placed at the subordinate level. A subsequent study of the attributes subjects believed to be associated with the concepts at each level indicated that the superordinate concepts had fewer common attributes (because they can be applied to a wide variety of instances) than the subordinate concepts, as Rosch's model predicts.

Cantor and Mischel's work can be criticised for not studying person concepts that are in everyday use. They included some rather obscure terms (e.g. acrophobic, hydrophobic), and only nine of the thirty-six categories they used were coded in the form of single nouns – the majority were noun phrases (e.g. supporter of the community orchestra). Their work highlights the distinction between personality nouns and traits. Nouns categorise people whereas traits categorise behaviours. The English language contains many more traits than nouns (Goldberg, 1982), and most personality theories have focused on trait-dimensions as opposed to personality types.

Rosch's model has been extended to traits by Hampson (1982) and Hampson, John and Goldberg (1986). In this model, traits are viewed as categories for behaviours. Behaviours are characterised by attributes which include situational and motivational components as well as motor movements. Each trait category has an associated set of attributes, and behaviour is assigned to a category on the basis of its prototypicality with respect to these attributes. Traits are viewed as being hierarchically organised; broad, superordinate traits (e.g. extraverted) are subsumed by narrow, subordinate traits describing the same aspect of personality (e.g. talkative).

Although it is intuitively reasonable to suppose that traits vary on a breadth dimension, establishing their relative breadth is an empirical question. Hampson *et al.* (1986) developed two converging measures of breadth based on subjects' judgments. Some of the broadest traits identified so far include active, competent, emotional, extraverted, irresponsible, sensitive, and unpredictable; some of the narrowest traits are fault-finding, fidgety, jittery, miserly, overstudious, punctual, musical, and wordy.

In addition, Hampson *et al.* have established that hierarchical class-inclusion relations are judged to exist between some traits differing in breadth. Using an asymmetry task to measure degree of class-inclusion (e.g. 'To be talkative is a way of being extraverted' is judged by most subjects as more meaningful than 'To be extraverted is a way of being talkative'), several hierarchies of traits describing the same aspect of personality at differing levels of breadth have been located. These hierarchies are composed of two levels (e.g. stable [broad] – calm [narrow]) and three levels (e.g. kind [broad] – generous [middle] – charitable [narrow]), and have been found for desirable and undesirable traits describing the five main areas of personality (i.e. the Big Five).

The finding that people organise at least some of their knowledge about personality traits in a hierarchical fashion raises the question of whether or not there is a basic level of personality description in the same way that Rosch has argued for a basic level of object description (Rosch *et al.*, 1976). John, Hampson and Goldberg (1986) found that subjects preferred to use relatively broad traits in a personality description task where they chose between traits at different levels. Subjects may prefer broad traits because they see them as causal, thus providing a more powerful explanation and understanding of a person than narrow traits, which are seen as the effects of the broad traits (John, 1986).

Both the work by Cantor and Mischel and by Hampson *et al.* are examples of new approaches to personality concepts inspired by the recognition of the value of taking lay beliefs about personality into account. The long-term goal of this type of work is to develop more effective assessment and communication about personality both by lay persons and by psychologists. The benefits of the constructivist influence on personality assessment are already beginning to be seen.

Personality assessment

Buss and Craik's act frequency approach is an example of an extension of Rosch's model to the assessment of personality traits (Buss and Craik, 1980, 1981, 1983, 1984). They define traits as summaries of general trends in behaviour, which they call act frequencies, and traits refer to a range of acts that vary in prototypicality. Buss and Craik have investigated the structure of various trait categories by having subjects generate acts that are representative of the traits and then having other subjects rate these acts for prototypicality. In this way, traits are defined in terms of the sets of partially overlapping behaviours which they categorise.

The act lists that subjects generated for traits were used to assess individuals' act trends. One hundred acts per trait were selected and adapted for questionnaires in which respondents reported how often they performed each act. From these reports it was possible to compare trait levels, defined in terms of act frequencies, both across and within individuals.

The act frequency approach suggests a solution to one aspect of the behavioural consistency problem. Act trend assessment allows for the possibility that two people could have the same level of a trait and yet express it through two non-overlapping sets of behaviour. Thus one person could report acts 1–50 and another could report acts 51–100. Both reports would yield the same trait score. Similarly, the same person could achieve the same trait score on two different occasions by reporting two non-overlapping sets of acts. In this way, the act frequency approach incorporates the idea of psychological equivalence of behaviours.

Buss and Craik's approach combines the lay perspective and the personality theorist's perspective by using the systematic analysis of lay beliefs about trait-behaviour relations as the foundation of a personality assessment procedure. An example of implications of the constructivist approach for personality assessment emphasising the role of the self perspective is given by Herriot's work on graduate recruitment (Herriot, 1984). He identified the self perspective as being of major significance in a young person's career choice and in the selection process. In particular, it is important that a young person develops a strong sense of possible future selves (Markus and Nurius, 1986). These future selves are of interest to both employers and applicants. Are the applicant's current self concept and possible future self concept compatible with the ethos of the firm? Herriot (1984) conceptualised selection as a social exchange process, and advocated what amounts to a more constructivist view of personality by emphasising the assessment of the self concept over the more traditional personality assessment procedures derived from the personality theorist's perspective.

Conclusions

The aim of this chapter has been to serve as both an overview of the first three parts of this book and a demonstration that the three perspectives can be united to form a coherent approach to the study of personality. The view of personality that has emerged as a result of examining these three different perspectives and then combining them is very different from the definition of personality with which this book began. The most important consequence of the arguments that have been presented here is that personality is no longer viewed as residing exclusively within the individual. Instead, personality is viewed as the product of a process involving the conversion of the individual actor's behaviour into socially significant acts by the observer and the self-observer. In this sense, personality should not be located *within* persons, but *between* or *among* persons.

In the remaining part of this book, two substantive areas of personality research, personality over the life-span and criminal personality, are examined and discussed from the constructivist approach.

Part Four

Applications of the Constructivist Approach

9 Personality over the life-span

The preceding three parts of this book have contained chapters presenting relatively independent streams of personality research conducted from different perspectives. However, the boundaries between these approaches are hard to maintain, and from a constructivist point of view the study of personality is made all the richer by encouraging their merger. In this final part, two topics in personality will be described which illustrate the value of adopting the wider, constructivist view: personality over the life-span and the so-called 'criminal' personality (chapter 10). Most life-span research has been the product of the personality theorist's perspective, although there are some more recent studies which also take account of the lay and self perspectives.

From the personality theorist's perspective (e.g. Eysenck or Cattell) the aim of life-span research has been to demonstrate continuity in its strongest form: that personality, once formed, remains stable. The stability of traits over time and across situations is the central assumption of the personality concept, as we saw in chapter 4. Therefore, one of the most powerful ways to demonstrate the validity and utility of personality constructs is to demonstrate intra-individual consistency over time intervals as long as years or even decades. Life-span studies which have adopted a more constructivist approach by making use of data obtained from a combination of perspectives have tended to be less committed to continuity and are more willing to countenance change. In particular, the constructivist approach has favoured the view that personality proceeds through a series

210 Applications of the Constructivist Approach

of developmental stages which continue right through the life-span and which may necessitate change in order to be negotiated (e.g. Erikson, 1963). Instead of focusing on particular personality traits, the constructivist approach considers the whole person as perceived from two or more perspectives.

Life-span research, irrespective of its ruling perspective, has a choice of three main classes of research designs: longitudinal, cross-sectional or sequential. Each type of design raises its own particular methodological problems (Nunnally, 1973; Schaie, 1965, 1973). Therefore, in order to be in a position to evaluate the studies to be described later in the chapter, the first section will describe these designs and their attendant advantages and disadvantages.

Research designs in life-span psychology

Life-span psychology is concerned with mapping the changes that occur in psychological characteristics, particularly intellectual and personality variables, as individuals grow older (Baltes, Reese and Lipsitt, 1980). It is a forward extension of developmental psychology, which has traditionally only been concerned with development during childhood and adolescence and has regarded the biologically mature adult as of no further interest. Life-span psychology, with its stress on the adult years, may also be seen as a backward extension of gerontology which has picked up the developmental story in old age to study the decline of physical and psychological powers. Life-span psychology does not regard development as a journey towards an end state of biological maturity beyond which, like the fading of a prize bloom, it is downhill all the way. Instead, no distinction is made between development and ageing: life-span psychology regards the human being as continually developing from birth to death.

The purpose of life-span psychology is to study developmental change, the aims being to describe the changes and to explain them. Usually the investigator wants to explain developmental change in terms of age, but often there are methodological weaknesses in the research design which prevent a confident explanation in terms of age alone (Nunnally, 1973; Schaie, 1965, 1973). There are three factors which could explain developmental change: ageing, the nature of the cohort, and time of measurement (Schaie, 1965). Ageing refers to the amount of time elapsed from the birth of the organism to the point in time of the investigation. The term 'cohort' refers to the total population of individuals born at approximately the same point in time, which is usually taken to mean born during the same calendar year (e.g. everyone born in 1969 belongs to the 1969 cohort). Time of measurement is probably the most difficult of the three factors to grasp. As time goes by two things may be said to be happening: people are growing older (the age factor) and the world they experience – their environment – is changing. At any moment in time a particular constellation of environmental factors will impinge upon the individual: the world in 1980 is different from the world in 1970, it will be different tomorrow from the way it is today. 'Time of measurement' is a shorthand term suggested by Schaie (1965) to sum up this notion of the impact of the current environment.

The difficulty facing life-span researchers is to determine which of these three factors is the source of an observed developmental change. Before a change may be attributed to age the effects of cohort and time of measurement must be ruled out. None of the research designs are entirely successful in this respect, and hence it is important to know where each succeeds and fails. The strategy adopted by longitudinal and cross-sectional designs is to keep one of the factors constant thus leaving the other two free to vary. As a result, the explanation of an observed developmental change is always problematic because of the confounding of two of the three factors. Confounding is the primary methodological problem of these two designs. In addition, they each suffer from a secondary problem created by holding the third factor constant. In each case, by ruling out the effects of one factor these effects remain unexplored, and therefore the findings cannot be generalised beyond the one condition investigated in the study.

Longitudinal designs

In longitudinal studies, the same group of individuals is studied over an extended period of time. Generally the group is not studied continuously, but is measured on the variables under investigation at various points in time. The group may be established initially at any age and studied for as short or as long a time as is appropriate for the variables in question. For example, in the longitudinal research carried out at the Fels Institute (Kagan and Moss, 1962), the subjects were contacted in their first year of life and studied through to their mid-twenties; in the longitudinal research carried out by the Institute for Human Development, Berkeley (Block, 1971) the subjects were followed from school up to mid-life. Longitudinal designs are represented by the rows in Table 9.1.

		Time of measurement				
Cohort		A 1975	B 1976	C 1977	D 1978	E 1979
1954	1	21	22	23	24	25
1955	2	20	21	22	23	24
1956	3	19	20	21	22	23
1957	4	18	19	20	21	22
1958	5	17	18	19	20	21
1959	6	16	17	18	19	20

Table 9.1 Age of cohorts measured at six ages with annual measurement intervals indicating the variety of life-span research designs (adapted from Schaie, 1973)

Row 1 represents a group of subjects all born in 1954 who were studied over a period of five years between the ages of 21 and 25. Because the subjects were all born in the same year they may be said to be members of the same cohort. To illustrate, imagine that row 1 represents a longitudinal study of locus of control. The 1954 cohort were measured in 1975, when they were aged 21, and then every year for four years thereafter until they were aged 25. Assume that the results indicated a steady increase in external locus of control over this five-year period. Is it possible to conclude from this study that people typically become more external as they grow older? It is impossible to draw this conclusion with any confidence because of the potential influence of another factor on the sample's locus of control scores, namely the prevailing environmental influences at the times of measurement. It could be that the 1970s, a decade of rising inflation and world recession, provided a climate to which people responded with increasing feelings of powerlessness, thus causing the steady increase in externality in the same individuals over this period.

The problem of interpretation of age changes is rooted in the fact that longitudinal designs confound age changes with time of measurement. Not only is the sample growing older over the period, but also the times are changing. If the 1954 cohort could be allowed to age naturally and yet to look every day at a world identical to the one which existed in the year they were born, then we could confidently attribute any change in locus of control to age. Of course, such an experiment is impossible; as time passes people grow older and the world they live in changes. Any age changes observed in a longitudinal study could be due to environmental changes (i.e. time of measurement) rather than the process of ageing.

A secondary problem in longitudinal designs is that since only one cohort has been sampled, it may be that the developmental changes are specific to this particular cohort and would not generalise to other cohorts. In terms of Table 9.1, the scores in row 1 might be different from the scores for rows 2, 3 and 4, etc. Unless other cohorts are studied, it cannot be assumed that the results are applicable to people from earlier or later cohorts who have lived through a different set of environmental experiences.

Cross-sectional designs

One way of extricating the influences of age and time of measurement is to use cross-sectional designs. Here, several groups of different ages are studied at the same point in time: age is varied, while the time of measurement – and hence the environment – is held constant. This design is represented by the columns of Table 9.1. Thus column A represents a study conducted in 1975 in which, let us imagine, locus of control was measured in groups of subjects born in 1954, 1955, 1956, 1957, 1958 and 1959 who were aged 21, 20, 19, 18, 17 and 16. Any differences in scores among the various age groups could not be attributed to the time of measurement factor, as was the case in longitudinal designs, because the time of measurement factor has been held constant. All the subjects looked out on the same world on the day they were tested even though they were of different ages.

The cross-sectional design thus solves the problem inherent in longitudinal research by unconfounding age change and environmental change. However, it brings with it another and equally serious confounding. Imagine that the cross-sectional investigation of locus of control demonstrated that the older subjects were more external than the younger ones. Would such an observation be conclusive support for the hypothesis that people become more external as they grow older? Again, the answer is not straightforward. Cross-sectional designs confound age and cohort. Each of the different age groups tested at the same point in time have been drawn from different cohorts. Thus if persons aged 21 are more external than persons aged 16 when both are tested in 1975, the older group may be more external as a result of the accumulated environmental impact experienced by the cohort born in 1954 rather than merely as a result of being older. For example, an adolescence dominated by the Vietnam war may have had a unique influence in the 1954 cohort, rendering this group more external than a group born in 1959, who were still children in the late 1960s and early 1970s. Age differences in cross-sectional research cannot be attributed to the process of ageing because of the confounding of age and cohort. The psychological differences between the groups could be due to differences in age or to the difference in cohort.

The secondary problem in cross-sectional designs is that the observed age differences may be due to the particular environmental impact at the point in time the investigation was conducted. Thus, different cohorts may react differently to the time of measurement, which makes it invalid to conclude that if the investigation were to be repeated at another time of measurement (e.g. as represented by columns B, C, D, etc.) the same age differences would emerge.

Neither longitudinal nor cross-sectional designs are satisfactory; both hold one of the three factors in life-span research constant, leaving the effects of the other two confounded. Longitudinal designs hold the cohort constant, leaving age and time of measurement confounded; cross-sectional designs hold time of measurement constant, leaving age and cohort confounded. In addition, neither design permits the generalisation of its findings because of the secondary problems created by leaving the effects of one factor unexplored.

Sequential designs

There are three varieties of sequential design, all of which may be seen as extensions of the straightforward longitudinal and cross-sectional designs. Essentially, sequential designs involve carrying out simultaneously either a sequence of longitudinal studies, a sequence of cross-sectional studies, or a sequence of both longitudinal and cross-sectional studies. The advantage of sequential designs is that they permit the investigation of two of the factors determining developmental change within the same study, and thus they are able to overcome the secondary problems encountered in the conventional designs although, unfortunately, the primary problems still remain.

In the cohort-sequential design, two or more longitudinal studies are carried out simultaneously. Thus, cells 2B, 2C, 3C and 3D of Table 9.1 represent the minimal case of this design. The same age sequence is studied in two cohorts. The advantage of the cohort-sequential design is that it allows developmental changes observed in one cohort to be compared with those observed in another cohort, thus permitting the factors of both age and cohort to be investigated in the same study. As a result, the investigator can discover whether the developmental change observed in one cohort generalises to other cohorts in a straightforward way or whether age and cohort interact. For example, the 1955 and 1956 cohorts may both show increases in externality with age, but the 1955 cohort may be consistently more external than the 1956 cohort at both times of measurement. Such a result would suggest that while externality probably does increase with age, the environmental experiences unique to a given cohort are liable to enhance or diminish this age change. The disadvantage of the cohort-sequential design is the same as that of a regular longitudinal design, namely that time of measurement remains confounded. Thus it should only be used where the investigator is confident that the impact of the environment is irrelevant to the psychological variable under study.

The sequential design which involves running two or more cross-sectional studies simultaneously is known as the time-sequential design. Thus an investigation represented by cells 4B, 5B, 5C and 6C of Table 9.1 would give the minimum condition for a time-sequential design. This design permits the investigator to make a comparison among groups with the same differences in age at several different points in time. It will be recalled that a single cross-sectional study only allows for differences among age groups to be observed at one point in time. The time-sequential method permits the comparison to be made across at least two points in time, thus allowing for the impact of time of measurement to be assessed in addition to observing developmental change between the age groups. The disadvantage of the time-sequential design is the same as that of the conventional cross-sectional design: that the effects of cohort have not been controlled. Developmental change could be due to cohort differences and not to the influence of age and time of measurement, which have been assessed by the design. The time-sequential design is therefore only appropriate in those circumstances where the investigator can be confident that cohort effects are unimportant.

The final research design to be described is the cross-sequential design. The minimal case of this design is represented by cells 4D, 4E, 5D and 5E in Table 9.1. The two factors investigated here are cohort and time of measurement: several cohorts are studied over several times of measurement. The cross-sequential design is a mixture of both the conventional longitudinal design and the conventional cross-sectional design. Each cohort is measured on several occasions (longitudinal); different age groups are measured at the same point in time (cross-sectional). The cross-sequential design also incorporates the advantages of the cohort-sequential and the time-sequential designs by studying several cohorts at several times of measurement.

Cross-sequential designs allow the investigator to tease out the relative contributions of cohort and time of measurement to developmental change. However, while this design has a certain logical appeal, it is probably the least satisfactory in so far as the life-span psychologist is concerned because it does not allow for the age factor. Notice that cells 4D, 4E, 5D and 5E contain several different ages. Thus it is only suitable where the investigator can be certain that age is irrelevant. It is possible that cross-sequential designs would be appropriate in studies of adulthood where biological development is no longer important for the variable under study, but where cohort and time of measurement may be critical.

In all the research designs described so far, age has been treated as an independent variable: it is regarded as one of the factors that can explain developmental change. In other words, researchers have been trying to obtain results such as that people aged 25 are more external than people aged 21, or children aged 12 have a larger digit span than children aged 8. There is one developmental psychologist who disagrees with this approach and has proposed a radical alternative. Wohlwill (1970, 1973) has argued that age should not be regarded as an independent variable, but as a dependent variable. The consequence of adopting Wohlwill's view of age is that age differences are not the object of investigation but are regarded as inherent characteristics of behaviour. There are other areas in psychology where change is not studied for its own sake but is regarded as an inherent aspect of the behaviour in question (e.g. the processes of habituation, adaptation and forgetting), and Wohlwill argues that developmental change should be regarded in the same light. Thus, instead of studying different age groups to discover differences in locus of control or digit span, age changes in these variables are assumed and the influence of other factors, such as environmental conditions, should be investigated. The application of Wohlwill's approach to personality involves studying developmental functions of personality variables: instead of comparing different age groups, the variables' patterns of change over the life-span are studied. The developmental function of a personality variable may be estimated using the research designs described above.

Life-span research and the personality theorist's perspective

The stability model

Life-span psychology has been characterised by three contrasting models of development: the stability model, the ordered change model and the dialectical model (Gergen, 1977). In the main, the personality theorist's perspective has adopted the stability model, which assumes that, once formed, personality will not undergo major changes and hence long-term predictions may be made on the basis of personality measurement. The most prominent example of a personality theorist operating with a stability model is Freud. He proposed that the experiences of the first six years of life leave an indelible mark on an individual and lay the foundations of the adult personality. The adult's career choice, sexual preferences, eating habits, hobbies and indeed any behaviour of social significance are all determined by early childhood experiences.

Freudian theory proposes that there are three adult personality types: the oral, anal and phallic. These correspond to the three early stages of development, which are centred on each of the erotogenic zones. There are three ways in which the adult's personality reflects the infant's experiences of gratification during these stages. Gratification may be perpetuated into adulthood (e.g. the adult who smokes is perpetuating oral gratification), sublimated (e.g. socially unacceptable anal gratification may be sublimated into an adult passion for collecting things which is seen as equivalent to retention of faeces), or subject to reaction formation (e.g. the hatred of waste may be a reaction formation against gratification associated with the expulsion of faeces).

The Freudian theory of psychosexual personality syndromes has been summarised by Kline (1972, 1984). The oral personality is believed to be formed as a result of the frustration or satisfaction of two sorts of oral gratification, sucking and biting. Thus, impatience is an adult oral trait believed to be the result of frustrated sucking, whereas sociability is the result of satisfied sucking. Since oral eroticism is permissible in Western society, few oral traits are the results of sublimation or reaction formation. The anal personality is characterised by the three key traits of obstinacy, parsimony and orderliness. Anal characteristics are believed to derive from the act of expulsion of faeces and from interest in the faeces. Anal eroticism, being less acceptable, is prone to sublimation and reaction formation in the adult. The phallic personality is said to be characterised by recklessness, self-assurance and resolute courage often accompanied by intense pride and vanity.

Kline (1972, 1984) has indicated two major hypotheses which may be derived from this theory. First, adult personality will be characterised by clusters of traits corresponding to the psychosexual syndromes described by Freud. Second, the occurrence of these adult clusters can be related to childhood experiences during these stages. Research investigating these hypotheses provides some evidence for the existence of the oral and anal personality syndromes (Kline, 1969, 1972; Kline and Storey, 1977, 1980), but the phallic syndrome has received no support. Attempts to relate the adult syndromes to early childhood, particularly weaning and toilet training, have not proved illuminating. Kline (1972, 1984) comments on the methodological weaknesses of many of these studies. For example, information on child-rearing practices is often obtained retrospectively by asking adults to recall how they themselves were brought up or how they brought up their own children, and these data are prone to distortions and inaccuracies. Nevertheless, the hypothesised relation between childhood experience and adult personality cannot be discounted, since there remains the possibility that methodologically superior studies would provide the necessary evidence.

Whereas Freud's theory is an excellent example of one in which personality is assumed to remain stable over the life-span, much of the life-span research investigating stability has been conducted within the framework of trait theories such as Cattell's or Eysenck's, presumably because of the reliable personality measures associated with these theories. This research will be presented according to the type of design employed: longitudinal, cross-sectional, or sequential.

Longitudinal research

Prior to 1940 there were virtually no longitudinal studies concerned specifically with personality. The emphasis of the pre-1940 work was on intelligence. An example of this early work is the study of gifted children by Terman and his colleagues (Terman and Oden, 1959) in which it was discovered, contrary to popular belief, that high IQ (135–200) does not 'burn itself out', but that the gifted child grows up to become the gifted and successful adult. It was also found that the person blessed with a high IQ also tends to be well endowed in other ways such as having good physical health, artistic talents, being of good character and popular. This all-round superiority was retained in comparison with a normal IQ control group throughout the length of the study, from the first testing when the subjects were aged 11 years, to the last testing when they had reached their mid-forties.

The longitudinal research carried out at the Fels Institute was an early study with an emphasis on personality (Kagan and Moss, 1962). The development of social behaviours such as dependence, aggression and achievement was studied in boys and girls from the first year of life through to their mid-twenties. The data gathered in the early stages consisted of observations and ratings made during home visits, and included the mother's behaviour towards the child as well as the child's behaviour. Assessment at later stages was predominantly via ratings of social behaviour (e.g. dependence, aggression, heterosexual behaviour, fear of physical harm, passivity and withdrawal). One of the ways the rating data were analysed was by correlating ratings obtained when the children were young with the same ratings made when they were older. If there was a high correlation between the two sets of ratings then the behaviour in question had shown no marked change from childhood to adulthood, but if the correlation was low it suggested that the developmental path had taken a dramatic twist or turn.

These analyses were carried out separately for males and females and some interesting differences emerged. For males, measures of aggression taken when they were aged 6 to 10 years did correlate with adult measures, whereas early measures of dependency and passivity did not correlate with later measures. For females, the reverse pattern emerged: aggression did not remain stable across the two measuring points, whereas dependency and passivity did. These findings suggest that the developmental paths taken by males and females diverge fairly early on in childhood, resulting in adult sex differences in social behaviour. What this study cannot tell us is whether these diverging paths are the result of biological maturation, the intervention of socialisation, or a combination of the two.

The Kagan and Moss study is typical of earlier longitudinal research in that it was concerned with the continuity between childhood and adulthood. There is now a growing interest in continuity over the whole life-span, with an emphasis on patterns of stability or change during the adult years. One such study is Kelly's longitudinal inquiry into the personality of married couples (E. L. Kelly, 1955). Three hundred engaged couples were contacted between 1935 and 1938 and each person was given extensive interviewing and testing, including measures of interest, values, personality and intelligence. The subjects were followed up annually until 1941, and seen finally in 1953–4. The intra-individual correlations between scores obtained at initial testing and scores obtained twenty years later showed a marked consistency in values and vocational interests (which correlated around .50), rather less consistency in personality as measured on the Beunreuter Personality Inventory and self-ratings on various traits (correlations for these measures were all around .30), and the least consistency was observed in attitude measures (which correlated around .10).

There is now a sequel to this study (Conley, 1984, 1985). The couples were contacted again between 1979 and 1981 and, although 161 of the original participants were deceased by this time, 183 men and 205 women were located and completed the Cornell Medical Index. Consequently, data for this group were available at three times of measurement across forty years of adult life. Not surprisingly in view of the changes in psychometrics over this period, different measurements were taken at each of the three times of measurement and none directly assessed traits of contemporary interest.

Conley solved this problem by factor analysing the data obtained at each of the three times. In all three data sets, he identified two currently familiar personality factors, neuroticism and social introversion, which emerged despite the variation in tests across the three occasions. Therefore, he was able to examine the longitudinal stability of these personality dimensions by comparing subjects' scores over the forty-year period. The results strongly supported the stability model. The mean of the three correlations (time 1 and time 2, time 2 and time 3, and time 1 and time 3) for the men was .45 for neuroticism and .40 for social introversion, and the equivalent correlations for the women were .42 and .41.

Is adult personality equally stable from young adulthood through to old age, or are some age groups within adulthood more susceptible to personality changes than others? Findings from the Baltimore Longitudinal study add to the body of support for the overall stability of adult personality. Costa, McCrae and Arenberg (1980) studied the stability of self-ratings on the Guilford-Zimmerman Temperament Survey over a twelve-year period. They compared the magnitude of test-retest correlations in three age groups: young, middle-aged and old adults. They obtained extremely high levels of personality stability in all three groups. Indeed, the test-retest correlations were so high in the young adults that it was impossible for the comparisons with the older groups to show any increase in stability.

Are there any dissenters among longitudinal researchers who are prepared to challenge the accumulating evidence in favour of personality stability in adulthood? Two reviewers (Bloom, 1964; Livson, 1973) concluded that despite the preponderance of evidence in favour of stability, a detailed inspection of the studies reveals some variability in the stability of different traits. This conclusion is confirmed by a recent longitudinal study reported by Finn (1986). He studied two cohorts, aged 21 years and 45 years at the beginning of the study, over a thirty-year period from 1947 to 1977. Test-retest reliability coefficients on fifteen trait scales of the MMPI were compared across the thirty-year interval. Variations in stability for different traits were observed. For example, the Depression scale demonstrated low levels of stability in both cohorts, and traits related to the higher-order factor of Constraint were more stable in the older than the younger cohort. However, over all the scales, the mean coefficient of .53 for the older cohort (45 to 75 years), in which middle to late adulthood was compared, was significantly higher than the corresponding coefficient of .38 for the younger cohort (20 to 50), in which young to middle adulthood was compared.

How can Finn's finding of greater stability from middle to old age than from young to middle age be reconciled with Costa *et al.*'s findings? Finn (1986) explained the discrepancy in terms of attrition rates. In Costa *et al.*'s study, the attrition rate was 66 per cent with some evidence that the unstable subjects were more likely to have dropped out. In Finn's study, the attrition rate was 45 per cent and he claimed that there was no evidence of selective attrition. The definitive answer to the question of variations in stability between different portions of adulthood awaits a cross-sequential study in which the age-related findings cannot be explained away as cohort-specific, a confound common to both Finn's and Costa *et al.*'s studies.

Cross-sectional research

A considerable amount of cross-sectional research has been carried out using the personality measures derived from Eysenck's and Cattell's personality theories, with the intention of validating these theories by demonstrating their applicability to all age groups. These theories are based on a stability model of personality in which it is assumed that the structure of adult personality will demonstrate continuity with that of the child. Cross-sectional studies of this kind are not concerned with finding high correlations between trait scores of different age groups; rather, the concern is to demonstrate similarity in factor structure in personality studies of different age groups. Thus, while young people may, for example, be considerably more extraverted than old people, the important finding would be that extraversion emerged as a major factor in studies of both old and young people.

Within the framework of Eysenck's theory, the personality of children has been investigated and appears to be similar to that of adults. Both extraversion and neuroticism have been assessed in children using a special form of the Eysenck Personality Inventory, the Junior Personality Inventory (S.B.G. Eysenck, 1965) which is reliable for use with children as young as 8 years (S.B.G. Eysenck, 1969). In his review, Rachman (1969) concluded that extraversion remains

Table 9.2 Mean scores on extraversion (E), neuroticism (N) and psychoticism (P) for three age groups shown separately for males and females (from S.B.G. Eysenck and H.J. Eysenck, 1969)

		E	N	P
under 30	M	13.46	8.34	2.60
	F	13.02	9.71	1.92
30–49	M	11.81	6.68	2.15
	F	11.72	7.62	1.73
over 50	M	11.55	5.79	2.90
	F	11.40	6.50	2.33

stable during childhood and early measures reliably predict adolescents' scores. Neuroticism is less stable and boys tend to have lower scores than girls. Cross-sectional studies within the adult age range (S.B.G. Eysenck and H.J. Eysenck, 1969) have demonstrated that extraversion, neuroticism and psychoticism may be measured in young, middle-aged and old people. Young people (below 30) were more extraverted, neurotic and psychotic than middle-aged (30–49) and old (over 50) people. These differences were not so large as to imply a discontinuity, but large enough to be significant given the big samples (see Table 9.2).

The same pattern of continuity between childhood and adult personality factors has been observed within the framework of Cattell's personality theory (Cattell, 1973; Dreger, 1977). There are versions of the 16PF for three school ages: the High School Questionnaire, the Children's Personality Questionnaire and the Early School Personality Questionnaire. In addition, there is even a questionnaire for pre-school children now available. The results of studies of children of various age groups using these different questionnaires indicate that nearly all the adult personality factors are to be found in children (Cattell and Kline, 1977). At present there remain eight adult factors which have not been identified, and it has yet to be established whether they are genuinely not present in children or whether, once suitable items have been constructed, they will emerge.

Cross-sectional and longitudinal studies from the personality theorist's perspective have tended to confirm that there is continuity in the structure of personality across age groups and long-term stability for some traits. However, other traits show considerable variability, and there may be different levels of stability between different adult age groups. Owing to the inherent limitations of longitudinal and cross-sectional designs, the question of personality stability is best resolved by conducting sequential research.

Sequential research

Sequential designs have been widely adopted in the study of intelligence (e.g. Schaie, 1973, 1974), but they are still comparatively rare in personality. One of the most extensive personality investigations to date based on sequential designs is that conducted by Schaie and Parham (1976). In his investigation of intelligence Schaie had already succeeded in dispelling one myth (that intelligence declines with age), and in investigating personality he hoped to dispel another – that adult personality remains stable.

Schaie and Parham hypothesised that there would be three types of traits each characterised by a particular form of developmental change: biostable traits, which either through genetics or learning remain relatively stable throughout life and therefore show systematic sex differences but no age differences; acculturated traits, which are primarily determined by the environment and may therefore show age differences related to cohort and time of measurement effects but no sex differences; and biocultural traits, which are determined by genetics, yet are susceptible to environmental influences, and hence show no age differences but cohort differences and time of measurement effects. Personality measures were obtained using a questionnaire constructed especially for the study, which measured thirteen of Cattell's personality factors and six attitudes. The data were obtained in such a way as to permit a cross-sequential analysis with independent samples and a time-sequential analysis with

Table 9.3 The design used by Schaie and Parham (1976)

Cohort (mean time of birth)	Samples A	A_1	B
1 1889	a	a_1	b
2 1896	a	a_1	b
3 1903	a	a_1	b
4 1910	a	a_1	b
5 1917	a	a_1	b
6 1924	a	a_1	b
7 1931	a	a_1	b
8 1938	a	a_1	b
Time of measurement	1963	1970	1970

independent samples. This was achieved by testing two independent samples of subjects, one in 1963 (sample A) and the other in 1970 (sample B). In addition, the sample tested in 1963 was also retested in 1970 (sample A_1). In each sample the subjects ranged in age from their early twenties to their late seventies and were grouped into eight cohorts (a cohort being defined broadly as a seven-year span). The youngest cohort was aged 21–28 and the oldest 71–77 years. The design is represented in Table 9.3.

The scores obtained for samples A and A_1 provided the data for the cross-sequential repeated measures analysis; scores obtained for samples A and B provided the data for the cross-sequential analysis with independent samples and for the time sequential analysis. The results of this study, as can be imagined, are exceedingly complex. At the risk of over-simplification, the conclusions that may be drawn from the three sequential analyses are that within cohorts there was considerable evidence for the stability of personality traits, despite some differences between cohorts and across the two times of measurement. These findings are particularly impressive in view of the various sequential analyses employed, which all confirmed the overall trend of stability.

In addition to reporting the main findings, Schaie and Parham also discussed how far their results supported the threefold model of personality traits which they had proposed initially. In the light of their findings they extended this model to a total of thirteen different subtypes of adult personality traits: four types of biostable traits, six types of acculturated traits and three types of biocultural traits. However, it is difficult to see how this highly complex extension of the model of adult personality development will be helpful for future investigators.

Schaie and Parham's study demonstrated that even with the benefit of the more rigorous sequential designs adult personality traits appear, on the whole, to remain stable over the life-span. Stability proved, after all, to be more fact than fantasy. Support for stability was also obtained in a subsequent recent study by Siegler, George and Okun (1979). In this study 16PF scores were obtained from men and women ranging in age from 46 to 69. A cross-sequential design was used, and each cohort was assessed four times over an eight-year period. The average correlation for all the trait scores between different times of measurement was around .50, which is as stable as the short-term test-retest reliability of the 16PF. The more complex analyses of the results confirmed the overall pattern of stability, and also showed greater similarity between cohorts than had been observed by Schaie and Parham.

The final study to be described in this section (Woodruff and Birren, 1972) is representative of the personality theorist's perspective in so far as a personality inventory was used but it could also be said to illustrate the self perspective because a measure of the subjects' self-perceived personality stability was also obtained. In the late 1960s Woodruff and Birren obtained access to some data which at first sight could not have looked very promising. The data consisted of a group of 19-year-olds' scores on the California Test of Personality (CTP), the time of testing being over twenty years earlier, in 1944. However, Woodruff and Birren used these scores as the basis of a sequential design. By following up the group tested in 1969 they were able to obtain some valuable longitudinal data, and by testing a group of contemporary 19-year-olds they were able to make cross-sectional comparisons. Only a portion of the rather complex study will be described here; the relevant part of the design is set out in Table 9.4.

Table 9.4 Age of cohorts measured at one or more times of measurement by Woodruff and Birren (1972)

Time of measurement	Cohort	
	1924	1948
1944	19	—
1969	45	19

When retested in 1969, the 1924 cohort filled out the CTP twice: first they were asked to respond as they currently saw themselves, and then in the way they thought they had responded when they were 19-year-olds. Thus there were three sets of CTP scores available for the 1924 cohort: their scores when 19-year-olds in 1944; their scores when in their forties obtained in 1969; and their retrospective perceptions of themselves as 19-year-olds also obtained in 1969.

The CTP is primarily a measure of personal and social adjustment and, although it contains several subscales, it yields a single composite score (higher scores represent better adjustment). When the 1924 longitudinal data were analysed there were no significant differences for either men or women between their 1944 and 1969 test scores: their responses had remained stable over the twenty-five-year interval. Interestingly, the retrospective scores showed that the subjects' self-perceptions lacked this stability. The 1924 cohort remembered themselves as being less well-adjusted at 19 years than they actually were. It is rather alarming to think that we could have such inaccurate views of what we were like twenty-five years ago. However, Linton (1978) argued that we have forgotten the majority of the significant events that happened to us only six years ago, and Nisbett and Wilson (1977) cited evidence suggesting that attitudes are recalled inaccurately over intervals of no more than a few weeks.

Where had the 1924 cohort picked up such a negative and inaccurate view of themselves as 19-year-olds? Woodruff and Birren were able to provide a partial answer to this question because they had obtained a set of CTP scores from a group of people aged 19 years in 1969. This 1950 cohort was selected to be as similar as possible in background to the 1924 cohort. The 1950 cohort turned out to have significantly lower adjustment scores than the 1924 cohort at 19 years. Young people in 1969 saw themselves more negatively than did young people in 1944. The negative self-view that emerged in the 1924 retrospective scores was more similar to the self-view of the 1950 cohort than to the actual self-view of the 1924 cohort obtained at 19 years. One interpretation of these findings is that adults in 1969 were remembering themselves at 19 years as being more like the 19-year-olds they saw around them than they really were. Another interpretation is that both the 1924 cohort and the 1950 cohort were responding in 1969 on the basis of a widely held stereotype of what 19-year-olds are like.

Woodruff and Birren concluded from the longitudinal aspect of their study that there is personality stability, and from the cross-sectional element that there was a marked generation gap, with the 1950 cohort seeing itself as less well adjusted than the 1924 cohort. The difference between the 1924 cohort's actual and retrospective scores is intriguing and could be interpreted as adaptive. Objectively there were marked differences between the two generations, but subjectively the gap was narrower.

The results of longitudinal, cross-sectional and sequential research conducted from the personality theorist's perspective generally support a stability model of personality. Longitudinal studies support stability by indicating that individuals' personality scores do not undergo marked changes over the course of their adult lives, and cross-sectional studies support continuity by demonstrating that the structure of personality remains essentially the same from childhood to adulthood. Sequential designs have supported the overall pattern of stability, although some traits appear to be more susceptible to change than others. In contrast, the studies to be discussed in the next section, conducted from the constructivist viewpoint, have stressed the evidence for personality change as opposed to stability.

Life-span research and the constructivist approach

The studies to be described in this section have made use of a combination of perspectives on personality. The personality theorist's perspective is represented by the use of various forms of psychometric tests of personality. The lay perspective is represented by the data collected from the subjects' peers and family. However, it is the self perspective that is given the most prominence in many of the studies to be described in this section. There is an emphasis on long and detailed interviews in which the subjects are asked to give their *own* account of their personality development.

Two of the studies to be described used conventional longitudinal designs following the same group of subjects for time-spans of twenty to thirty years or more. Block (1971) has data from the junior high school years through to mid-life, and Vaillant (1977) followed his subjects from their college years through to mid-life. The third study (Levinson, 1978) may also be described as longitudinal, with the qualification that the data were obtained retrospectively in a series of interviews with subjects in mid-life. Levinson's study is therefore based primarily on the self perspective.

The change model

The most striking feature of all three studies is the stress on personality change. The ordered change model in life-span psychology regards development as involving a sequence of changes over time. These changes may be qualitative or quantitative in nature. Where change is regarded as quantitative there is continuity between earlier and later stages in the sequence, and there is a sense in which quantitative, orderly change is a weak form of the stability model, since the early stages may be used to predict the later stages. Freud has already been introduced to exemplify the stability model, but he defies precise categorisation since he may also be used to represent the quantitative, orderly change model. We have seen how he believed that personality develops over a series of clearly defined stages during early childhood, and that the experiences during these stages will determine the personality of the adult.

The Freudian model has been used by Overton and Reese (1973) in their discussion of models of development to illustrate the mechanistic model, which is a version of the quantitative, orderly change model. Mechanistic models set out to describe the state of the organism which, like a machine, is inherently at rest and it only begins to operate when it is acted upon by external forces. Since complete description of the organism at any stage is believed possible, if the nature of the external forces is understood then the prediction of future states of the organism is also possible. Another example of the mechanistic or quantitative, orderly change model would be the behaviouristic approach of developmentalists such as Baer (1970), in which it is assumed that change is the consequence of learning and present behaviour can be explained in terms of previous learning.

Overton and Reese (1973) also discuss their equivalent of the qualitative, orderly change model, which they call the organismic model. Here the living organism serves as the guiding metaphor. The organism is regarded as an organised whole which is in continuous transition from one state to another. The organism is active; its behaviour is the consequence of internally generated purpose rather than the consequence of the action of external forces. Because of this teleological element, complete description and prediction is impossible. Overton and Reese cite Piaget's theory of cognitive development as exemplifying the organismic model; however, more relevant here is the personality theorist Erik Erikson, since his ideas have strongly influenced the three studies to be described.

Erikson's (1963) view of personality is an extension of Freudian theory. Although Erikson made use of many Freudian concepts, he regarded personality as subject to change throughout the life-span, whereas Freud regards the adult as a puppet controlled by strings which reach back into childhood. According to Erikson there are eight developmental stages:

1 Trust *vs.* basic mistrust
2 Autonomy *vs.* shame and doubt   early childhood
3 Initiative *vs.* guilt
4 Industry *vs.* inferiority
5 Identity *vs.* role diffusion   adolescence
6 Intimacy *vs.* isolation
7 Generativity *vs.* stagnation   adulthood
8 Ego identity *vs.* despair

The stages' bipolar titles indicate that each stage contains a conflict which has to be resolved. At any point in the life-span, personality is the product of the way these conflicts have been resolved. As a result of the way each stage is resolved the personality undergoes qualitative change. With Erikson, as with Freud, we have to contend with a major theory which defies categorisation. Erikson's theory is not only illustrative of the ordered change model, but also contains the essential feature of the dialectical model in which development is seen as the product of the resolution of thesis and antithesis. This takes place in the context of the developmental task confronting the person in each stage.

The first three stages are akin to the Freudian oral, anal and phallic stages. During the first stage (oral), the infant's task is to learn that the mother may be trusted to return as the source of comfort. The second stage (anal) is centred on the task of anal muscular control – learning when it is appropriate to hold back and when to let go. Like Freud, Erikson regarded the task of the third stage (phallic) as the development of conscience. The title of the third stage implies Erikson's view that a child may acquire too strict a conscience at this time, which will result in excessive guilt and a corresponding crippling of initiative.

During the two adolescent stages the tasks involve learning to win recognition by producing things and the integration of experience and expression into a career. During the first adult stage the task involves establishing an intimate relationship with another person, which requires having enough confidence to be able to lose a part of the self in the merging with another. If achieved, such a relationship will foster the release of creative and productive powers, and in stage 7 these powers can be directed towards establishing and guiding the next generation. The task of the final stage is one of reviewing life's successes and failures and preparing for death. Erikson believed that these stages are pan-cultural: the conflicts remain the same although every culture will have its own particular ways of resolving them.

Erikson's theory describes personality change in terms of the different conflicts that preoccupy each developmental stage. Do people perceive their own personality changes in this way? Ryff and Heinke (1983) studied subjectively perceived personality change in three adult groups: young, middle-aged and old-aged. All subjects filled out several personality scales, including two which measured the Eriksonian concepts of integrity (associated with old age) and generativity (associated with middle age). What makes this study particularly interesting is that subjects completed concurrent, retrospective and prospective self-reports on these measures. Consistent with Erikson, all the age groups awarded themselves higher integrity at old age and perceived themselves as being most generativity-oriented at middle age.

Support for Erikson's view that establishing an identity in adolescence is essential for later successful intimate relationships was obtained in a longitudinal study by Kahn, Zimmerman, Csikszentmihaly and Getzels (1985). They related art students' identity scores taken in 1963 with their marital status nearly twenty years later in 1981. Some interesting sex differences emerged. For men, there was a strong relationship between low identity and remaining single. For women, identity scores were not related to whether they had ever been married; however, women with low identity scores were likely to experience more marital instability (i.e. divorce and separation) than women with high identity scores.

The studies by Block, by Vaillant and by Levinson (to be described below) reflect the influence of several aspects of Erikson's ideas. First, these investigators all believe that personality changes take place during the adult years. Second, they conceptualise development as a series of tasks which may be executed successfully or unsuccessfully. This second point is the basis of the third, more general point that development is viewed as the process of adaptation to life. The way a person resolves the conflicts of each stage is the major determinant of that person's psychological adjustment. Their work is therefore not only about the development of personality, but also the origins of mental illness and mental health as seen within the context of the life-span.

Popular interest in life-span research has been growing of late (e.g. Sheehy, 1976). Adults are eager to read about the developmental stages they are supposed to be experiencing and those which lie ahead. An explanation for this current interest is the enthusiasm, particularly in the United States, for the idea that adults can change themselves. Encounter and T-groups, meditation, jogging, the Reverend Moon and the like are all believed to hold the key to positive change. More than ever before, we seem to be fascinated with the malleability of human nature. However, the research described so far in this chapter has generally supported the stability model rather than a change model. The constructivist approach appears to have identified changes ignored by the personality theorist's perspective.

Block

The first study to be described is the work reported in Block's book *Lives Through Time* (Block, 1971). This report is based on data obtained in two studies carried out at the Institute for Human Development, Berkeley, one of which began in 1929, the other in 1932. Together they involved 500 subjects, approximately half male and half female. By now these subjects have been studied from childhood to their mid-forties, although *Lives Through Time* only reports the findings up to and including the testing in the mid-thirties.

When Block began to tackle the job of making sense of the mountain of data amassed over the years, he was confronted by a series of virtually overwhelming problems typical of longitudinal research. He had not been involved with the research from its inception and there had been no continuity in the personnel concerned. As a result the data had been collected without a guiding hypothesis or theory in mind. A bewildering mass of varied information had built up over the years on each subject, including such diverse material as school reports, personality test scores, parents' reports, college records, unstructured interviews with the subjects and even newspaper cuttings referring to the subjects' exploits. Each subject's file contained a unique conglomeration of information.

Block approached his daunting task with two goals in view. He believed that adolescence is a critical time in personality development, so he wanted to see how personality at adolescence demonstrated continuity or change when compared with personality at an earlier or later point in life. Adolescence has long been regarded by psychologists as a period of rapid change and of accompanying difficulties of adjustment, and Block hoped that a longitudinal analysis would show how this period of apparent upheaval made sense in terms of a longer time perspective.

A second goal of Block's work was to see if there were groups of subjects each characterised by their own particular form of development. We have already had a hint of the importance of different paths of development in the Kagan and Moss study, where males and females showed different development of certain social behaviours. Block wanted to see whether, in addition to sex differences within the male and female groups, there would be subgroups which could be distinguished from one another. For example, it could be that some individuals go through a stormy adolescence but emerge as well-adjusted adults whereas others have an easy passage into a disturbed adulthood. There may be several different routes all leading to the same end point, or there may be as many end points as paths. Block's interest in individual differences in developmental paths is unusual; most longitudinal studies have been aimed at describing a single, generally applicable course of development. However, the range of developmental paths we can imagine if we compare some of our own long-standing friends and acquaintances suggests that the many end points, many paths model is nearer to the truth.

Block's first decision concerned which points in time to choose for comparison. Since he was particularly interested in adolescence he chose one time point during the subjects' senior high school years and compared this with two other time points: the junior high school years and the mid-thirties. In this way he was able to compare pre-adolescence, adolescence and adulthood. His next problem was to decide which of the available data to use and how best to compare data from these time points.

He hit on an excellent solution which reduced the bulk of the data without losing too much of the detail contained within it. The solution was to use a Q sort. As was outlined in chapter 7, a Q sort consists of a series of personality statements such as 'Is a popular person', 'Is dominant' or 'Quick to become angry' which a judge places in rank order from the most to the least applicable to the subject in question. Where there are many statements the judge may be asked to sort them into a small number of categories, ranging from very characteristic to very uncharacteristic, with a fixed number to be allocated to each category. For example, in one of the Q sorts used in Block's study there were one hundred statements which had to be sorted into nine categories according to the following distribution:

5 8 12 16 18 16 12 8 5

very characteristic   very uncharacteristic

The advantage of using Q sorts in this particular study was that the mass of varied data could be boiled down to a description consisting of a particular sorting of a series of statements. Exactly the same procedure could be applied to all the subjects, who could then be compared. Comparisons within subjects at different time points could also be made. It was a brilliant solution to the problem created by the fact that for no subject had exactly the same set of data been collected, and anyway the sheer bulk of the material prevented its detailed analysis.

The Q sorts became the basic data for all subsequent analyses, so it was essential that they were obtained in a methodologically sound manner. A file of raw data for each subject for each of the three time points was prepared. A Q sort was then obtained for each subject at each of these time points. Three judges read the data file and made their own Q sorts. No judge performed more than one Q sort for the same subject. If there was high agreement between the three judges' sorts, a composite Q sort consisting of the average of the three was constructed. Where judges did not agree, a fourth judge would be called in, and if agreement could still not be reached then that subject was dropped from the study. Checks were made to ensure that judges were not basing their Q sorts on stereotypes of hypothetical persons of the three ages. As a result of this elaborate judging process, each subject was described by three Q sorts: one for their junior high school years, one for their senior high school years, and one for their mid-thirties.

Block proceeded to analyse the Q sorts in two ways. First, in keeping with most longitudinal research, he looked for general trends. He wanted to find out if there were any clear patterns in male and female development. Second, he looked at the data more closely to see if there were any subgroups of subjects which could be described by distinct developmental paths which differed from the other subjects.

In order to analyse the data for general trends, he looked in particular at the continuity or change between the junior and senior high school Q sorts and the senior high school and adult Q sorts. The broad picture which emerged was not very informative. For both males and females the Q sorts for the two time points during the school years were highly similar, but there was considerably less correspondence between the senior high school and adult Q sorts. No clear sex differences emerged from this general analysis.

The general analysis had hinted at personality change between adolescence and the mid-thirties, but the details of this change were unclear. Block's second analysis involved looking for groups of subjects characterised by particular developmental paths. It could be that the differences between subgroups were cancelling each other out in the general analysis. The technique he used to locate subgroups characterised by similar developmental paths was inverted, or Q, factor analysis (Stephenson, 1953). So far, we have seen how factor analysis may be used to identify clusters of highly intercorrelating *variables*. In Q factor analysis, clusters of highly intercorrelating *subjects* are identified. The initial correlation matrix is composed of measures of similarity between each subject and every other. In Block's analysis the measures of similarity consisted of the correlations between pairs of subjects' combined adult and adolescent Q sorts. The factors obtained in Q factor analysis identify subgroups of highly similar subjects. In Block's analysis, the Q factors identified subjects who had followed similar developmental paths as indexed by their profiles on their combined adolescent and adult Q sorts.

Q factor analysis resulted in five subgroups for the males and six for the females. In order to get a full picture of the characteristics of each group, he used other data available on the subjects, such as their pre-adolescent Q sorts and material not used in the Q sorting process. The five male and six female types revealed the diversity of developmental paths which had been obscured when the sample was considered as a whole. For example, the best-adjusted male type was the 'Ego Resilient', of which there were nineteen instances. They were characterised by intelligence, good health and good family background. They showed maturity even in their junior high school years and this developed steadily over the next two time points. Their development was untroubled, predictable and continuous. In contrast there were eleven 'Anomic Extraverts'. These men had bad family backgrounds with dominant mothers and weak fathers. They conformed to the adolescent stereotype, being gregarious, vigorous, self-confident and rebellious. However, this early vigour had burnt out by adulthood, leaving tense, anxious and repressive men who were surprisingly empty after such a promising adolescence.

The female types were entirely different from the male types, with no equivalent to the successful and positively evaluated male Ego Resilients. The largest subgroup consisted of nineteen Female Prototypes. These women are described by Block as having led smoothly progressive and satisfying lives. They had been poised and pretty as teenagers and had matured into replicas of the all-American housewife. The greatest change was observed in fourteen Cognitive Copers. As adolescents these women were maladjusted but by adulthood they had grown into mature, well-educated and well-adjusted women. The least well-adjusted of the female types were the ten Hyper-feminine Repressives. These women had been moderately inadequate as adolescents but by adulthood Block describes them as being in a shambles. The father played more of a part in their upbringing than their working mothers (which Block regarded as a bad start). These women were physically voluptuous as adults, trying to be conventional but displaying all the symptoms of a hysterical personality: preoccupied with their health, complaining, devious and whiny.

The major difficulty with producing a typology is making sense of the individual types. A subjective bias will unavoidably invade the interpretations in the effort to produce a meaningful picture. Early on, Block acknowledges a debt to psychoanalytic thinking which becomes apparent at the final stage of the book, when he presents the subtypes.

He stresses the importance of parental characteristics for future development, and uses psychoanalytic terms such as 'repression' and 'ego strength' to portray the qualities of the types. As well as introducing a subjective element, typological findings can also be criticised for being limited to the particular sample studied. Only eighty-three males and eighty-five females were available at the end of the follow-up period for the typological analysis, and it is doubtful whether subgroups composed of ten to twenty individuals will be replicated in subsequent samples.

How do the results of Block's analyses relate to the two main goals he set at the outset, namely to examine the importance of adolescence in the life-span and to see if development followed distinct paths for different subgroups? The two goals became fused in the actual analysis, since the distinctive developmental paths adopted by the subgroups were frequently characterised by the nature of the continuity or change between adolescence and adulthood. Block's research has demonstrated that, within this particular sample, there were distinctive subgroups characterised by particular developmental pathways.

Vaillant

The aim of Vaillant's (1977) work has been to further the understanding of the nature of human adjustment. He was not interested merely in how adults develop, but how they develop successfully to be fully adjusted, psychologically healthy adults.

The subjects of the study were ninety-five men from each of the classes of 1942, 1943 and 1944 from Harvard University. When they were at college they participated in intensive testing and interviewing, amounting to about twenty hours in all. After they had graduated they completed a questionnaire every year until 1955, and Vaillant himself interviewed forty-four of them in 1967. Vaillant discusses the findings from two viewpoints: first he was interested in seeing to what extent these men's biographies revealed a series of developmental stages through which they had all passed, and second he was interested to see if any characteristics at an early stage predicted the sorts of outcomes at later stages.

In assessing the data for evidence of stages Vaillant was influenced by Erikson's theory. In the years immediately following college the men were concerned with establishing intimate relationships in the form of marriage and friends (Erikson's stage 6: intimacy *vs.* isolation). They were also working hard, particularly between the ages of 25 and 30 years. During this time they were very conforming, and, in Vaillant's words, had lost their capacity to play. When they were in their forties the men went through a kind of second adolescence: a period of questioning and reappraisal which led either to a more relaxed attitude towards their work and a new-found non-conformity leading to a more adventurous approach to life, or to depression and an inability to grow in new directions. This period is equivalent to Erikson's stage of generativity *vs.* stagnation.

Since Vaillant was primarily interested in the nature of human adjustment, he compared the men who by 1967 had the best outcomes with those who had the worst outcomes (as assessed by his adult adjustment scale). He then explored their past histories to discover the characteristics of successful and unsuccessful lives. There were a number of surprises, and some old beliefs were challenged. For example, the Worst Outcomes were not predicted by the symptoms of maladjustment at college: shyness, ideational thinking, introspection, inhibition and absence of purpose. The characteristics of the college student that were found in the Best Outcomes were being well-integrated, practical and organised. These are not features of the stereotype of the adolescent. The Best Outcomes were found to have achieved stable marriages before the age of 30 and to have remained married until 50. The Worst Outcomes had either married very young, after 30, or were separated before 50. The men who by mid-life had become company presidents (a recognised index of success in the United States) had the best marriages and friendships.

In his careful study of the biographies of these men Vaillant came to the conclusion that they had *all* had to cope with experiences which were enough to precipitate a mental breakdown, even though only a small proportion had actually become mentally ill. He believes adult adjustment to be the result of experiencing trials as well as blessings. Using Erikson's terminology, he regards varied experience of positive and negative kinds as an aid to ego development. In Terman's longitudinal study of intellectually superior individuals it turned out that they were better adjusted than a normal IQ control group. Vaillant would not agree that intelligence alone is enough to guarantee adjustment. He argues that adjustment is achieved by developing healthy defence mechanisms. For example, one of his subjects who was a wartime bomber pilot now writes poetry as an outlet for his feelings of guilt.

Levinson

The final study to be described is the retrospective longitudinal study conducted by Levinson (1978). In contrast to Block, who was particularly interested in adolescence, Levinson was motivated to carry out his research by his fascination with the difficulties of middle age – partly inspired, as he acknowledges, by his own experiences during this period. Levinson, like Vaillant, was interested in charting the stages of adult development and was influenced by Erikson's views on adult personality development.

Levinson studied forty males all born between 1923 and 1934, and therefore aged between 35 and 45 years at the time the study was carried out in 1969. They were drawn from four different occupational groups: industrial workers, business executives, university biologists and novelists. Levinson and his colleagues spent many hours with each subject obtaining an extensive biography. They then sifted through these biographies to see if a general developmental pattern emerged. Levinson was impressed by the similarity between all his subjects' biographies despite their varied economic, racial, religious and educational backgrounds. Although the particular events differed from person to person, Levinson claimed that all his subjects went through periods of major upheaval and transition at remarkably similar ages. On the basis of his observations, Levinson (1978, 1986) proposed that everyone passes through a sequence of developmental periods and transitional stages which can be depicted as a series of steps, as is shown in Figure 9.1.

On the right of the staircase there are the eras which Levinson likens to the seasons of spring, summer, autumn and winter. On the left there are the transitional periods between eras. These are the periods of life crisis. During a transitional period one era has to be terminated and another begun. This process always took about five years for Levinson's subjects, and occurred within specific age limits. Each era and its associated transitions is characterised by a series of tasks. For example, in the young adult era a young man has to carry out four tasks: form a dream of what he wants out of life, form a mentor relationship to aid in the realisation of that dream, form an occupation, and form love relationships, marriage and a family.

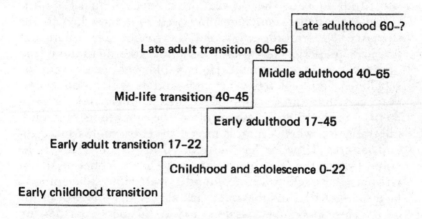

FIGURE 9.1 *Levinson's theory of developmental periods and transitional stages*

Around the middle of the young adult era comes the crucial transitional period. It occurs within the same era, not as a step between eras. Nevertheless Levinson regarded it as the most traumatic of all the transitional phases. He called it the Age 30 transition, and it occurs between the ages of 28 and 33 years. It is a period of upheaval because it is the time when the initial experimentation with young adult life draws to a close and a man settles down to making a variety of commitments which will shape his future life, commitments in his occupation and his family. The next time of upheaval after the Age 30 transition is the mid-life transition. It is not always as chaotic as the Age 30 transition, and some fortunate people will hardly notice it slip by, but for others it too can be a period of exceptional difficulty.

The sources of difficulty in these transitional periods are different for everyone; but they will be centred on the significant areas in the person's life, which are usually work, family and relationships and, for some, a hobby or spare-time activity. For example, a young man may have married during his early adult transition when he was busy rejecting his parents and all they stood for. His wife may have represented the alternative set of values he wanted to identify with and yet, at the same time, provided a form of mother substitute to ease the separation anxiety induced by the transition. Such a marriage may well founder when it hits the Age 30 transition, argued Levinson. The man has finished his period of exploration and experimentation, and now seeks real commitment. He is a different person from the rebellious youth of ten years ago and it will be an elastic marriage that can accommodate this change and develop-ment. Marital difficulties are often the symptoms of a mid-life transition when a man is forced to reflect on his successes and failures. How far has he realised his dream? How is he going to face the fact that he has not won a Nobel prize nor written a best-selling yet profound novel? How is he going to face the fact that his marriage has slowly dissolved from the early closeness and passion to a business partnership between acquaintances?

A radical solution to the mid-life crisis may require cutting out aspects of the previous era in order to come to terms with what lies ahead. Erikson referred to adulthood as a period of generativity versus stagnation, and Levinson regards middle adulthood as a time to accept one's successes and failures and give way to a younger generation, serving them as a source of wisdom via mentor and parental relationships. One reason why the mid-life transition can be so difficult to accept is that it involves stepping out into another generation. The man of 45 is no longer one of the boys, and must accept and find rewards in being a member of the older generation.

Levinson's book is absorbing and non-technical and makes excellent reading. He describes in detail the biographies of four of his subjects, one from each of the occupational groups he studied, showing how they conform to his stages of development. However, he does not present any quantified analyses of his findings and, as a piece of psychological research, his work may be questioned in many respects.

The sample is small (N = 40), and was drawn from the Boston area of the United States, which is highly unrepresentative; it attracts a large proportion of intelligent and talented people. (The same criticism may be levelled against Vaillant's study of Harvard men.) The data were retrospective, and therefore subject to the biases of selective memory. Not only will people forget and distort events that occurred twenty years ago, they will also imbue their past with a meaning and organisation that was absent at the time. Levinson commented that it was only by looking back over long time periods that the structure of an individual's life became apparent, but with the aid of hindsight it is easy to make the course of an individual's life appear purposeful and directed. Since there was no attempt to derive the sequence of developmental stages in an objective and quantifiable fashion, it is impossible to evaluate Levinson's claim that all his subjects passed through these stages. They did in Levinson's eyes, but would another researcher have reached the same conclusion? (Again the same criticism may be levelled against Vaillant's work.) Levinson includes little theoretical discussion about the status of these stages, but he does propose that they are universal and that they are the product of biological maturation and environmental pressures produced by a complex social system.

Throughout this book Levinson seems to be confused about the origin of the developmental tasks. For example, when commenting on the fact that most people get married during their twenties, the period of early adulthood, he says, 'It is astonishing that nature's timing is so bad: we must choose a partner and start a family before we quite know what we are doing or how to do it well' (Levinson, 1978, p. 107). To attribute the age of marriage in Western society to the force of nature is unconvincing since the typical age of marriage varies culturally and historically. It would be more appropriate to blame the pressure of Western society for expecting people to marry in their twenties. A similar confusion arises in his discussion of young adulthood, when he describes the young man as experimenting with life and not really settling down until he reaches his thirties. Such experimentation is surely a luxury restricted to certain privileged groups in industrialised society; it is not found in more primitive cultures or in earlier periods of our history, where usually an individual's occupation is not a matter of choice and there is no room for experimentation.

Both Levinson's and Vaillant's studies were concerned exclusively with male development. However, the appearance of Levinson's (in press) new work on the seasons of a *woman's* life is eagerly awaited. Meanwhile, a recent investigation into the Age 30 crisis in women presents some evidence to suggest that this particular life crisis also occurs in females, and is chronologically precipitated as opposed to role-related. Reinke, Holmes and Harris (1985) conducted retrospective interviews with sixty middle-class women representing four cohorts: 30, 35, 40 and 45 years. The interviews focused on events and self-perceived change, and were subsequently coded for age of occurrence of changes (e.g. births, divorces), and major psychosocial transitions were identified by clinicians. The main finding was clear evidence for an Age 30 crisis: 78 per cent of subjects reported starting a transition between 27 and 30 years, and this percentage was consistent across cohorts. Interestingly, there was no relation between the transitions and any particular phase in reproduction and parenting. These women's Age 30 crises cannot be explained as a panic reaction to the ticking of the biological clock. It occurred in women with children of any age and in women without children.

Stability or change?

Of these three studies, Block's is the only one to conform to acceptable standards of quantitative, empirical research, and for this reason it would be unwise to give the findings as a whole too much weight. Nevertheless it is worth considering why these studies, particularly Vaillant's and Levinson's, have stressed change: they studied the development of personality during adulthood showing how the personality at mid-life can be traced back through a series of transitions to the personality of the young person. Why should these studies find evidence of personality change whereas the studies from the personality theorist's perspective have stressed stability?

The material collected in the studies by Block, Vaillant and Levinson covered a wide range, including data from the lay perspective (i.e. parental and peer reports) and the self perspective, as well as conventional test data of the type used by the personality theorist's perspective. This suggests that while test data may yield evidence of stability, a person's self-perceptions and others' perceptions of that person indicate personality development and change. This change is not inexplicable, but appears reasonable in the light of the developmental tasks that have been tackled. Ask yourself whether you are the same as you were ten years ago and it is likely that you will perceive yourself to have changed in some ways since then, although the changes will make sense to you in the light of your experiences. However, self-perceived change and change perceived by others can be misleading because they may be wrongly attributed to the person when in fact they should be attributed to the situation. Perhaps perceived change is yet another example of the fundamental attribution error (Ross, 1977): the tendency to overestimate the importance of personality dispositions at the expense of situation variables.

Both Vaillant and Levinson imply that there are periods of particularly intense personality change, and that these are during the major transitional periods (e.g. from adolescence to adulthood, from young adulthood to middle age). These transitory periods are marked by specific developmental tasks such as breaking away from the ties of the family and establishing an independent identity, or switching from the younger to the older generation. It could be that in carrying out the tasks more or less successfully our personalities are actually changed. Alternatively, it could be that our personalities remain the same but we have to apply ourselves to a different set of tasks, and this creates a sense of change in ourselves. Other people see us behaving in the necessary ways to adapt to a new stage and consequently they perceive us as having changed. For example, the novice parent is the subject of comments such as 'I never knew he could be so good with babies', and personality changes are attributed when it may only be the circumstances which have changed.

According to this argument life-span research carried out with a constructivist approach, in which the subjects' personalities are assessed from all three perspectives, will be likely to yield evidence of personality change because the material obtained from the subjects themselves and from the subjects' families and peers will contain assertions of change. In contrast, research carried out from the personality theorist's perspective, in which only personality test data are obtained, will produce a more stable picture of personality. It is of course impossible to answer the question of which view, stability or change, is the more accurate. It may be more objective to argue on the basis of the personality theorist's studies that personality remains stable, but if this view contradicts the beliefs and intuitions of the lay person and the self-perceiver it will not be particularly helpful in the understanding of life-span development to ignore these contradictory views.

10 Criminal personality

Particularly in Western industrialised society, we value individuality and cherish the fact that everyone is unique. However, there is a limit to our tolerance and admiration for idiosyncrasies, and there comes a point at which eccentricity becomes abnormality. This point is extremely difficult to define. Despite our implicit understanding of the concept of deviant personality, attempts at making it explicit are only partially successful. Nevertheless, it is valuable to consider some of the attempts at an explicit definition of deviance because they give a greater awareness of the conditions under which a person or a behaviour is branded as having passed the limit of acceptability. In achieving a greater understanding of those conditions perhaps we learn as much about ourselves and the society in which we live as we do about the concept of deviance itself. After considering the problems of defining deviance, the rest of this chapter will focus on one form of deviance – criminality – and discuss it from each of the three perspectives on personality.

Defining deviance

Deviance as non-conformity

Attempts at defining deviance by concentrating on the qualities of the person or the behaviour identified as deviant are generally unsuccessful. Thus, deviance has been defined as that which is statistically rare. But rarity alone does not guarantee deviancy; having red hair, playing the bagpipes and being a cross-channel swimmer are all relatively rare qualities, but a person would not be branded as deviant for possessing one of them (although being characterised by all three might raise an eyebrow). Deviance has been defined as that which causes distress to the deviant or to the victim; but psychopaths are capable of highly deviant behaviour which causes them no distress, and deviant behaviour does not always distress those at the receiving end. Indeed, sometimes it is quite the reverse: the musical genius's deviant ability to play the piano exquisitely may give pleasure to millions. Behaviour with which others cannot empathise has been defined as deviant, but non-deviants can empathise with the person found guilty of speeding or driving over the alcohol limit ('There but for the grace of God go I'). The deviant has been defined as someone who causes a problem for society. For example, in the Soviet Union political dissidents present a problem for society and are labelled mentally ill (deviant), which solves the problem by allowing the removal of the dissident to a mental hospital (Lader, 1977). However, dissidence itself cannot be said to be deviant since in other societies critical appraisal of existing social structures is tolerated or even encouraged.

Searching for the hallmark of deviance within the person or the behaviour is continually hampered by the unavoidable fact of cultural relativism and all its implications. Cultural relativism refers to the fact that different societies place different values on the same behaviour. For example, we abhor the killing of newborn babies, but it has been reported by anthropologists that certain societies regard infanticide as an acceptable form of population control. A person who claims to be able to see and hear things unseen and unheard by others is regarded in our society as suffering from hallucinations and may well end up in a mental hospital, whereas the same person in another social context could well become the most revered member of the group. Societies differ not only on what forms of behaviour are regarded as antisocial deviance, but also in the definition of prosocial deviance. For example, independence and individuality are cultivated in the United States, whereas dependence and the submerging of the self beneath the state is expected in modern-day China (Munro, 1977).

The inevitable consequence of acknowledging cultural relativism is that no behaviour or person may be regarded as inherently deviant in the pro- or antisocial sense. There will always be a society somewhere in the world today, or one that has existed in the past, capable of invalidating a claim for the universal evaluation of a behaviour as deviant. However, the significance of cultural relativism should not be exaggerated, for it must be acknowledged that societies show a considerable degree of consistency in outlawing certain behaviours such as murder, rape and theft (Lemert, 1972; Welford, 1975). Does this mean, after all, that certain behaviours are inherently deviant? Not necessarily. Such behaviours may be universally proscribed because they are disruptive of human social life which, although capable of superficial variation, is restricted by certain biological limitations.

Despite the similarities between many societies, we can never arrive at a satisfactory definition of deviance. We are forced to end up by saying that deviance, positive or negative, is that which a particular society has chosen to evaluate as such at a particular point in time. The definition of deviance does not depend upon some quality inherent in a person or a behaviour, but on the rules of society which determine the boundary between deviance and conformity. Recognising the importance of social rules in defining deviance has resulted in a shift in attention away from the person and the behaviour onto the conditions under which a person or behaviour comes to be regarded as deviant.

Given that deviance must be defined in terms of the social context in which it occurs, it follows that deviance may be defined as non-conformity to accepted social norms. When a given culture has categorised a particular behaviour as deviant then, generally speaking, the performance of that behaviour is usually fairly rare. We do not typically commit infanticide, have more than one spouse or steal the weekly groceries. However, these behaviours do occur, and when they do they are regarded as deviant. In other words, most people most of the time conform to society's explicit and implicit rules; when people fail to conform they are labelled as deviant. Defining deviance as non-conformity is illuminating because it incorporates the idea that deviant behaviour is frequently unexpected or unpredictable; it is not the way most people would behave in the circumstances.

The three perspectives on deviance

Deviance may be studied from any of the three perspectives on personality. From the personality theorist's perspective deviance is primarily the result of internal characteristics of the person which cause him or her to behave in a deviant fashion. From the lay perspective the interesting questions about deviance are not how it is caused, but which behaviours and people come to be evaluated as deviant by others, under what circumstances and why. The subject matter of the lay perspective is the process by which some members of society attribute deviance to others. The self perspective is concerned with self-attributions of deviance. Here the focus of attention is on the deviant's self-perceptions, in particular on how a deviant identity is acquired and its effects on subsequent behaviour.

Deviance may work to the benefit or the detriment of society and therefore be encouraged or discouraged accordingly. In this chapter the focus will be on criminality, which is generally considered to be a form of antisocial deviance, although (as we shall see below) it has been argued that it has beneficial effects. Criminality will be considered from each of the three perspectives.

The personality theorist's perspective on criminality

Attention throughout the following discussion will be on the person who commits crimes as opposed to the actual criminal behaviours themselves, which are the special interest of criminologists and sociologists. Some psychologists (e.g. Feldman, 1977) have chosen to focus on criminal behaviours, arguing that they are learned in the same way that non-deviant behaviours are learned, and that the best way to arrive at an explanation of criminality is to understand the contingencies controlling the performance of criminal activities. However, the focus here is on the person rather than the behaviour because whereas virtually all of us have engaged in a technically criminal activity at some time, only a few of us have become hardened criminals in the sense that we are continually engaged in criminality as a way of life. The hardened criminal commits hundreds or even thousands of crimes in his lifetime and is extremely resistant to any attempts at therapeutic change.

The research to be described in this chapter is about male criminality, and therefore only the male personal pronoun will be used. Although certain forms of female criminality may be on the increase, at present it is still the case that the vast majority of apprehended criminals are male. There remains a regrettable paucity of theory and research on female criminality (but see Box, 1983; and Heidensohn, 1985). In view of women's meagre contribution to the criminal statistics, it has been argued that the study of female criminality is a waste of resources. However, such reasoning is misguided. Consider the case of a sex-linked deadly disease. Research into both the vulnerable sex and the invulnerable sex will be illuminating. Similarly, in the case of criminality, the intriguing question is why women are so successfully inoculated against crime, while men are at such a high risk.

The personality theorist's perspective emphasises the role of person variables at the expense of situational variables in the determination of behaviour, and in theories of criminal personality this bias is strongly apparent. The aim of theories of criminal personality is to demonstrate that people who commit crimes are characterised by a particular constellation of personality traits that differentiate them from people who do not commit crimes. Implicit in this aim is the view that these traits are the underlying cause of the criminal behaviour. The research from this perspective falls into two categories: studies either compare criminals with non-criminals, or they look for different criminal subtypes within the criminal population. In most of these studies the criminal subjects are drawn from the population of 'official' criminals: those who have been apprehended by the police and who are subsequently found guilty of an offence and entered into criminal statistics.

There are two important disadvantages associated with the use of official criminals. First, official criminal statistics not only grossly underestimate the amount of crime that actually takes place (Wootton, 1959), but they are also unrepresentative of the total population of criminals and their crimes (Box, 1981; Feldman, 1977). The incarcerated criminal, although providing the ideal captive subject, cannot be said to be representative of criminals in general. Investigators who limit themselves to studying official criminals are in danger of developing theories that are only applicable to the highly atypical criminal – the one who gets caught. Although attempts to make statements about criminals in general on the basis of findings obtained from such a biased sample must be highly speculative, the findings may be generalised with reasonable confidence to other official criminals. The criminal statistics do not vary dramatically from year to year, which indicates that the official criminal population remains fairly constant. However, research on unofficial criminals, such as self-reported offenders, is essential in order that the generality of these theories may be tested.

The second disadvantage of studying the official criminal is that any personality characteristics found to distinguish the apprehended criminal may be the result of his present imprisonment and recent experiences rather than indications of enduring qualities which were present before arrest and were causally related to the criminal behaviour. While this possibility cannot be excluded, it does seem rather tenuous in connection with the relatively enduring personality traits such as those measured by Cattell's and Eysenck's questionnaires which, as longitudinal studies have shown, remain relatively stable over the adult life-span. The point is more relevant where measures of less stable characteristics such as attitudes are involved.

Criminals versus non-criminals

In general, the results of studies in which criminals have been compared with non-criminals on personality measures have suggested that the differences between the two are less clear-cut than the personality theorist's perspective would have assumed. In 1950, Schuessler and Cressey reviewed all the investigations of the previous twenty-five years and found that of the 113 studies only 42 per cent obtained results differentiating between criminals and non-criminals. A review of the ninety-four studies conducted between 1950 and the mid-1960s (Waldo and Dinitz, 1967) indicated an improvement, with 81 per cent of the studies differentiating between criminals and non-criminals. This could well be due to the increased sophistication of personality assessment techniques during this period.

Multi-trait theories have featured in particular in the more recent studies of criminals versus non-criminals. As was described in chapter 3, Eysenck elaborated a theory of criminal personality in which criminals are believed to have failed to acquire the constraints of a conscience as a result of defective learning. He predicted that criminals are characterised by high scores on all of his three personality factors: extraversion, neuroticism and psychoticism. Since psychoticism is a recent addition to the theory, most of the studies only provide data on extraversion and neuroticism. In two comprehensive reviews (Cochrane, 1974; Passingham, 1972) it was concluded that whereas there is some support for the hypothesis that criminals are highly neurotic, the evidence for the hypothesis that they are also highly extraverted is inadequate. Cochrane reviewed twenty studies, and in five of these the results were actually in the reverse direction, with criminals scoring significantly lower than non-criminals on extraversion (reported in Hoghughi and Forrest, 1970; S.B.G. Eysenck and H.J. Eysenck, 1971).

In his defence, Eysenck has pointed out that some of the items on the extraversion scale may be unsuitable for a prison population (e.g. an item referring to whether the respondent likes going to parties is inappropriate in a context where parties do not take place). The presence of unsuitable items could lead to the artificial lowering of prisoners' extraversion scores. Eysenck was also critical of the control groups used in some studies, and stressed the importance of matching the criminals and non-criminals on variables such as age, sex, social class and intelligence, all of which are themselves related to extraversion.

Burgess (1972) proposed that an appropriate test of Eysenck's theory must take account of extraversion and neuroticism scores simultaneously. This is done by dividing the subjects into four groups on the basis of their scores corresponding to the four quadrants formed by the two orthogonal dimensions of extraversion (E) and neuroticism (N) (i.e. high E, high N; high E, low N; low E, high N; low E, low N). He demonstrated that although there may be no significant differences between the two groups when the means for the two dimensions were analysed separately, if the number of criminals appearing in the high E high N quadrant was compared with the corresponding number in the non-criminal group, significant differences may be obtained. However, a study by Shapland and Rushton (1975), which met all the necessary methodological requirements, including quadrant analysis, failed to support Eysenck's theory. Using self-reported delinquency, a high delinquency group and an appropriately matched low delinquency group were compared for the frequency of highly extraverted and neurotic subjects. The results showed no tendency for the high delinquency group to contain an excess of extraverted neurotics.

In sum, there is no conclusive support for Eysenck's theory that criminals are highly neurotic and highly extraverted. The evidence as regards psychoticism is limited, but does support the theory (H.J. Eysenck, 1979, 1974). In view of the criticism of Eysenck's theory concerning the relations between personality and learning (see chapter 3), it is not surprising that the hypothesised personality characteristics of criminals, which are intended to account for their supposed defective learning ability, have failed to emerge.

The other major multi-trait theorist who has been involved in the investigation of differences between criminals and non-criminals is Cattell. Unlike Eysenck, Cattell did not develop a specific theory of criminal personality. However, given that his representation of the structure of personality is relatively complex, it is possible to compare criminals and non-criminals on Cattell's personality tests to see if criminals emerge with a distinctive profile. As with Eysenck's theory, the results using Cattell's theory are inconclusive. Cattell, Eber and Tatsuoka (1970) reported the personality profile, derived from a sample of 800 prisoners. They were found to be below average in superego and ego strength (low G and low C) and low on self-sentiment (low Q3). They were also characterised by desurgency (low F) and guilt-proneness (high O). They were not dominant (low E) and they had high autistic imagination (high M). Other studies have obtained different results even on such presumably key factors as G, superego strength (e.g. Warburton, 1965, found that a sample of highly dangerous psychopaths had near-average scores on G), which makes it impossible to draw any firm conclusions.

The reviews of earlier studies using a variety of personality measures and the more recent studies using Eysenck's and Cattell's questionnaires indicate that clear-cut personality differences between criminals and non-criminals are not easy to find. Perhaps the lack of evidence in the personality domain can be offset by greater success in other areas of psychological functioning. Two other dimensions of individual variation, neither of which are strictly regarded as personality variables but which would seem to be likely candidates, are intelligence and moral reasoning.

It might be expected that official criminals would be less intelligent than non-criminals. Such a hypothesis could be based on the assumption either that all criminals are less intelligent than non-criminals or that only the less intelligent criminals are likely to get caught. However, the evidence does not provide strong support for either hypothesis. In Caplan's (1965) review of delinquency studies, he concluded that delinquents typically scored around eight points less than non-delinquents. There was also some evidence for a discrepancy between delinquents' performance subtest scores versus their verbal subtest scores in the direction of higher performance scores. The evidence, such as there is, suggests that the differences in intelligence are small and could be due to the effects of institutionalisation, as opposed to intelligence being a significant precursor to criminality. Caplan recommended that more studies be carried out on unofficial, self-reported criminals. In just such a study, West and Farrington (1973, 1977) found slightly lower intelligence scores and poorer educational achievement in their high delinquency group than in their low delinquency group. Thus, there is some evidence for an association between marginally lower intelligence and delinquency, but the difference in intelligence is smaller than expected and has yet to be thoroughly investigated in the adult criminal.

Theories of moral development (Piaget, 1932; Kohlberg, 1964) propose that children and adults pass through a series of developmental stages beginning with a stage characterised by egocentricity, in which morally right behaviour is regarded as that which avoids breaking rules and the motivation to behave correctly is a desire to avoid punishment. The end point of moral development will vary among individuals, with some attaining a higher level of moral maturity than others. In Kohlberg's theory, the highest stage (stage six) is characterised as one in which a person governs his or her behaviour according to a set of self-chosen ethical principles which are universal in the sense that they transcend culture-specific legal rules and regulations. Kohlberg's six stages are divided into three levels: the preconventional (stages one and two), conventional (stages three and four) and postconventional (stages five and six). Most adults reach the conventional level of moral reasoning, in which the individual is recognised as being part of a social system that has to be preserved by following rules and regulations. Only about 10 per cent of adults are believed to attain stage six. Research into moral reasoning involves presenting subjects with moral dilemmas which the subjects have to resolve, giving a full account of their reasoning. Their responses are then categorised as indicative of one of the six stages.

Criminal behaviour typically involves violating society's rules and regulations and hence also involves violating most individuals' moral principles, since stage four morality is composed of a respect for authority and avoidance of censure. Hence, it could be expected that official criminals would be at a lower stage of moral development than their non-criminal counterparts. This possibility is discussed by Feldman (1977), who cites two studies investigating the association between morality and criminal behaviour. Kohlberg (1969) argued that prisoners demonstrated a morality at levels one and two in their statements about the morality of criminal behaviour. Fodor (1972) found that official delinquents were significantly lower than matched non-delinquents on a quantitative measure of morality even though both groups fell within the range of stage four moral reasoning. More recently Griffore and Samuels (1978), using Rest's defining issues test (Rest, 1974), found that residents of a maximum security prison in the United States were predominantly at Kohlberg's stage four.

As with intelligence, the evidence for differences in moral reasoning between criminals and non-criminals does not appear substantial enough to provide an adequate explanation of criminality. Although more research might be helpful, there are a number of limitations to the study of moral development. When people are asked to give their opinions about moral dilemmas in a paper-and-pencil task it is their moral attitudes which are being assessed, and attitudes are notorious for not correlating with behaviour. A person may respond in a stage five manner on Kohlberg's task, but when confronted with a real-life moral dilemma behave at stage two. The interaction between individual differences in moral reasoning and the complex situational factors associated with moral decisions must be taken into account (Kurtines, 1986).

Another series of problems is concerned with the degree to which a person will apply the same level of moral reasoning to different aspects of his or her life. For instance, a person may have attained stage six ethical principles but still behave in a stage two way in certain contexts. The extent to which moral development proceeds uniformly in different domains requires further investigation. This point will be developed later in the chapter when we come to take a closer look at the criminal mind.

The search for distinguishing characteristics, be they personality traits or other psychological dimensions of individual variation, has not proved particularly successful. Few clear-cut findings can be reported. One possible explanation for the absence of results is the heterogeneity of official criminals. A sample of incarcerated criminals will be a mixture of people of different ages with different criminal records. It is possible that there are homogeneous subgroups within the broad category of official criminals which are similar with respect to personality variables, but the differences among these subgroups may be of such an order as to cancel out any characteristics for the category as a whole. The importance of heterogeneity has been recognised by Eysenck, Rust and Eysenck (1977), who recommend that subgroups be studied.

Criminal subgroups

The most striking source of heterogeneity within the criminal population is the variety of offences for which criminals have been convicted. There has been a tendency for investigators to assume that criminals specialise in particular sorts of offences. For example, the property offender is usually non-violent, and the child molester is typically law-abiding in most other respects. Hence, offence-based typologies have been developed (e.g. Gibbons and Garrity, 1962; Hayner, 1961). Such typologies are based on intuition and past experience and, although they can be applied to criminal groups to see how well they account for the heterogeneity, they are not as satisfactory as empirically derived typologies.

Using multivariate techniques such as factor analysis or cluster analysis it is possible to feed in a profile of information on each subject and discover which subgroups share similar profiles and so arrive at an empirical typology. We have already come across an example of this approach in Block's longitudinal study, where Q factor analysis was used to identify subgroups which had undergone similar long-term personality development. Similar techniques have been applied with some success to criminal groups. The main disadvantage of empirically based typologies is that they are limited by the nature of the sample from which they are derived. For example, if the sample contained no violent offenders then no indication as to whether violent offenders form a subgroup could be obtained. Ideally, empirically derived typologies should be tested out on additional samples to check on their generality. Additionally, the results from different studies can be compared to see if the same subgroups have been found by different investigators. Studies of heterogeneous prison samples of adult offenders in Britain and America have produced some consistent findings on criminal subtypes. The two most reliable types appear to be the active aggressive type (characterised by a long history of impulsive violence) and the inadequate type (characterised by passivity and lack of social skills) (Carlson, 1972; Marcus, 1960; Sinclair and Chapman, 1973; West, 1963).

In view of the immense variety of individuals to be found in the prison population, some researchers have turned their attention to studying subgroups within a specific subsection of official criminals. In particular, the subsection of violent offenders has attracted considerable interest. Much of this work has been stimulated by Megargee's theory that there are two types of aggressive person: overcontrolled and undercontrolled (Megargee, 1966). He proposed that the most extreme acts of violence were performed by overcontrolled people without any history of violence; they keep all their hostility bottled up, and when they eventually allow it to escape the effects are disastrous. Undercontrolled people commit numerous but relatively minor violent acts. Megargee (1966) obtained moderate support for this typology in a study of delinquents, but Blackburn's work on Broadmoor patients provided more conclusive evidence (Blackburn, 1968a, 1968b, 1970). The MMPI profiles of patients convicted for extremely violent acts were different from those of patients convicted for moderately violent offences, the differences being on scales relating to overcontrol such as Repression (R), Ego control (Eo) and Mania (Ma).

In Britain, violent offenders are sometimes sent to special hospitals (e.g. Broadmoor) as opposed to prison, because they have been deemed mentally abnormal by the courts and hence regarded as in need of custodial treatment rather than imprisonment. Not all mentally abnormal offenders have committed violent crimes, and the less dangerous offenders are sent to regular psychiatric hospitals for their treatment. For a criminal to be deemed mentally abnormal the court must be satisfied that he is either mentally ill, of subnormal intelligence or psychopathic. Mentally abnormal offenders are therefore a legally created subsection of official criminals based on a psychological rationale. They are particularly worthy of investigation because they are supposed to be receiving treatment, and yet little is known about the nature of their problems or the best way to help them.

One subtype of mentally abnormal offender to receive considerable attention from both professionals and the public is the psychopath. The validity of this diagnostic category is dubious (Wootton, 1959), and it has been described as a waste-paper category which is used to dispose of patients who do not fit into any other category. Clinical descriptions of the psychopath are varied, but usually include references to an abnormal absence of guilt for antisocial behaviour, an inability to form lasting bonds of affection and a failure to learn by experience (Cleckley, 1964; Craft, 1966; McCord and McCord, 1964). Some studies of criminal subtypes have generated a type resembling the clinical description of a psychopath, and the MMPI is able to locate those diagnosed as psychopathic by their distinctive 4–9 profile (high scores on the Psychopathic and Mania scales).

In Hampson and Kline's (1977) investigation into subtypes of mentally abnormal offenders, criminals and matched non-criminals were analysed together to see if subtypes would emerge which both differentiated within the criminal group and between the criminals and non-criminals. The subjects were given a battery of tests including personality questionnaires, objectively scored projective tests, and variables derived from lengthy interviews and the subjects' life histories. Subjects' profiles based on the projective test and interview data were Q factor analysed. In three separate analyses of three different samples of mentally abnormal offenders and appropriately matched non-offender controls, subgroups composed exclusively of offenders were obtained. These subtypes were identified with the aid of the questionnaire and life history data not used in the Q factor analyses.

Although the subtypes found within each offender sample did not replicate perfectly, there were many points of similarity. In the first two samples, which were both drawn from the same institution and contained a high proportion of mentally subnormal offenders, two offender subtypes in each sample were obtained. Within each sample the subtypes distinguished between inadequate, immature offenders with authoritarian attitudes and the more insecure, egocentric and aggressive offenders. These subtypes are reminiscent of the inadequate and aggressive subtypes found in other studies. The third sample was drawn from Broadmoor patients, who are typically of approximately average intelligence. The two offender subtypes which emerged contrasted those who were impulsive and psychopathic with the more anxious and pessimistic individuals. These investigations demonstrated that with the use of highly detailed personality data it is possible to differentiate certain criminals from non-criminals and to draw distinctions within a criminal sample.

In conclusion, the research on criminal personality characteristics indicates that it is unlikely that any single personality trait will unerringly differentiate between criminals and non-criminals. Such a conclusion is not particularly surprising in view of the opening discussion of the definition of deviance, which implied that crimes are defined by society rather than by inherent properties of behaviour, and also in view of the evidence that official criminals are a highly biased sample of the criminal population as a whole (to be discussed below). The research indicates that criminals are a heterogeneous group and that the study of offender subgroups is a more promising approach, particularly when a wide variety of personality measures is used. However, any studies of official criminals' personality characteristics are circumscribed by the uncertainty of their applicability to the wider, non-official criminal population.

Conclusions

Viewed from the personality theorist's perspective the

criminal is expected to be characterised by distinguishing personality traits. This perspective is based on the assumption that personality determines behaviour so, since criminals engage in forms of antisocial behaviour, they should demonstrate personality differences when compared with non-criminals. These differences may be the result of genetic factors, environmental factors, or a combination of both. However, the evidence for a 'Mark of Cain' is far from convincing. Certainly there are no straightforward differences between criminals and non-criminals, but it may be that there are complex combinations of personality measures which will yield differences within samples of official criminals. The aetiology of such refined and complex differences has yet to be explored.

The personality theorist's perspective cannot claim much success in the prevention of crime or the treatment of criminals. This failure has been one of the reasons for the shift in emphasis in criminology away from the criminal, who appears to be much the same sort of person as the rest of us, to the processes by which some people come to be labelled as criminals while others do not. Under what conditions is a criminal attribution made and what effect will it have on the person so labelled? These are questions which have been asked mainly by sociologists and criminologists, but they are relevant here because they may be viewed as representative of the lay and self perspectives.

The lay and self perspectives on criminality

The lay and self perspectives refer to people's perceptions of the personalities of other people and themselves. In the context of criminality, the lay perspective refers to the study of the processes by which people come to be regarded as criminals by others, and the self perspective is concerned with how people come to perceive themselves as criminals. Investigations from these points of view are comparatively recent developments in sociology and criminology, and the approach is known as social labelling theory.

Social labelling theory

Social labelling theory (Becker, 1963; Box, 1981; Schur, 1971) is composed of four major propositions.

1 No behaviour is inherently deviant.
2 The official criminal statistics give a biased and unrepresentative impression of crimes and criminals.
3 The processes by which certain people are selected and labelled as official criminals serve the function of maintaining social order.
4 People labelled as official criminals may as a result acquire a criminal identity and continue to commit crimes.

The first proposition of social labelling theory states that no behaviour is inherently deviant. In other words, a behaviour is neither pro- nor antisocial until society has evaluated it as such.

The labelling theorists' claim that no behaviour is inherently deviant has been challenged in the light of the evidence that crimes such as murder, rape and theft are considered antisocial by virtually all societies (Lemert, 1972; Welford, 1975). However, just because a behaviour is regarded as antisocial by most societies does not make it 'inherently deviant'. Indeed, it is difficult to appreciate what precisely is meant by the concept of 'inherent deviance', since it is impossible to distinguish operationally between a behaviour which is universally regarded as antisocial and one which is inherently deviant. Since the concept of inherent deviance is unsatisfactory, arguments about whether or not it exists are unhelpful. Fortunately, even though social labelling theorists have insisted on the proposition that no behaviour is inherently deviant, the other elements of the theory do not appear to depend critically on this confused concept.

The second point, that official criminals are unrepresentative of those who commit crimes, is well substantiated (Feldman, 1977). Official criminal statistics include figures on both crimes and criminals, and both are probably highly inaccurate. For a crime to appear in the official statistics it has to be reported, which means it must either be observed by the police or reported to them by a witness or the victim. It follows that crimes which are not reported are those which are invisible to the police or witnesses (e.g. drug abuse in the home), or those in which the victim is unaware of his or her victim status (e.g. confidence tricks), or where there is no obvious victim (e.g. tax embezzlement). Additionally, victims may not report crimes because they fear embarrassment and distress, as in the case of sexual assaults.

Some idea of the amount of unreported crime can be obtained by asking people whether they have been the victim of an unreported crime and whether they have committed crimes which have not come to official attention. Winslow's (1969) survey in Boston revealed that three times as many serious crimes had been committed as were actually reported by their victims, and Wallerstein and Wyle (1947) found that 99 per cent of New Yorkers admitted to undetected offences. Belson's study of self-reported delinquency in London revealed that virtually every member of a random sample of 1,445 boys admitted to some form of prosecutable offence (Belson, 1975). Recently, Radzinowicz has confirmed his estimate that only about 15 per cent of the total number of crimes actually committed are ever both reported to the police *and* 'cleared up' by achieving a conviction (Radzinowicz and King, 1977).

The statistics on the people who commit crimes are misleading because they imply that the majority of criminals are male members of the lower classes and minority ethnic groups. Investigations using self-report techniques have shown that the proportion of people from the lower classes and ethnic minorities appearing in the official statistics is far higher than is representative of the actual distribution of social class and race in the criminal population as a whole (Belson, 1975; Box, 1981; Gold, 1966; Wadsworth, 1975; Wolfgang, Figlio and Sellin, 1972).

Although the evidence supports the claim that working-class people and ethnic minorities are discriminated against, social labelling theory does not specifiy how this discrimination comes about. Do the police actively seek out these people, ignoring middle-class white criminals? Perhaps they have their own lay perspective on criminality, a 'police theory' (Rock, 1973), which determines where they look. Or does the bias occur after the alleged criminal is apprehended, with the middle-class white being better equipped in social skills and general knowledge of the 'system' to extricate himself before a prosecution takes place? These two questions were recently investigated by Bennett (1979) in the London Metropolitan Police District. He studied the operations of the Juvenile Bureau and found that significantly more middle-class than working-class children were let off with a caution, thus avoiding being sent to court.

On interviewing the officers concerned, Bennett was satisfied that they were not operating with a stereotype of working-class delinquency. In order to test the other hypothesis, that the middle classes are better able to negotiate their way out of a prosecution, Bennett studied the reports of home visits made routinely in these juvenile cases. The reports suggested that middle-class families were able to create a considerably more favourable impression on the officer than were the working-class families. Bennett concluded that the police should not be blamed for the unrepresentativeness of official criminals and implied that it is the result of the inferior interactional skills of working-class people. Considerably more research of a more precise nature is needed before this conclusion can be accepted.

The third and fourth propositions of labelling theory may be presented in terms of the three perspectives on personality. The personality theorist's perspective has been rejected in the first two propositions by saying that there is nothing special about criminals, particularly official ones, since they are victims of a biased labelling process. Instead, in proposition three, the lay perspective is advocated. What is it that causes one group of people to identify others as deviant and put them through an elaborate labelling process? What functions does labelling serve for those who engage in it? The self perspective is also regarded as important because labelling theorists are interested in the effects of the label (see proposition four). Does it serve to reduce deviance or, paradoxically, could labels actually enhance the very qualities they were designed to eradicate?

The lay perspective: the function of labels

According to social labelling theory, the process of apprehending and punishing criminals makes little impact on the bulk of criminal activity. Therefore, the interesting question to ask is, why does the process continue? Sociologists have challenged ∂ the traditional view that crime is mainly dysfunctional and disruptive. Instead, they propose that crime acts to preserve social order, and is useful and desirable to those in control over society (Box, 1981, 1983; K.T. Erikson, 1962; Quinney, 1970). The process of apprehending and punishing criminals serves to clarify and maintain the boundaries between unacceptable and acceptable behaviour: it serves to remind us of the rules and hence binds society together. It is therefore not the criminal behaviour itself that is of importance, but the response in others to that behaviour. This means that information about crime and the consequences of criminality must be salient. In the past this was done by visible punishments such as public hangings; today it is achieved by the media. For example, even the relatively serious-minded newspaper the *Guardian* gave front-page coverage to an account of the execution by electric chair of the convicted murderer John Spenkelink. It included a step-by-step description of the entire procedure and such graphic details as the singe to the right calf produced by the first surge of shock (*Guardian*, 26 May 1979).

Box (1981) argued that it is not only those in power who feel uncertain about the nature of social reality and strive to find ways of preserving their particular definition. He believes that insecurity afflicts us all. We need to impose order on the chaos of life by clinging to our definitions of what is normal, right and good. By being sanctimonious about the deviance of others we can suppress the nagging doubts we may have about ourselves. The public labelling of criminals helps us to preserve the consensus about social reality. Theorists like Box and Quinney argue that the scapegoats who are legally 'processed' are likely to be the least powerful members of society, which explains the bias towards the working class and ethnic minorities. Those in control are unlikely to label themselves as criminal. In order to function effectively as scapegoats official criminals should not be portrayed as being different from the rest of us. It follows that those in power would be resistant to the idea that criminals have distinguishing psychological characteristics. If criminals are different from non-criminals then the latter would not have anything to learn from the former.

Social labelling theory is generally seen as sensitising us to the evils of capitalist society which makes scapegoats out of innocent victims. In contrast, the personality theorist's perspective on criminality is regarded as an attempt to divert the responsibility for crime away from the evils of society and onto the criminal's shoulders. However, the personality theorist's perspective is a potentially powerful means of attacking the use of crime for social control. By demonstrating that criminals are different from non-criminals, the non-criminal population would have no need to be anxious about their own normality and would not see themselves as having a lesson to learn from the criminal scapegoats.

Social labelling theory represents the lay perspective on criminality at the societal level. At the individual level, the lay perspective on criminality is the study of people's beliefs about the nature of crime and criminals. For example, Furnham and Henderson (1983) investigated lay explanations of delinquency. Subjects were asked to rate the importance of thirty factors, both psychological and sociological, for explaining delinquency. Although subjects rated societal explanations as most important overall, Conservative voters emphasised educational failure whereas Labour voters emphasised societal injustice.

The self perspective: the effect of labels

The self perspective encompasses the final proposition in labelling theory: the effects of labelling on the recipient of the label. The theory argues that persons labelled as criminals, either officially by the authorities or unofficially by their family and peers, will commence on a process of identification with that label which will eventually result in the adoption of a criminal identity and its accompanying lifestyles (Box, 1981; Matza, 1969). It is assumed that the imposition of a label is likely to raise identity doubts, and that the processes of conviction, imprisonment and return to society are all likely to increase rather than decrease these doubts (Goffman, 1961). As a result the person acquires a new identity, that of being a criminal, and behaves in ways consistent with this new identity. The irony is that the label was intended to reduce criminality, and yet may actually increase it.

The proposition is highly speculative, and the psychological processes by which identity changes take place have not been spelled out by social labelling theorists. However, as was discussed in chapter 8, there is now plenty of empirical evidence in the psychological literature for the powerful effects of prior beliefs and expectations on behaviour and subsequent self perceptions (Darley and Fazio, 1980; Snyder, 1984). Although these studies were typically conducted using non-deviant subjects under laboratory conditions, they do provide support for the social labelling theorists' arguments.

An integration of the three perspectives

There is an inconsistency between the last proposition of labelling theory and the earlier ones. Labelling theorists are adamant that there is nothing special about the criminal, and argue that the focus of attention should be directed away from the criminal to the labelling process. However, in proposing that one of the effects of labelling is that criminals acquire deviant identities which cause them to continue behaving deviantly, the theorists are now arguing that there is something distinctive and special about people who adopt crime as a way of life. The distinction between primary and secondary deviance is useful here (Matza, 1969). Primary deviants are those who do not acquire a criminal identity and for whom crime does not become a way of life. They return to the fold of law-abiding society after a brief spell of deviancy. Secondary deviants are those who adopt criminal identities and the associated lifestyle.

Early in this chapter it was stated that the focus of attention would be on the 'hardened criminal' or secondary deviant. As a result of working through the lay and self perspectives incorporated in social labelling theory we can now see that labelling theory is not incompatible with the personality theorist's perspective in so far as secondary deviants are concerned, even though the theory is internally inconsistent. Labelling theory proposes that the way secondary deviants see themselves will be different from the way both primary deviants and non-criminals see themselves.

A combination of the three perspectives on criminality suggests that the place to look for psychological characteristics which will differentiate reliably between criminals and non-criminals and within the criminal population is in the area of self-perception. There has been little work adopting such a point of view, but there is one extensive clinical study which contains much relevant material (Yochelson and Samenow, 1976). Another source of information is the accounts of criminality given either by criminals themselves or by their biographers. Both sources will be drawn upon in the next section.

Another look at criminal personality

It is puzzling that studies from the personality theorist's perspective have failed to locate differences between criminals and non-criminals with respect to self-perception if, as the lay and self perspective suggest, this is the best area in which to look for such differences. A possible solution to the puzzle is provided by Yochelson and Samenow (1976; Samenow, 1984), who have proposed a new approach to criminality every bit as revolutionary as that put forward by the social labelling theorists. They argue that criminals, particularly 'hard-core' ones (i.e. secondary deviants), are psychologically distinct from non-criminals, but not in the ways explored in the previous, inconclusive studies. What distinguishes the hard-core criminal are his typically criminal thinking patterns. Yochelson and Samenow use the term 'thinking patterns' to include emotions and attitudes as well as styles of information processing. They believe that these patterns are central in aiding the criminal in his pursuit of crime. Yochelson and Samenow argue that a criminal is totally immersed in criminality in the same way that an alcoholic is immersed in drinking. As a consequence of this view, they are convinced that the only way to change a hard-core criminal is to eradicate every last vestige of those criminal thinking patterns and replace them with normal ones. The criminal must be persuaded to abandon every aspect of criminality; even a stray thought about crime is as dangerous to the criminal as one drink is for the alcoholic.

At the outset it must be acknowledged that Yochelson and Samenow's theory of criminality is based on research flawed by numerous methodological weaknesses. Therefore it would be foolish to claim any strong scientific validity for their ideas, but their arguments are compelling, despite the absence of quantitative evidence. For those who find the ideas repugnant or ill-founded, as well as for those who find them fascinating and insightful, the conclusion is the same: the theory needs translating into testable hypotheses and the appropriate research needs to be conducted.

Yochelson and Samenow's views of criminal personality are the result of fourteen years' investigations of criminal subjects in the United States. Over 240 male official criminals were involved, many of whom were detained in psychiatric hospitals as the US equivalent of the mentally abnormal offender. Most of the subjects were hard-core adult criminals with histories of repeated violations. The method of study was intensive interviewing amounting to considerable periods of time spent with each subject (e.g. twelve of the subjects each received 5,000 hours of interviewing). The aim of the study was to gain some understanding of criminal personality in order that an effective treatment could be evolved. The treatment programme which emerged from the study is novel in its approach and, on the basis of the ten-year follow-up of some subjects, Yochelson and Samenow claim that it has been 100 per cent effective in some cases. The critical reader will have already noticed the major design flaws: no control group, a total reliance on interviewing and no attempt at controlled assessment of the treatment programme. Suspending our critical faculties for a while, let us look at what emerged from this fourteen-year-long enterprise.

Yochelson and Samenow called the first chapter of their

book 'The reluctant converts'. Contrary to expectations, the title does not refer to the criminal subjects of the study, but to the investigators. They had started out on the project with an extensive knowledge of the psychological and sociological literature, and therefore were committed to the belief that criminals are the victims of their psychological defects and sociological deprivations. Through their prolonged and intense contact with criminals, the investigators were reluctantly forced to come to the conclusion that the model of the criminal as victim is a subversive myth cultivated by the machinations of the criminal mind and nurtured by the gullibility of social scientists.

Social labelling theory argues that the official criminal is liable to acquire a deviant identity and hence see himself and his behaviours as deviant: he tells himself he is a 'bad' person and proceeds to live up to his expectations about himself. Yochelson and Samenow's findings are entirely the reverse. They argue that the criminal does not see himself as a criminal but as an exceptionally superior and good person. 'The apprehended criminal believes that, although he broke the law, he is inherently not criminal. He thinks he is a good person who should not be punished' (Yochelson and Samenow, 1976, p.486). They believe that criminals are totally lacking in any kind of insight into the immorality of their way of life. No wonder the personality theorist's perspective failed to find evidence to support the labelling theorist's view that criminals would have negative self-perceptions – they do not! The criminal views himself in a particularly positive light.

If Yochelson and Samenow are right, how can the criminal reconcile himself to the unavoidable fact that he has behaved in ways which society deplores? Yochelson and Samenow argue that this mental somersault is achieved with the aid of criminal thinking patterns. These patterns help him to commit crimes and yet maintain a positive self-image. Yochelson and Samenow compiled their description of criminal thinking patterns on the basis of their clinical experience, and they provide no quantitative evidence to support their identification of these patterns. While the patterns must therefore be regarded as speculative, it is

interesting to note that several have been identified independently in autobiographical and biographical accounts of
criminality, as will be indicated by drawing on the accounts
of the lives of crime led by McVicar, the Kray twins and
Mackay.

John McVicar was a professional thief with a reputation
for violence. He became widely known to the general public
in 1968 when he made a sensational escape from the
notorious maximum security wing of Durham Prison. He
was at large for two years and, when finally recaptured,
faced a cumulative sentence of twenty-six years' imprisonment. He was released on parole in 1978, having spent the
previous eight years studying for A-levels and a degree.
McVicar (1979) gives an account of his escape and a brief
autobiography in which he attempts to explain his criminality.

Ronald and Reginald Kray were also professional criminals, but on a much larger scale than McVicar. During the
1950s and 1960s they contrived to build up a network of
control over the criminal activity in London akin to the
operations of the Mafia (Pearson, 1972). Eventually they
were convicted and sent to prison to serve life sentences for
murder.

Patrick Mackay was labelled as a dangerous psychopath
when only a teenager, and at 23 was sentenced to life
imprisonment for three murders. His is a disturbing story of
lack of communication between the police and medical and
social services to whom he had been well known since
childhood (Clark and Penycate, 1976).

Criminal thinking patterns

The first cluster of criminal thinking patterns to be described
by Yochelson and Samenow are those concerned with the
criminal's emotional life. Providing a basis for everything
else is the criminal's tremendous supply of energy, which
gets translated into both physical and mental activity. His
continual need for excitement is charged by these seemingly
limitless energy reserves. Next most important is the cluster
of emotions associated with what McVicar (1979) called
'machismo', although Yochelson and Samenow do not use

the term. Central to the concept of machismo is fear. In particular, the criminal finds the fear of being humiliated the hardest to tolerate; yet humiliations large and small, referred to by Yochelson and Samenow as 'putdowns', loom in every aspect of his life. 'For the criminal, emerging from all situations on top is an overriding concern. Both in everyday situations and fantasy, the criminal must be a winner every time' (Yochelson and Samenow, 1976, p. 281). When a criminal experiences a major putdown he is in what Yochelson and Samenow describe as a 'zero state'. From being a mega-success he becomes a mega-failure and sinks into a deep depression centred on intense feelings of worthlessness. Putdowns must be avoided in order that machismo be maintained.

The preoccupation with maintaining machismo is illustrated in McVicar's autobiography, which reveals that even as a child he considered it his number one priority. His only fear when first going to primary school was that he might not be tough enough to win the fights. 'I believed not only that fighting was the best method of settling any dispute, but that courage and success in showing aggression provided the only true basis for self-esteem' (McVicar, 1979, p.145). A similar pattern is revealed in the biography of the Kray twins. As children they ruled over their own gang and kept rival gangs at bay by fighting. As teenagers the Krays trained to become professional boxers, and McVicar seriously considered the idea of making a career out of sport.

Physical superiority remains a way of maintaining machismo in adulthood, although by then it is enhanced in other ways such as through sexual conquests, money and possessions. Also associated with machismo are the emotions of anger (when machismo is threatened) and pride (when machismo is enhanced), both of which are believed to be present in excess in the criminal. According to Yochelson and Samenow, the criminal's pride in his self-image as all-powerful and self-determining prevents him from accepting any form of authority.

In contrast to the aggressive and fiercely masculine self-image associated with machismo, the criminal is characterised by another set of emotions relating to sentimentality.

Yochelson and Samenow claim to have found sentimentality in every hardened criminal they have worked with, often directed towards helpless objects such as the elderly, the disabled and animals. In addition, criminals are prone to excessive sentimentality about their mothers; certainly this appeared to be true of McVicar and the Krays. It would seem contradictory for the criminal to be both sentimental and to cultivate machismo, but he accommodates these apparently conflicting clusters of emotions because being sentimental conforms with his self-image of being a good person.

The turbulent emotional life of the criminal is only part of the syndrome of deviant thinking patterns identified by Yochelson and Samenow. Just as important are the deviant cognitive processes they have ascribed to the criminal mind, for these essential processes could underlie a wide range of criminal activity. Of these, two seem crucial: the criminal's vivid imagination and the fragmentation of his thinking.

According to Yochelson and Samenow, the criminal's energies are liable to be directed to mental as well as physical activity. His mind is constantly fantasising about crime and rehearsing criminal escapades; it is 'a reservoir of criminal ideas' (1976, p. 411). It is difficult for a non-criminal to imagine what this must be like, but Yochelson and Samenow insist that the criminal is forever weighing up the criminal potential of every situation he is in and fantasising about the rewards and costs of committing crime. Singer (1976) has described how one significant function of fantasy is to prepare the individual for action by mental rehearsal, and the criminal is apparently well versed in this piece of psychology. One of the most powerful fantasies for the professional thief is that of the 'big score'. One day he will carry out a robbery of such proportions that he will be able to retire forever on the proceeds. The imagination of the criminal, including the concept of the 'big score', is portrayed expertly in one of Ed McBain's novels, *Doors* (1978). More direct evidence that criminals are characterised by vivid imaginations is to be found in Cattell's studies, where criminals have been found to be high scorers on factor M (autistic imagination) (Cattell, Eber and Tatsuoka, 1970).

It is because of the criminal's fertile imagination that Yochelson and Samenow argue that there is no such thing as a crime of passion. The criminal has repeatedly thought about the act he eventually commits: 'In our experience, no criminal has ever suddenly done something that he has not *repeatedly* considered before' (Yochelson and Samenow, 1976, p. 450, their emphasis). However, there are probably many people who engage in fantasies they would never translate into reality, so what makes the criminal different? The answer, say Yochelson and Samenow, lies in the fragmented nature of the criminal mind and his ability to operate a 'cut-off'. Fragmentation is present to some extent in us all: it refers to the inconsistency between attitudes and behaviours. However, it occurs on a massive scale in criminals. We have seen signs of fragmentation already: criminals revere their mothers and yet they cause them grief; they are sentimental about the helpless and yet they exploit them ruthlessly when it suits them; they believe they are morally superior and yet engage in acts of gross immorality. Fragmentation permits the maintenance of a positive self-image in the face of contradictory evidence.

Fragmentation, along with all the other deviant thinking patterns, becomes most relevant when the criminal is engaged in committing a crime. His fertile imagination aids in planning the crime and the fragmentation and cut-off prevent him from dwelling on the long-term consequences and the short-term fear associated with the criminal activity. The successful execution of a crime is tremendously rewarding, confirming the criminal's high opinion of himself and enhancing his machismo. Criminals describe the experience of excitement and pleasure associated with criminality as a 'charge', and it is graphically portrayed in Mackay's account of his horrific killing of an elderly priest. Although the murder had been planned in advance, when Mackay began to hack at the priest's head with knives and an axe he became possessed by a frenzy of excitement.

While Yochelson and Samenow have discussed many other aspects of supposed criminal thinking, the essentials have been summarised here. The criminal's emotional life is believed to be dominated by machismo and his thought processes are at the mercy of his vivid imagination and ability to cut out the unwanted. Yochelson and Samenow do not attempt to explain how it is that the criminal comes to be characterised by these patterns; they dismiss purely genetic or environmental explanations. Indeed, they go so far as to dismiss the whole enterprise of searching for causes because they believe that it detracts from the responsibility of the individual criminal. They argue that the only way to change the criminal is to alter his criminal thinking patterns, and that this can only be achieved if he is made to feel responsible for his behaviour.

The approach to rehabilitation advocated by Yochelson and Samenow is based on the assumption that the criminal has to undergo an entire change in identity if he is to give up criminality. Telling him he is like he is because of his unhappy childhood, or his position in society, or analysing the reinforcement contingencies for a specific criminal act, will all bypass the critical problem. The criminal has to be persuaded to abandon criminal values and adopt the ethical standards of normal society. It is a question of moral education. Yochelson and Samenow demanded a total abstinence from all criminal activity, be it fantasy or reality, and required a rigid adherence to conventional morality. In their own rehabilitation programme they worked with criminals individually and in groups with these goals in view. They used what they described as a phenomenological approach, in which criminals were required to report comprehensively on their thoughts during the previous day and the therapists pointed out where these thoughts were deviant and constituted evidence of criminal thinking patterns. Before being allowed to begin the programme the criminal gave an undertaking that all his current criminal activity would cease. (It is a sobering thought that incarcerated offenders are frequently engaged in as much criminal activity while in prison or hospital as they are outside.)

It is interesting to note that McVicar (1979) recommends a form of rehabilitation on much the same lines as that proposed by Yochelson and Samenow. He argues that criminals require ethical indoctrination to bring about what amounts to an identity crisis as the way to jolt them out of their criminal lifestyles. He writes bitterly of his wasted youth and the complete failure of any 'punishment' he has received:

> At almost any time anyone who understood the psycho-dynamics of crime, who could relate them to my own life, who commanded my respect and attention in conditions that were designed to promote them, could have exposed my criminality for what it was and crushed it. (McVicar, 1979, p. 140)

Conclusions on criminal personality

Yochelson and Samenow's ideas are provocative and remain essentially speculative, requiring empirical investigation rather than wholesale rejection or acceptance. Their theory of the criminal mind is worthy of careful consideration because it seems to solve a number of riddles and is consistent with both biographical and clinical data.

The theory resolves the contradictions between the personality theorist's perspective, the lay perspective and the self perspective. The personality theorist's perspective hypothesises that differences between the personalities of criminals and non-criminals will be found, and yet the evidence is far from conclusive. The lay perspective, as presented within social labelling theory, hypothesises that hard-core criminals will be characterised by negative or deviant identities, whereas the self perspective, as suggested by Yochelson and Samenow, indicates that the criminal's self-image is highly positive. As yet there is no direct evidence to support Yochelson and Samenow's view, and such evidence would be difficult to obtain by conventional testing methods. The criminal would probably not be fooled into responding honestly on self-esteem questionnaires, and instead would conform to the image he perceived was expected by the investigator, which would be one of low self-esteem. By taking the self perspective into account, it looks as though the social labelling theorists have been misled into thinking that criminals acquire deviant identities. Future research from the personality theorist's perspective should concentrate on investigating the possibility that criminals have positive and inflated self-perceptions.

The self perspective also resolves the contradictions posed by the findings on criminals' moral development. Although more studies are needed, it is likely that criminals are not less moral than non-criminals, since they are capable of average moral thinking. Nevertheless, there is a discrepancy between their moral thinking and their actual behaviour. This discrepancy can be accommodated in Yochelson and Samenow's theory by the concept of fragmentation. While the criminal shows normal moral development in some respects (e.g. he may be a model father and husband), he is able to cut out any ethical considerations when he carries out a crime because of the fragmentation which characterises his thinking patterns.

The application of the constructivist approach has shed some light on the mysteries of criminal personality and has pointed to new directions for future research. Criminal personality and personality over the life-span are just two examples of where the constructivist approach can be useful in the application of personality theory to issues of social importance. The integration of explicit and implicit understandings of personality has proved beneficial for both theory and practice in personality.

Bibliography

Adorno, T.W., Frenkel-Brunswick, E., Levinson, D.J. and Sanford, R.N. (1950), *The Authoritarian Personality*, New York, Harper & Row.

Alker, H.A. (1972), 'Is personality situationally specific or intraphysically consistent?', *Journal of Personality*, vol. 40, pp. 1–16.

Alker, H.A. (1977), 'Beyond ANOVA psychology in the study of person-situation interactions', in D. Magnusson and N.S. Endler (eds), *Personality at the Crossroads: Current Issues in Interactional Psychology*, Hillsdale, New Jersey, Lawrence Erlbaum Associates.

Allport, G.W. (1937), *Personality: A Psychological Interpretation*, New York, Holt, Rinehart & Winston.

Allport, G.W. and Odbert, H.S. (1936), 'Trait-names: a psycho-lexical study', *Psychological Monographs*, vol. 47, whole no. 211.

Alston, W.P. (1975), 'Traits, consistency and conceptual alternatives for personality theory', *Journal for the Theory of Social Behaviour*, vol. 5, pp. 17–47.

Anastasi, A. (1982), *Psychological Testing*, 5th edn, London, Collier Macmillan.

Anderson, N.H. (1962), 'Application of an additive model to impression formation', *Science*, vol. 138, pp. 817–18.

Anderson, N.H. (1965), 'Averaging versus adding as a stimulus-combination rule in impression formation', *Journal of Experimental Psychology*, vol. 70, pp. 394–400.

Anderson, N.H. (1974), 'Cognitive algebra', in L. Berkowitz (ed.), *Advances in Experimental Social Psychology*, vol. 7, pp. 1–101, New York, Academic Press.

Anderson N.H. (1976), 'Equity judgments as information integration', *Journal of Personality and Social Psychology*, vol. 33, pp. 291–9.

Anderson, N.H. (1978), 'Progress in cognitive algebra', in L. Berkowitz (ed.), *Cognitive Theories in Social Psychology*, New York, Academic Press.

Angleitner, A., John, O.P. and Löhr, F. (1986), 'It's *what* you ask and *how* you ask it: an itemmetric analysis of personality questionnaires', in A.

Angleitner and J.S. Wiggins (eds), *Personality Assessment via Questionnaires: Current Issues in Theory and Measurement*, Berlin, Springer-Verlag.

Apter, M.J. (1984), 'Reversal theory and personality: a review', *Journal of Research in Personality*, vol. 18, pp. 265–88.

Argyle, M. and Little, B.R. (1972), 'Do personality traits apply to social behaviour?', *Journal for the Theory of Social Behaviour*, vol. 2, pp. 1–35.

Asch, S.E. (1946), 'Forming impressions of personality', *Journal of Abnormal and Social Psychology*, vol. 41, pp. 258–90.

Asch, S.E. (1956), 'Studies of independence and conformity: I. A minority of one against a unanimous majority', *Psychological Monographs*, vol. 70, whole no. 416.

Asch, S.E. and Zukier, H. (1984), 'Thinking about persons', *Journal of Personality and Social Psychology*, vol. 46, pp. 1230–40.

Ashton, S.G. and Goldberg, L.R. (1973), 'In response to Jackson's challenge: the comparative validity of personality scales constructed by the external (empirical) strategy and scales developed intuitively by experts, novices, and laymen', *Journal of Research in Personality*, vol. 7, pp. 1–20.

Averill, J.R. (1973), 'The dis-position of psychological dispositions', *Journal of Experimental Research in Personality*, vol. 6, pp. 275–82.

Baer, D.M. (1970), 'An age-irrelevant concept of development', *Merrill-Palmer Quarterly of Behavior and Development*, vol. 16, pp. 238–46.

Bales, R.F. (1951), *Interaction Process Analysis*, Cambridge, Massachusetts, Addison-Wesley.

Bales R.F. (1970), *Personality and Interpersonal Behaviour*, New York, Holt, Rinehart & Winston.

Baltes, P.B., Reese, H.W. and Lipsitt, L.P. (1980), 'Lifespan developmental psychology', *Annual Review of Psychology*, vol. 31, pp. 65–110.

Bandura, A. (1977), 'Self-efficacy: toward a unifying theory of behavioral change', *Psychological Review*, vol. 84, pp. 191–215.

Becker, H.S. (1963), *Outsiders*, New York, Free Press.

Belson, W. (1975), *Juvenile Theft: The Causal Factors*, New York, Harper & Row.

Bem, D.J. (1967), 'Self-perception: an alternative interpretation of cognitive dissonance phenomena', *Psychological Review*, vol. 74, pp. 183–200.

Bem, D.J. (1972), 'Self-perception theory', in L. Berkowitz (ed.), *Advances in Experimental Social Psychology*, vol. 6, pp. 1–62, New York, Academic Press.

Bem, D.J. (1983), 'Constructing a theory of the triple typology: some (second) thoughts on nomothetic and idiographic approaches to personality, *Journal of Personality*, vol. 51, pp. 566–77.

Bem, D.J. and Allen, A. (1974), 'On predicting some of the people some of the time: the search for cross-situational consistencies in behavior', *Psychological Review*, vol. 81, pp. 506–20.

Bem, D.J. and Funder, D.C. (1978), 'Predicting more of the people more of the time', *Psychological Review*, vol. 85, pp. 485–501.

Bem, S.L. (1974), 'The measurement of psychological androgyny', *Journal of Consulting and Clinical Psychology*, vol. 42, pp. 155–62.

Bem, S.L. (1981), 'Gender schema theory: a cognitive account of sex typing', *Psychological Review*, vol. 88, pp. 354–64.

Bennett, T. (1979), 'The social distribution of criminal labels: police, "proaction" or "reaction"', *British Journal of Criminology*, vol. 19, pp. 134–45.

Berg, I.A. (ed.) (1967), *Response Set in Personality Assessment*, Chicago, Aldine Press.

Berger, P.L. and Luckmann, T. (1971), *The Social Construction of Reality*, Harmondsworth, Penguin.

Berman, J.S. and Kenny, D.A. (1976), 'Correlational bias in observer ratings', *Journal of Personality and Social Psychology*, vol. 34, pp. 263–73.

Berman, J.S., Read, S.J. and Kenny, D.A. (1983), 'Processing inconsistent social information', *Journal of Personality and Social Psychology*, vol. 45, pp. 1211–24.

Berry, J.W. (1966), 'Temne and Eskimo perceptual skills', *International Journal of Psychology*, vol. 1, pp. 207–29.

Blackburn, R. (1968a), 'Personality in relation to extreme aggression in psychiatric offenders', *British Journal of Psychiatry*, vol. 114, pp. 821–8.

Blackburn, R. (1968b), 'Emotionality, extraversion and aggression in paranoid and nonparanoid schizophrenic offenders', *British Journal of Psychiatry*, vol. 115, pp. 1301–2.

Blackburn, R. (1970), 'Personality types among abnormal homicides', *Social Hospitals Report*, no. 1.

Blass, T. (ed.) (1977), *Personality Variables in Social Behaviour*, Hillsdale, New Jersey, Lawrence Erlbaum Associates.

Block, J. (1971), *Lives Through Time*, Berkeley, California, Bancroft Books.

Block, J. (1977), 'Correlational bias in observer ratings: another perspective on the Berman and Kenny study', *Journal of Personality and Social Psychology*, vol. 35, pp. 873–80.

Block, J. (1981), 'Some enduring and consequential structures of personality', in A.I. Rabin, J. Aronoff, A.M. Barclay and R.A Zucker (eds), *Further Explorations in Personality*, New York, Wiley.

Block, J., Weiss, D.S. and Thorne, A. (1979), 'How relevant is a semantic similarity interpretation of personality ratings?', *Journal of Personality and Social Psychology*, vol. 37, pp. 1055–74.

Bloom, B.S. (1964), *Stability and Change in Human Characteristics*, New York, Wiley.

Borgatta, E.F., Cottrell, L.S. and Mann, J.H. (1958), 'The spectrum of individual interaction characteristics: an inter-dimensional analysis', *Psychological Reports*, vol. 4, pp. 279–319.

Borkenau, P. (1986), 'Toward an understanding of trait interrelations: acts as instances for several traits', *Journal of Personality and Social Psychology*, vol. 51, pp. 371–81.

Bowers, K.S. (1973), 'Situationism in psychology: an analysis and critique', *Psychological Review*, vol. 80, pp. 307–36.

Box, S. (1981), *Deviance, Reality and Society*, 2nd edn, London, Holt, Rinehart & Winston.

Box, S. (1983), *Power, Crime, and Mystification*, London, Tavistock.

Brand, C (1984), 'Personality dimensions: an overview of modern trait psychology', in J. Nicholson and H. Beloff (eds), *Psychological Survey* 5, Leicester, British Psychological Society, pp. 175–209.

Briggs, S.R., Cheek, J.M. and Buss, A.H. (1980), 'An analysis of the self-monitoring scale', *Journal of Personality and Social Psychology*, vol. 38, pp. 679–86.

Bromley, D.B. (1977), 'Natural language and the development of the self', in C.B. Keasey (ed.) *1977 Nebraska Symposium on Motivation*, vol. 25, pp. 117–67, Lincoln, Nebraska, University of Nebraska.

Brown, R. (1986), *Social Psychology*, 2nd edn, New York, Free Press.

Bruner, J.S. and Tagiuri, R. (1954), 'The perception of people', in G. Lindzey (ed.), *Handbook of Social Psychology*, Cambridge, Massachusetts, Addison-Wesley.

Bruner, J.S., Shapiro, D. and Tagiuri, R. (1958), 'The meaning of traits in isolation and in combination', in R. Tagiuri and L. Petrullo (eds), *Person Perception and Interpersonal Behaviour*, Stanford, California, Stanford University Press.

Burger, J.M. (1985), 'Desire for control and achievement-related behaviours', *Journal of Personality and Social Psychology*, vol. 48, pp. 1520–33.

Burgess, P.K. (1972), 'Eysenck's theory of criminality: a new approach', *British Journal of Criminology*, vol. 12, pp. 74–82.

Burisch, M. (1984), 'Approaches to personality inventory construction: a comparison of merits', *American Psychologist*, vol. 39, pp. 214–27.

Burke, P.A., Kraut, R.E. and Dworkin, R.H. (1984), 'Traits, consistency, and self-schemata: what do our methods measure?', *Journal of Personality and Social Psychology*, vol. 47, pp. 568–79.

Burton, R.V. (1963), 'Generality of honesty reconsidered', *Psychological Review*, vol. 70, pp. 481–99.

Buss, A.H. (1980), *Self-Consciousness and Social Anxiety*, San Francisco, Freeman.

Buss, A.H. and Briggs, S.R. (1984), 'Drama and the self in social interaction', *Journal of Personality and Social Psychology*, vol. 47, pp. 1310–24.

Buss, D.M. (1985), 'The temporal stability of acts, trends, and patterns', in C.D. Spielberger and J.N. Butcher (eds), *Advances in Personality Assessment*, vol. 5, pp. 165–96.

Buss, D.M. and Craik, K.H. (1980), 'The frequency concept of disposition: dominance and prototypically dominant acts', *Journal of Personality*, vol. 48, pp. 379–92.

Buss, D.M. and Craik, K.H. (1981), 'The act frequency analysis of interpersonal dispositions: aloofness, gregariousness, dominance, and submissiveness', *Journal of Personality*, vol. 49, pp. 174–92.

Buss, D.M. and Craik, K.H. (1983), 'The act frequency approach to personality', *Psychological Review*, vol. 90, pp. 105–26.

Buss, D.M. and Craik, K.H. (1984), 'Acts, dispositions, and personality', in B.A. Maher and W.B. Maher (eds), *Progress in Experimental Personality Research: Normal Personality Processes*, vol. 13, pp. 241–301, New York, Academic Press.

Byrne, D. (1964), 'Repression-sensitization as a dimension of personality', in B.A. Maher (ed.), *Progress in Experimental Psychology Research*, vol. 1, New York, Academic Press.

Cantor, N. and Mischel, W. (1979), 'Prototypes in person perception', in L. Berkowitz (ed.), *Advances in Experimental Social Psychology*, vol. 12, pp. 3–52, New York, Academic Press.

Caplan, N.S. (1965), 'Intellectual functioning', in H.C. Quay (ed.), *Juvenile Delinquency Research and Theory*, Princeton, New Jersey, Van Nostrand.

Carlson, K.A. (1972), 'Classes of adult offenders: a multivariate approach', *Journal of Abnormal Psychology*, vol. 79, pp. 84–93.

Cattell, R.B. (1946), *Description and Measurement of Personality*, London, George Harrap.

Cattell, R.B. (1947), 'Confirmation and clarification of primary personality factors', *Psychometrika*, vol. 12, pp. 197–220.

Cattell, R.B. (1957), *Personality and Motivation Structure and Measurement*, Yonkers-on-Hudson, World Books.

Cattell, R.B. (1966), 'The meaning and strategic use of factor analysis', in R.B. Cattell (ed.), *Handbook of Multivariate Psychology*, Chicago, Rand McNally.

Cattell, R.B. (1973), *Personality and Mood by Questionnaire*, San Francisco, Jossey-Bass.

Cattell, R.B. and Child, D. (1975), *Motivation and Dynamic Structure*, London, Holt, Rinehart & Winston.

Cattell, R.B. and Kline, P. (1977), *The Scientific Analysis of Personality and Motivation*, New York, Academic Press.

Cattell, R.B. and Scheier, I.H. (1961), *The Meaning and Measurement of Neuroticism and Anxiety*, New York, Ronald Press.

Cattell, R.B. and Warburton, E.W. (1967), *Objective Personality and Motivation Tests*, Urbana, Illinois, University of Illinois Press.

Cattell, R.B., Eber, H.W. and Tatsuoka, M.M. (1970), *Handbook for the Sixteen Personality Factor Questionnaire*, 3rd edn, Champaign, Illinois, Institute for Personality and Ability Testing.

Chaplin, W.F. and Goldberg, L.R. (1984), 'A failure to replicate the Bem and Allen study of individual differences in cross-situational consistency', *Journal of Personality and Social Psychology*, vol. 47, pp. 1074–90.

Child, D. (1970), *The Essentials of Factor Analysis*, London, Holt, Rinehart & Winston.

Child, I.L. (1968), 'Personality in culture', in E.F. Borgatta and W.W. Lambert (eds), *Handbook of Personality Theory and Research*, Chicago, Rand McNally.

Claridge, G.S. (1967), *Personality and Arousal*, Oxford, Pergamon Press.

Clark, T. and Penycate, J. (1976), *The Case of Patrick Mackay*, London, Routledge & Kegan Paul.

Cleckley, H. (1964), *The Mask of Sanity*, 4th edn, St Louis, Missouri, Mosby.

Coates, S.W. (1972), *Preschool Embedded Figures Test*, Palo Alto, California, Consulting Press.

Cochrane, R. (1974), 'Crime and personality: theory and evidence', *Bulletin of the British Psychological Society*, vol. 27, pp. 19–22.

Collins, A.M. and Loftus, E.F. (1975), 'A spreading activation theory of semantic processing', *Psychological Review*, vol. 82, pp. 407–28.

Comrey, A.L. (1970), *The Comrey Personality Scales*, San Diego, Educational and Industrial Testing Service.

Conley, J.J. (1984), 'Longitudinal consistency of adult personality: self-reported psychological characteristics across 45 years', *Journal of Personality and Social Psychology*, vol. 47, pp. 1325–33.

Conley, J.J. (1985), 'Longitudinal stability of personality traits: a multitrait-multimethod-multioccasion analysis', *Journal of Personality and Social Psychology*, vol. 49, pp. 1266–82.

Cooley, C.H. (1902), *Human Nature and the Social Order*, New York, Scribner.

Coopersmith, S. (1967), *The Antecedents of Self-Esteem*, San Francisco, Freeman.

Costa, P.T., McCrae, R.R. and Arenberg, D. (1980), 'Enduring dispositions in adult males', *Journal of Personality and Social Psychology*, vol. 38, pp. 793–800.

Couch, A. and Keniston, K. (1960), 'Yeasayers and naysayers: agreeing response set as a personality variable', *Journal of Abnormal Social*

Psychology, vol. 60, pp. 151–74.

Craft, M. (ed.) (1966), *Psychopathic Disorders and their Assessment*, London, Pergamon Press.

Crandall, V.C., Katkovsky, W. and Crandall, V.J. (1965), 'Children's beliefs in their control of reinforcements in intellectual-academic achievement situations', *Child Development*, vol. 36, pp. 91–109.

Cronbach, L.J. (1957), 'The two disciplines of scientific psychology', *American Psychologist*, vol. 12, pp. 671–84.

Cronbach, L.J. (1975), 'Beyond the two disciplines of scientific psychology', *American Psychologist*, vol. 30, pp. 116–27.

Cronbach, L.J. and Gleser, G.C. (1957), *Psychological Tests and Personnel Decisions*, Urbana, Illinois, University of Illinois.

Cronbach, L.J. and Snow, R.E. (1977), *Aptitudes and Instructional Methods: A Handbook for Research on Interactions*, New York, Irvington.

Crowne, D.P. and Marlowe, D. (1960), 'A new scale of social desirability independent of psychopathology', *Journal of Consulting Psychology*, vol. 24, pp. 349–54.

D'Andrade, R.G. (1965), 'Trait psychology and componential analysis', *American Anthropologist*, vol. 67, pp. 215–28.

D'Andrade, R.G. (1974), 'Memory and the assessment of behaviour', in H.M. Blalock Jr (ed.), *Measurement in the Social Sciences*, Chicago, Aldine-Atherton.

Darley, J.M. and Fazio, R.H. (1980), 'Expectancy confirmation processes arising in the social interaction sequence', *American Psychologist*, vol. 35, pp. 867–81.

Deluty, R.H. (1985), 'Consistency of assertive, aggressive, and submissive behavior for children', *Journal of Personality and Social Psychology*, vol. 49, pp. 1054–65.

Demo, D.H. (1985), 'The measurement of self-esteem: refining our methods', *Journal of Personality and Social Psychology*, vol. 48, pp. 1490–502.

Digman, J.M. and Inouye, J. (1986), 'Further specification of the five robust factors of personality', *Journal of Personality and Social Psychology*, vol. 50, pp. 116–23.

Doherty, W.J. and Baldwin, C. (1985), 'Shifts and stability in locus of control during the 1970s: divergence of the sexes', *Journal of Personality and Social Psychology*, vol. 48, pp. 1048–53.

Dreger, R.M. (1977), 'Developmental structural changes in the child's personality', in R.B. Cattell and R.M. Dreger (eds), *Handbook of Modern Personality Theory*, New York, Halsted.

Durso, F.T., Reardon, R. and Jolly, E.J. (1985), 'Self-nonself segregation and reality monitoring', *Journal of Personality and Social Psychology*, vol. 48, pp. 447–55.

Duval, S. and Wicklund, R.A. (1972), *A Theory of Objective Self Awareness*,

New York, Academic Press.

Eaves, L.J. and Eysenck, H.J. (1975), 'The nature of extraversion: a genetical analysis', *Journal of Personality and Social Psychology*, vol. 30, pp. 102–12.

Edelmann, R.E. (1987), *The Psychology of Embarrassment*, Chichester, Wiley.

Edwards, A.L. (1957), *The Social Desirability Variable in Personality Assessment and Research*, New York, Dryden.

Ekehammar, B. (1974), 'Interactionism in personality from a historical perspective', *Psychological Bulletin*, vol. 81, pp. 1026–48.

Endler, N.S. (1973), 'The person versus the situation – a pseudo issue? A response to Alker', *Journal of Personality*, vol. 41, pp. 287–303.

Endler, N.S. (1975), 'A person-situation interaction model for anxiety', in C.D. Spielberger and I.G. Sarason (eds), *Stress and Anxiety*, vol. 1, Washington DC, Hemisphere.

Endler, N.S. (1983), 'Interactionism: a personality model, but not yet a theory', in *Nebraska Symposium on Motivation, Personality – Current Theory and Research*, pp. 155–200, Lincoln, Nebraska, University of Nebraska Press.

Endler, N.S. and Edwards, J. (1978), 'Person by treatment interactions in personality research', in L.A. Pervin and M. Lewis (eds), *Perspectives in Interactional Psychology*, New York, Plenum Press.

Endler, N.S. and Magnusson, D. (1976), 'Toward an interactional psychology of personality', *Psychological Bulletin*, vol. 83, pp. 956–74.

Epstein, S. (1979), 'The stability of behaviour: I. On predicting most of the people much of the time', *Journal of Personality and Social Psychology*, vol. 37, pp. 1097–126.

Epstein, S. (1982), 'The unconscious, the preconscious, and the self-concept', in J. Suls and A.G. Greenwald (eds), *Psychological Perspectives on the Self*, vol. 2, pp. 219–47, Hillsdale, New Jersey, Lawrence Erlbaum Associates.

Epstein, S. and O'Brien, E.J. (1985), 'The person-situation debate in historical and current perspective', *Psychological Bulletin*, vol. 98, pp. 513–37.

Erikson, E.H. (1963), *Childhood and Society*, 2nd edn, New York, Norton.

Erikson, K.T. (1962), 'Notes on the sociology of deviance', *Social Problems*, vol. 9, pp. 307–14.

Eysenck, H.J. (1944), 'Types of personality – a factorial study of 700 neurotic soldiers', *Journal of Mental Science*, vol. 90, pp. 851–961.

Eysenck, H.J. (1947), *Dimensions of Personality*, London, Routledge & Kegan Paul.

Eysenck, H.J. (1953), *The Structure of Personality*, London, Methuen.

Eysenck, H.J. (1967), *The Biological Basis of Personality*, Springfield, Illinois, C.C. Thomas.

Eysenck, H.J. (1974), 'Crime and personality reconsidered', *Bulletin of the British Psychological Society*, vol. 27, pp. 23–4.

Eysenck, H.J. (1977) *Crime and Personality*, London, Granada.

Eysenck, H.J. and Eysenck, M.W. (1985), *Personality and Individual Differences: A Natural Science Approach*, New York, Plenum Press.

Eysenck, H.J. and Eysenck, S.B.G. (1964), *Manual of the Eysenck Personality Inventory*, University of London Press.

Eysenck, H.J. and Eysenck, S.B.G. (1968), 'A factorial study of psychoticism as a dimension of personality', *Multivariate Behaviour Research*, All-clinical special issue, pp. 15–31.

Eysenck, H.J. and Eysenck, S.B.G. (1969), *Personality Structure and Measurement*, London, Routledge & Kegan Paul.

Eysenck, H.J. and Eysenck, S.B.G. (1975), *Manual for the Eysenck Personality Questionnaire*, London, Hodder & Stoughton.

Eysenck, H.J. and Eysenck, S.B.G. (1976), *Psychoticism as a Dimension of Personality*, London, Hodder & Stoughton.

Eysenck, S.B.G. (1965), 'A new scale for personality measurement in children', *British Journal of Educational Psychology*, vol. 35, pp. 362–7.

Eysenck, S.B.G. (1969), 'Personality dimensions in children', in H.J. Eysenck and S.B.G. Eysenck (eds), *Personality Structure and Measurement*, San Diego, Knapp.

Eysenck, S.B.G. and Eysenck, H.J. (1963), 'On the dual nature of extraversion', *British Journal of Social and Clinical Psychology*, vol. 2, pp. 46–55.

Eysenck, S.B.G. and Eysenck, H.J. (1967), 'Salivary response to lemon juice as a measure of introversion', *Perceptual and Motor Skills*, vol. 24, pp. 1047–53.

Eysenck, S.B.G. and Eysenck, H.J. (1968), 'The measurement of psychoticism: a study of factor stability and reliability', *British Journal of Social and Clinical Psychology*, vol. 7, pp. 286–94.

Eysenck, S.B.G. and Eysenck, H.J. (1969), 'Scores on three personality variables as a function of age, sex and social class', *British Journal of Social and Clinical Psychology*, vol. 8, pp. 69–76.

Eysenck, S.B.G. and Eysenck, H.J. (1971), 'A comparative study of criminals and matched controls on three dimensions of personality', *British Journal of Social and Clinical Psychology*, vol. 10, pp. 362–6.

Eysenck, S.B.G., Rust, J. and Eysenck, H.J. (1977), 'Personality and the classification of adult offenders', *British Journal of Criminology*, vol. 17, pp. 164–74.

Farina, A., Allen, J.G. and Saul, B.B.B. (1968), 'The role of the stigmatized in affecting social relationships', *Journal of Personality*, vol. 36, pp. 169–82.

Feldman, M.P. (1977), *Criminal Behaviour: A Psychological Analysis*, London, Wiley.

Fenigstein, A., Scheier, M.F. and Buss, A.H. (1975), 'Public and private self-consciousness: assessment and theory', *Journal of Consulting and Clinical Psychology*, vol. 43, pp. 522–7.

Finn, S.E. (1986), 'Stability of personality ratings over 30 years: evidence for an age/cohort interaction', *Journal of Personality and Social Psychology*, vol. 50, pp. 813–18.

Fiske, D.W. (1974), 'The limits for the conventional science of personality', *Journal of Personality*, vol. 42, pp. 1–11.

Flavell, J.H. (1963), *The Developmental Psychology of Jean Piaget*, Princeton, New Jersey, Van Nostrand.

Foa, U.G. and Foa, E.B. (1974), *Societal Structures of the Mind*, Springfield, Illinois, Charles C. Thomas.

Fodor, E.M. (1972), 'Delinquency and susceptibility to social influence among adolescents as a function of moral development', *Journal of Social Psychology*, vol. 86, pp. 257–60.

Fodor, J.A., Bever, T.G. and Garrett, M.F. (1974), *The Psychology of Language*, New York, McGraw-Hill.

Fong, G.T. and Markus, H. (1982), 'Self-schemas and judgments about others', *Social Cognition*, vol. 1, pp. 191–204.

Frank, B.M. and Noble, J.P. (1984), 'Field independence-dependence and cognitive restructuring', *Journal of Personality and Social Psychology*, vol. 47, pp. 1129–35.

Franks, C.M. (1956), 'Conditioning and personality: a study of normal and neurotic subjects', *Journal of Abnormal Social Psychology*, vol. 52, pp. 143–50.

Franks, C.M. (1957), 'Personality factors and the rate of conditioning', *British Journal of Psychology*, vol. 48, pp. 119–26.

Frederiksen, N. (1972), 'Toward a taxonomy of situations', *American Psychologist*, vol. 27, pp. 114–23.

Froming, W.J. and Carver, C.S. (1981), 'Divergent influences of private and public self-consciousness in a compliance paradigm', *Journal of Research in Personality*, vol. 15, pp. 159–71.

Fulker, D.W. (1981), 'The genetic and environmental architecture of psychoticism, extraversion and neuroticism', in H.J. Eysenck (ed.), *A Model for Personality*, Berlin, Springer-Verlag.

Furnham, A.F. (1984), 'Lay conceptions of neuroticism', *Personality and Individual Differences*, vol. 5, pp. 95–103.

Furnham, A.F. and Henderson, M. (1983), 'Lay theories of delinquency', *European Journal of Social Psychology*, vol. 13, pp. 107–120.

Gale, A. (1973), 'Individual differences: studies of extraversion and EEG', in P. Kline (ed.), *New Approaches in Psychological Measurement*, London, Wiley.

Gallup, G.G. (1970), 'Chimpanzees: self-recognition', *Science*, vol. 167, pp. 86–7.

Gangestad, S. and Snyder, M. (1985), 'To carve nature at its joints: on the existence of discreet classes in personality', *Psychological Review*, vol. 92, pp. 317–49.

Gardner, R.A. and Gardner, B.T. (1969), 'Teaching sign language to a chimpanzee', *Science*, vol. 165, pp. 664–72.

Geizer, R., Rarick, D.L. and Soldow, G.P. (1977), 'Deception and judgment accuracy: a study in person perception', *Personality and Social Psychology Bulletin*, vol. 3, pp. 446–9.

Gergen, K.J. (1973), 'Social psychology as history', *Journal of Personality and Social Psychology*, vol. 26, pp. 309–20.

Gergen, K.J. (1977), 'Stability, change and chance in understanding human development', in N. Datan and H.W. Reese (eds), *Life-span Developmental Psychology: Dialectical Perspectives on Experimental Research*, New York, Academic Press.

Gergen, K.J. (1984), 'Theory of the self: impasse and evolution', in L. Berkowitz (ed.), *Advances in Experimental Social Psychology*, vol 17, pp. 49–115.

Gergen, K.J. (1985), 'The social constructionist movement in modern psychology', *American Psychologist*, vol. 40, pp. 266–75.

Gergen, K.J. and Davis, K.E. (eds) (1985), *The Social Construction of the Person*, New York, Springer-Verlag.

Gibbons, D.C. and Garrity, D.L. (1962), 'Definition and analysis of certain criminal types', *Journal of Criminal Law and Police Science*, vol. 53, pp. 27–35.

Goffman, E. (1955), 'On face-work: an analysis of ritual elements in social interaction', *Psychiatry: Journal for the Study of Interpersonal Processes*, vol. 18, pp. 213–31.

Goffman, E. (1959), *The Presentation of Self in Everyday Life*, New York, Doubleday.

Goffman, E. (1961), *Asylums*, New York, Anchor Books.

Gold, M. (1966), 'Undetected delinquent behavior', *Journal of Research in Crime and Delinquency*, vol. 3, pp. 27–46.

Goldberg, L.R. (1971), 'A historical survey of personality scales and inventories', in P. McReynolds (ed.), *Advances in Psychological Measurement*, vol. 2, pp. 293–336, Palo Alto, California, Science and Behavior Books.

Goldberg, L.R. (1981a), 'Language and individual differences: the search for universals in personality lexicons', in L. Wheeler (ed.), *Review of Personality and Social Psychology*, vol. 2, pp. 141–65, Beverly Hills, Sage.

Goldberg, L.R. (1981b), 'Developing a taxonomy of trait descriptive terms', in D. Fiske (ed.), *New Directions for Methodology of Social and Behavioural Science*, no. 9, pp. 43–69, San Francisco, Jossey-Bass.

Goldberg, L.R. (1982), 'From Ace to Zombie: some explorations in the language of personality', in C.D. Spielberger and J.N. Butcher (eds), *Advances in Personality Assessment*, vol. 1, pp. 203–44, Hillsdale, New Jersey, Lawrence Erlbaum Associates.

Golding, S. (1975), 'Flies in the ointment: methodological problems in the analysis of the percentage variance due to persons and situations', *Psychological Bulletin*, vol. 82, pp. 278–88.

Goodenough, D.R. (1978), 'Field dependence', in H. London and J.E. Exner (eds), *Dimensions of Personality*, New York, Wiley.

Gray, J.A. (1970), 'The psychophysiological nature of introversion–extraversion', *Behaviour Research and Therapy*, vol. 8, pp. 249–60.

Gray, J.A. (1972), 'The psychophysiological nature of introversion–extraversion: a modification of Eysenck's theory', in V.D. Neblitsyn and J.A. Gray (eds), *Biological Bases of Individual Behaviour*, New York, Academic Press.

Gray, J.A. (1983), 'Anxiety, personality and the brain', in A. Gale and J.A. Edwards (eds), *Physiological Correlates of Human Behaviour*, pp. 31–43, London, Academic Press.

Gray, J.A. (1985), 'A whole and its parts: behaviour, the brain, cognition and emotion', *Bulletin of the British Psychological Society*, vol. 38, pp. 99–112.

Griffore, R.J. and Samuels, D.D. (1978), 'Moral judgment of residents of a maximum security correctional facility', *Journal of Psychology*, vol. 100, pp. 3–7.

Guilford, J.P. and Zimmerman, W.S. (1956), 'Fourteen dimensions of temperament', *Psychological Monographs*, vol. 70, whole no. 417.

Guttman, L.A. (1954), 'A new approach to factor analysis: the radex', in P.R. Lazarsfeld (ed.), *Mathematical Thinking in the Social Sciences*, Glencoe, Illinois, Free Press.

Hall, C.S. and Lindzey, G. (1978), *Theories of Personality*, 3rd edn, New York, Wiley.

Hammond, S.B. (1977), 'Personality studied by the method of rating in the life situation', in R.B. Cattell and R.M. Dreger (eds), *Handbook of Modern Personality Theory*, New York, Halsted.

Hampson, S.E. (1982), 'Person memory: a semantic category model of personality traits', *British Journal of Psychology*, vol. 73, pp. 1–11.

Hampson, S.E. (1983), 'Trait ascription and depth of acquaintance: the preference for traits in personality descriptions and its relation to target familiarity', *Journal of Research in Personality*, vol. 17, pp. 398–411.

Hampson, S.E. (1984), 'The social construction of personality', in H. Bonarius, G. van Heck and N. Smid (eds), *Personality Psychology in Europe: Theoretical and Empirical Developments*, Lisse, Swets & Zeitlinger.

Hampson, S.E. and Kline, P. (1977), 'Personality dimensions differentiating certain groups of abnormal offenders from non-offenders', *British Journal of Criminology*, vol. 17, pp. 310–31.

Hampson, S.E., John, O.P. and Goldberg, L.R. (1986), 'Category breadth and hierarchical structure in personality: studies of asymmetries in judgments of trait implications', *Journal of Personality and Social Psychology*, vol. 51, pp. 37–54.

Harman, H.H. (1967), *Modern Factor Analysis*, Chicago, University of Chicago Press.

Harré, R. (1979), *Social Being*, Oxford, Blackwell.

Harré, R. (1983), *Personal Being*, Oxford, Blackwell.

Harré, R. and Secord, P.F. (1972), *The Explanation of Social Behaviour*, Oxford, Blackwell.

Harris, P.L. and Hampson, S.E. (1980), 'Processing information within implicit personality theory', *British Journal of Social and Clinical Psychology*, vol. 19, pp. 235–42.

Hartshorne, H. and May, M.A. (1928), *Studies in the Nature of Character*, vol. 1, *Studies in Deceit*, New York, Macmillan.

Hayner, N.S. (1961), 'Characteristics of five offender types', *American Sociological Review*, vol. 21, pp. 96–102.

Hays, W.L. (1958), 'An approach to the study of trait implication and trait similarity', in R. Tagiuri and L. Petrullo (eds), *Person Perception and Interpersonal Behaviour*, Stanford, California, Stanford University Press.

Heidensohn, F. (1985), *Women and Crime*, London, Macmillan.

Heider, F. (1958), *The Psychology of Interpersonal Relations*, New York, Wiley.

Helmreich, R. and Strapp, J. (1974), 'Short forms of the Texas Social Behavior Inventory (TSBI), an objective measure of self-esteem', *Bulletin of the Psychonomic Society*, vol. 4, pp. 473–5.

Herriot, P. (1984), *Down from the Ivory Tower*, Chichester, Wiley.

Herrnstein, R.J. (1973), IQ in the Meritocracy, London, Allen Lane.

Hirschberg, N. (1978), 'A correct treatment of traits', in H. London (ed.), *Personality: A New Look at Metatheories*, New York, Macmillan.

Hoelter, J.W. (1985), 'The structure of self-conception: conceptualization and measurement', *Journal of Personality and Social Psychology*, vol. 49, pp. 1392–407.

Hoghughi, M.S. and Forrest, A.R. (1970), 'Eysenck's theory of criminality: an examination with approved-school boys', *British Journal of Criminology*, vol. 10, pp. 240–54.

Ickes, W., Patterson, M.L., Rajecki, D.W. and Tanford, S. (1982), 'Behavioral and cognitive consequences of reciprocal versus compensatory responses to pre-interaction expectancies', *Social Cognition*, vol. 1, pp. 160–90.

Immergluck, L. and Mearini, M.C. (1969), 'Age and sex differences in response to embedded figures and reversible figures', *Journal of Experimental Child Psychology*, vol. 8, pp. 210–21.

Jaccard, J.J. (1974), 'Predicting social behavior from personality traits', *Journal of Research in Personality*, vol. 7, pp. 358–67.

Jackson, D.N. and Paunonen, S.V. (1985), 'Construct validity and the predictability of behavior', *Journal of Personality and Social Psychology*, vol. 49, pp. 554–70.

Jackson, D.N., Chan, D.W. and Stricker, L.J. (1979), 'Implicit personality theory: is it illusory?', *Journal of Personality*, vol. 47, pp. 1–10.

Jackson, D.N., Messick, S. and Myers, C.J. (1964), 'Evaluation of group and individual forms of the embedded-figures measures of field independence', *Educational and Psychological Measurement*, vol. 24, pp. 177–92.

James, W.H. and Rotter, J.B. (1958), 'Partial and one hundred percent reinforcement under change and skill conditions', *Journal of Experimental Psychology*, vol. 55, pp. 397–403.

Jensen, A. (1971), 'The race × sex × ability interaction', in R. Cancro (ed.), *Intelligence: Genetic and Environmental Influences*, New York, Grune & Stratton.

John, O.P. (1986), 'Direction and type of causal explanations in trait hierarchies', unpublished manuscript, Eugene, Oregon, Oregon Research Institute.

John, O.P. and Block, L. (1986), 'The skills, motives, and consistency of self-presentation: a decade of self-monitoring research', unpublished manuscript, Eugene, Oregon, Oregon Research Institute.

John, O.P., Hampson, S.E. and Goldberg, L.R. (1986), 'Is there a basic level of personality description?' unpublished manuscript, Eugene, Oregon, Oregon Research Institute.

Johnson, T.J., Feigenbaum, R. and Weiby, M. (1964), 'Some determinants and consequences of the teacher's perception of causation', *Journal of Educational Psychology*, vol. 55, pp. 237–46.

Jones, E.E. and Davis, K.E. (1965), 'From acts to dispositions: the attribution process in person perception', in L. Berkowitz (ed.), *Advances in Experimental Social Psychology*, vol. 2, New York, Academic Press.

Jung, C.G. (1923), *Psychological Types*, London, Routledge & Kegan Paul.

Kagan, J. and Moss, H.A. (1962), *Birth to Maturity: A Study in Psychological Development*, New York, Wiley.

Kahn, S., Zimmerman, G., Csikszentmihaly, M. and Getzels, J.W. (1985), 'Relations between identity in young adulthood and intimacy at midlife', *Journal of Personality and Social Psychology*, vol. 49, pp. 1316–22.

Kahneman, D. and Tversky, A. (1973), 'On the psychology of prediction', *Psychological Review*, vol. 80, pp. 237–57.

Karabenick, S.A. and Srull, T.K. (1978), 'Effects of personality and situational variation in locus of control of cheating: determinants of the "congruence effect"', *Journal of Personality*, vol. 46, pp. 72–95.

Karp, S.A. (1977), 'Psychological differentiation', in T. Blass (ed.), *Personality Variables in Social Behavior*, Hillsdale, New Jersey, Lawrence Erlbaum Associates.

Kelley, H.H. (1967), 'Attribution in social interaction', in D. Levine (ed.), *Nebraska Symposium on Motivation*, vol. 15, Lincoln, Nebraska, University of Nebraska Press.

Kelly, E.L. (1955), 'Consistency of the adult personality', *American Psychologist*, vol. 10, pp. 659–81.

Kelly G.A. (1955), *The Psychology of Personal Constructs*, vols I and II, New York, Norton.

Kihlstrom, J.F. and Cantor, N. (1984), 'Mental representations of the self', in L. Berkowitz (ed.), *Advances in Experimental Social Psychology*, vol. 17, pp. 2–47, New York, Academic Press.

Kim, M.P. and Rosenberg, S. (1980), 'Comparison of two structural models of implicit personality theory', *Journal of Personality and Social Psychology*, vol. 38, pp. 375–89.

Kline, P. (1969), 'The anal character: a cross-cultural study in Ghana', *British Journal of Social and Clinical Psychology*, vol. 8, pp. 201–10.

Kline, P. (1972), *Fact and Fantasy in Freudian Theory*, London, Methuen.

Kline, P. (1984), *Psychology and Freudian Theory: An Introduction*, London, Methuen.

Kline, P. and Storey, R. (1977), 'A factor analytic study of the oral character', *British Journal of Social and Clinical Psychology*, vol. 16, pp. 317–28.

Kline, P. and Storey, R. (1980), 'The etiology of the oral character', *Journal of Genetic Psychology*, vol. 136, pp. 85–94.

Kogan, N. and Wallach, M.A. (1964), *Risk Taking: A Study in Cognition and Personality*, New York, Holt, Rinehart & Winston.

Kohlberg, L. (1964), 'The development of moral character', in M.L. Hoffman *et al.* (eds), *Child Development*, vol. 1, New York, Russell Sage Foundation.

Kohlberg, L. (1969), 'State and sequence: the cognitive developmental approach to socialization', in D.A. Gosler (ed.), *Handbook of Socialization Theory and Research*, New York, Rand McNally.

Kohlberg, L. (1976), 'Moral stages and moralization: the cognitive developmental approach', in T. Lickona (ed.), *Moral Development and Behavior: Theory, Research and Social Issues*, New York, Holt, Rinehart & Winston.

Kretschmer, E. (1948), *Korperbau und Charakter*, Berlin, Springer.

Kuiper, N.A. and Derry, P.A. (1981), 'The self as a cognitive prototype: an application to person perception and depression', in N. Cantor and J.F. Kihlstrom (eds), *Personality, Cognition and Social Interaction*, pp. 215–32, Hillsdale, New Jersey, Lawrence Erlbaum Associates.

Kurtines, W.M. (1986), 'Moral behavior as rule governed behavior: person and situation effects on moral decision making', *Journal of Personality and Social Psychology*, vol. 50, pp. 784–91.

Lader, M. (1977), *Psychiatry on Trial*, Harmondsworth, Penguin.

Lamiell, J.T. (1981), 'Toward an idiothetic psychology of personality', *American Psychologist*, vol. 36, pp. 276–89.

Lamiell, J.T. (1982), 'The case for an idiothetic psychology of personality: a conceptual and empirical foundation', in B.A. Maher and W.B. Maher (eds), *Progress in Experimental Personality Research*, vol. II, pp. 1–64, New York, Academic Press.

Lamiell, J.T., Foss, M.A. and Cavenee, P. (1980), 'On the relationship between conceptual schemes and behaviour reports: a closer look', *Journal of Personality*, vol. 48, pp. 54–73.

Landman, J. and Manis, M. (1983), 'Social cognition: some historical and theoretical perspectives', in L. Berkowitz (ed.), *Advances in Experimental Social Psychology*, vol. 16, pp. 49–123, New York, Academic Press.

Lawson, A. (1976), 'Formal operations and field independence in a heterogeneous sample', *Perceptual and Motor Skills*, vol. 42, pp. 981–2.

Lay, C.H. and Jackson, D.N. (1969), 'Analysis of the generality of trait-inferential relationships', *Journal of Personality and Social Psychology*, vol. 12, pp. 12–21.

Lefcourt, H.M. (1982), *Locus of Control: Current Trends in Theory and Research*, 2nd edn, Hillsdale, New Jersey, Lawrence Erlbaum Associates.

Lefcourt, H.M., Martin, R.A., Fick, C.M. and Saleh, W.E. (1985), 'Locus of control for affiliation and behavior in social interactions', *Journal of Personality and Social Psychology*, vol. 48, pp. 755–9.

Lefcourt, H.M., von Baeyer, C.L., Ware, E.E. and Cox, D.J. (1979), 'The multidimensional-multiattributional causality scale: the development of a goal specific locus of control scale', *Canadian Journal of Behavioral Science*, vol. 11, pp. 286–304.

Lemert, E. (1972), *Human Deviance: Social Problems and Social Control*, 2nd edn, Englewood Cliffs, New Jersey, Prentice-Hall.

Levenson, H. (1974), 'Activism and powerful others: distinctions within the concept of internal-external control', *Journal of Personality Assessment*, vol. 38, pp. 377–83.

Levinson, D.J. (1978), *The Seasons of a Man's Life*, New York, Knopf.

Levinson, D.J. (1986), 'A conception of adult development', *American Psychologist*, vol. 41, pp. 3–13.

Levinson, D.J. (in press), *The Seasons of a Woman's Life*, New York, Knopf.

Lewin, K. (1935), *A Dynamic Theory of Personality*, New York, McGraw-Hill.

Lewis, M. and Brooks, J. (1975), 'Infants' social perception: a constructivist view', in L.B. Cohen and P. Salapatek (eds), *Infant Perception: From*

Sensation to Cognition, vol. II, *Perception of Space, Speech and Sound*, New York, Academic Press.

Linton, M. (1978), 'Real-world memory after six years: an in vivo study of very long-term memory', in M.M. Gruneberg, P.E. Morris and R.N. Sykes (eds), *Practical Aspects of Memory*, London, Academic Press.

Livesley, W.J. and Bromley, D.B. (1973), *Person Perception in Childhood and Adolescence*, London, Wiley.

Livson, N. (1973), 'Developmental dimensions of personality: a lifespan formulation', in P.B. Baltes and K.W. Schaie (eds), *Life-span Developmental Psychology: Personality and Socialisation*, New York, Academic Press.

Loehlin, J.C. (1977), 'Psychological genetics from the study of human behaviour', in R.B. Cattell and R.M. Dreger (eds), *Handbook of Modern Personality Theory*, New York, Halsted.

London, H. and Exner, J.E. (eds) (1978), *Dimensions of Personality*, New York, Wiley.

Luria, A.R. (1976), *Cognitive Development: Its Cultural and Social Development*, Cambridge, Massachusetts, Harvard University Press.

McBain, E. (1978), *Doors*, London, Pan.

McClelland, D.C., Atkinson, J.W., Clark, R.A. and Lowell, E.L. (1953), *The Achievement Motive*, New York, Appleton-Century-Crofts.

Maccoby, E. and Jacklin, C. (1974), *The Psychology of Sex Differences*, Stanford, California, Stanford University Press.

McCord, W. and McCord, J. (1964), *The Psychopath: An Essay on the Criminal Mind*, Princeton, New Jersey, Nostrand.

McCrae, R.R. and Costa, P.T. (1985), 'Updating Norman's "adequate taxonomy": intelligence and personality dimensions in natural language and in questionnaires', *Journal of Personality and Social Psychology*, vol. 49, pp. 710–21.

McGowan, J. and Gormly, J. (1976), 'Validation of personality traits: a multicriteria approach', *Journal of Personality and Social Psychology*, vol. 34, pp. 791–5.

McGuire, W.T. and McGuire, C.V. (1982), 'Significant others in self-space: sex differences and developmental trends in the social self', in J. Suls (ed.), *Psychological Perspectives on the Self*, Hillsdale, New Jersey, Lawrence Erlbaum Associates.

Mackintosh, N.J. (1974), *The Psychology of Animal Learning*, New York, Academic Press.

Maclean, C. (1979), *The Wolf Children*, Harmondsworth, Penguin.

McVicar, J. (1979), *McVicar By Himself*, London, Arrow.

Magaro, P.A. and Ashbrook, R.M. (1985), 'The personality of societal groups', *Journal of Personality and Social Psychology*, vol. 48, pp. 1479–89.

Magnusson, D. (ed.) (1981), *Toward a Psychology of Situations: An Interactional Perspective*, Hillsdale, New Jersey, Lawrence Erlbaum Associates.

Magnusson, D. and Endler, N.S. (eds), (1977), *Personality at the Crossroads: Current Issues in Interactional Psychology*, Hillsdale, New Jersey, Lawrence Erlbaum Associates.

Mann, R.D. (1959), 'The relation between personality characteristics and individual performance in small groups', unpublished PhD dissertation, Ann Arbor, Michigan, University of Michigan.

Marcus, B. (1960), 'A dimensional study of a prison population', *British Journal of Criminology*, vol. 1, pp. 130–53.

Markus, H. (1977), 'Self-schemata and processing information about the self', *Journal of Personality and Social Psychology*, vol. 35, pp. 63–78.

Markus, H. and Nurius, P. (1986), 'Possible selves', *American Psychologist*, vol. 41, pp. 954–69.

Markus, H., Smith, J. and Moreland, R.L. (1985), 'Role of the self-concept in the perception of others', *Journal of Personality and Social Psychology*, vol. 49, pp. 1494–512.

Markus, H., Crane, M., Bernstein, S. and Siladi, M. (1982), 'Self-schemas and gender', *Journal of Personality and Social Psychology*, vol. 42, pp. 38–50.

Marsh, H.W., Barnes, J. and Hocevar, D. (1985), 'Self-other agreement on multidimensional self-concept ratings: factor analysis and multitrait-multimethod analysis', *Journal of Personality and Social Psychology*, vol. 49, pp. 1360–77.

Matza, D. (1969), *Becoming Deviant*, Englewood Cliffs, New Jersey, Prentice-Hall.

Mausner, B. and Graham, J. (1970), 'Field dependence and prior reinforcement as determinants of social interaction in judgment', *Journal of Personality and Social Psychology*, vol. 16, pp. 486–93.

Mead, G.H. (1934), *Mind, Self and Society*, Chicago, University of Chicago Press.

Medin, D.L. and Smith, E.E. (1984) 'Concepts and concept formation', *Annual Review of Psychology*, vol. 35, pp. 113–38.

Megargee, E.I. (1966), 'Undercontrolled and overcontrolled personality types in extreme antisocial aggression', *Psychological Monographs*, vol. 80, whole no. 611.

Miller, D.T. and Ross, M. (1975), 'Self-serving biases in the attribution of causality: fact or fiction?', *Psychological Bulletin*, vol. 82, pp. 213–15.

Millham, J. and Jacobson, L.I. (1978), 'The need for approval', in H. London and J.E. Exner (eds), *Dimensions of Personality*, New York, Wiley.

Mirels, H.L. (1976), 'Implicit personality theory and inferential illusions', *Journal of Personality*, vol. 44, pp. 467–87.

Mirels, H.L. (1982), 'The illusory nature of implicit personality theory:

logical and empirical considerations', *Journal of Personality and Social Psychology*, vol. 50, pp. 203–22.

Mischel, W. (1968), *Personality and Assessment*, New York, Wiley.

Mischel, W. (1973), 'Toward a cognitive social learning reconceptualization of personality', *Psychological Review*, vol. 80, pp. 252–83.

Mischel, W. (1977a), 'On the future of personality measurement', *American Psychologist*, vol. 32, pp. 246–54.

Mischel, W. (1977b), 'The interaction of person and situation', in D. Magnusson and N.S. Endler (eds), *Personality at the Crossroads: Current Issues in Interactional Psychology*, Hillsdale, New Jersey, Lawrence Erlbaum Associates.

Mischel, W. and Peake, P.K. (1982), 'Beyond déjà vu in the search for cross-situational consistency', *Psychological Review*, vol. 89, pp. 730–55.

Morris, S. and Messer, S.B. (1978), 'The effect of locus of control and locus of reinforcement on academic task persistence', *Journal of Genetic Psychology*, vol. 132, pp. 3–9.

Mower White, C.J. (1982), *Consistency in Cognitive Social Behaviour*, London, Routledge & Kegan Paul.

Mulaik, S. (1964), 'Are personality factors raters' conceptual factors?', *Journal of Consulting Psychology*, vol. 28, pp. 506–11.

Munro, D.J. (1977), *The Concept of Man in Contemporary China*, Ann Arbor, Michigan, University of Michigan Press.

Nagpal, M. and Gupta, B.S. (1979), 'Personality, reinforcement and verbal operant conditioning', *British Journal of Psychology*, vol. 70, pp. 471–6.

Nasby, W. (1985), 'Private self-consciousness, articulation of the self-schema, and recognition memory of trait adjectives', *Journal of Personality and Social Psychology*, vol. 49, pp. 704–9.

Nebelkopf, E.B. and Dreyer, A.S. (1973), 'Continuous–discontinuous concept attainment as a function of individual differences in cognitive style', *Perceptual and Motor Skills*, vol. 36, pp. 655–62.

Newcomb, T.M. (1929), 'The consistency of certain introvert–extravert behavior patterns in 51 problem boys', New York, Teachers' College, Columbia University, Contributions to Education, no. 382.

Newell, A. and Simon, H.A. (1972), *Human Problem Solving*, Englewood Cliffs, New Jersey, Prentice-Hall.

Nichols, S.L. and Newman, J.P. (1986), 'Effects of punishment on response latency in extraverts', *Journal of Personality and Social Psychology*, vol. 50, pp. 624–30.

Nisbett, R.E. and Wilson, T.D. (1977), 'Telling more than we can know: verbal reports on mental processes', *Psychological Review*, vol. 84, pp. 231–59.

Norman, W.T. (1963), 'Toward an adequate taxonomy of personality attributes: replicated factor structure in peer nomination personality ratings', *Journal of Abnormal Social Psychology*, vol. 66, pp. 574–88.

Norman, W.T. (1967), '2,800 personality descriptors: normative operating characteristics for a university population', unpublished manuscript, Ann Arbor, Michigan, University of Michigan.

Norman, W.T. and Goldberg, L.R. (1966), 'Raters, ratees, and randomness in personality structure', *Journal of Personality and Social Psychology*, vol. 4, pp. 681–91.

Nowicki, S. and Duke, M.P. (1974), 'A locus of control scale for non-college as well as college adults', *Journal of Personality Assessment*, vol. 38, pp. 136–7.

Nunnally, J.C. (1973), 'Research strategies and measurement methods for investigating human development', in J.R. Nesselroade and H.W. Reese (eds), *Life-span Developmental Psychology: Methodological Issues*, New York, Academic Press.

Olweus, D. (1977), 'A critical analysis of the "modern" interactionist position', in D. Magnusson and N.S. Endler (eds), *Personality at the Crossroads: Current Issues in Interactional Psychology*, Hillsdale, New Jersey, Lawrence Erlbaum Associates.

Osgood, C.E. (1962), 'Studies on the generality of affective meaning systems', *American Psychologist*, vol. 17, pp. 10–28.

Overton, W.F. and Reese, H.W. (1973), 'Models of development: methodological implications', in J.R. Nesselroade and H.W. Reese (eds), *Lifespan Developmental Psychology: Methodological Issues*, New York, Academic Press.

Passingham, R.E. (1972), 'Crime and personality: a review of Eysenck's theory', in V.D. Nebylitsyn and J.A. Gray (eds), *Biological Bases of Individual Behaviour*, New York, Academic Press.

Passini, F.T. and Norman, W.T. (1966), 'A universal conception of personality structure?', *Journal of Personality and Social Psychology*, vol. 4, pp. 44–9.

Passini, F.T. and Norman, W.T. (1969), 'Ratee relevance in peer nomination', *Journal of Applied Psychology*, vol. 53, pp. 185–7.

Peabody, D. (1967), 'Trait inferences: evaluative and descriptive aspects', *Journal of Personality and Social Psychology Monograph*, vol. 7, whole no. 644.

Peabody, D. (1968), 'Group judgments in the Philippines: evaluative and descriptive aspects', *Journal of Personality and Social Psychology*, vol. 10, pp. 290–300.

Peabody, D. (1970), 'Evaluative and descriptive aspects in personality perception: a reappraisal', *Journal of Personality and Social Psychology*, vol. 16, pp. 639–46.

Peabody, D. (1984), 'Personality dimensions through trait inferences', *Journal of Personality and Social Psychology*, vol. 46, pp. 384–403.

Peabody, D. (1987), 'Selecting representative trait adjectives', *Journal of Personality and Social Psychology*, vol. 52, pp. 59–71.

Peabody, D. and Goldberg, L.R. (1986), 'Variance and invariance in personality structures: three determinants of the size and location of factors based on personality-trait adjectives', unpublished manuscript, Eugene, Oregon, Oregon Research Institute.

Pearce-McCall, D. and Newman, J.P. (1986), 'Expectations of success following noncontingent punishment in introverts and extraverts', *Journal of Personality and Social Psychology*, vol. 50, pp. 439–46.

Pearson, J. (1972), *The Profession of Violence*, London, Granada.

Penner, L.A. and Wymer, W.E. (1983), 'The moderator variable approach to behavioral predictability: some of the variables some of the time', *Journal of Research in Personality*, vol. 17, pp. 339–53.

Pervin, L.A. (1983), 'The stasis and flow of behavior: toward a theory of goals', in M.M. Page (ed.) *Personality: Current Theory and Research, 1982 Nebraska Symposium on Motivation*, vol. 30, pp. 1–53, Lincoln, Nebraska, University of Nebraska Press.

Pervin, L.A. and Lewis, M. (eds) (1978), *Perspectives in Interactional Psychology*, New York, Plenum Press.

Phares, E.J. (1957), 'Expectancy changes in skill and chance situations', *Journal of Abnormal and Social Psychology*, vol. 54, pp. 339–42.

Phares, E.J. (1976), *Locus of Control in Personality*, Morristown, New Jersey, General Learning Press.

Phares, E.J. (1978), 'Locus of control', in H. London and J.E. Exner (eds), *Dimensions of Personality*, New York, Wiley.

Piaget, J. (1932), *The Moral Judgement of the Child*, London, Routledge & Kegan Paul.

Powell, G.F. (1979), *Brain and Personality*, Farnborough, Hampshire, Saxon House.

Powell, S.R. and Juhnke, R.G. (1983), 'Statistical models of implicit personality theory: a comparison', *Journal of Personality and Social Psychology*, vol. 44, pp. 911–22.

Price, R.H. (1974), 'The taxonomic classification of behaviors and situations and the problem of behavior-environment congruence', *Human Relations*, vol. 27, pp. 567–85.

Price, R.H. and Bouffard, D.L. (1974), 'Behavioral appropriateness and situational constraint as dimensions of social behavior', *Journal of Personality and Social Psychology*, vol. 30, pp. 579–86.

Quattrone, G.A. (1985), 'On the congruity between internal states and actions', *Psychological Bulletin*, vol. 98, pp. 3–40.

Quinney, R. (1970), *The Social Reality of Crime*, Boston, Little, Brown.

Rachman, S. (1969), 'Extraversion and neuroticism in childhood', in H.J. Eysenck and S.B.G. Eysenck (eds), *Personality Structure and Measurement*,

San Diego, Knapp.

Radzinowicz, L. and King, J. (1977), *The Growth of Crime*, London, Hamish Hamilton.

Reinke, B., Holmes, D.S. and Harris, R.L. (1985), 'The timing of psychosocial changes in women's lives: the years 25–45', *Journal of Personality and Social Psychology*, vol. 48, pp. 1353–64.

Rest, J. (1974), 'Manual for the defining issues test: an objective test of moral judgment', Minneapolis, University of Minnesota.

Rich, M.C. (1979), 'Verbal reports on mental processes: issues of accuracy and awareness', *Journal for the Theory of Social Behaviour*, vol. 9, pp. 29–37.

Riggio, R.E. and Friedman, H.S. (1982), 'The interrelationships of self-monitoring factors, personality traits, and nonverbal skills', *Journal of Nonverbal Behavior*, vol. 7, pp. 33–45.

Rock, P. (1973), *Deviant Behaviour*, London, Hutchinson.

Rogers, C.R. (1951), *Client-Centered Therapy*, Boston, Houghton-Mifflin.

Rogers, C.R. (1959), 'A theory of therapy, personality, and interpersonal relationships as developed in the client-centered framework', in S. Koch (ed.), *Psychology: A Study of Science*, vol. 3, New York, McGraw-Hill.

Rogers, C.R. (1961), *On Becoming a Person*, London, Constable.

Rogers, T.B. (1977), 'Self-reference in memory: recognition of personality items', *Journal of Research in Personality*, vol. 11, pp. 295–305.

Romer, D. and Revelle, W. (1984), 'Personality traits: fact or fiction? A critique of the Shweder and D'Andrade systematic distortion hypothesis', *Journal of Personality and Social Psychology*, vol. 47, pp. 1028–42.

Rosch, E. and Mervis, C.B. (1975), 'Family resemblances: studies in the internal structure of categories', *Cognitive Psychology*, vol. 7, pp. 573–605.

Rosch, E., Mervis, C.B., Gray, W.D., Johnson, D. and Boyes-Braem, P. (1976), 'Basic objects in natural categories', *Cognitive Psychology*, vol. 8, pp. 382–439.

Rosenberg, M. (1965), *Society and the Adolescent Self-Image*, Princeton, New Jersey, Princeton University Press.

Rosenberg, S. and Gara, M.A. (1985), 'The multiplicity of personal identity', in P. Shaver (ed.), *Review of Personality and Social Psychology*, vol. 16, pp. 87–113.

Rosenberg, S. and Olshan, K. (1970), 'Evaluative and descriptive aspects of personality perception', *Journal of Personality and Social Psychology*, vol. 16, pp. 619–26.

Rosenberg, S. and Sedlak, A. (1972a), 'Structural representations of implicit personality theory', in L. Berkowitz (ed.), *Advances in Experimental Social Psychology*, vol. 6, pp. 235–97, New York, Academic Press.

Rosenberg, S. and Sedlak, A. (1972b), 'Structural representations of perceived personality trait relationships', in A.K. Romney, R.N. Shepard and S.B. Nelson (eds), *Multidimensional Scaling: Theory and*

Applications in the Behavioral Sciences, Vol. II, Applications, pp. 133–62, New York, Seminar Press.

Rosenberg, S., Nelson, C. and Vivekananthan, P.S. (1968), 'A multidimensional approach to the structure of personality impressions', *Journal of Personality and Social Psychology*, vol. 9, pp. 283–94.

Ross, L. (1977), 'The intuitive psychologist and his shortcomings: distortions in the attribution process', in L. Berkowitz (ed.), *Advances in Experimental Social Psychology*, vol. 10, pp. 173–220, New York, Academic Press.

Rotter, J.B. (1954), *Social Learning and Clinical Psychology*, Englewood Cliffs, New Jersey, Prentice-Hall.

Rotter, J.B. (1966), 'Generalized expectancies for internal versus external control of reinforcement', *Psychological Monographs*, vol. 80, whole no. 609.

Rotter, J.B. (1975), 'Some problems and misconceptions related to the construction of internal versus external control of reinforcement', *Journal of Consulting and Clinical Psychology*, vol. 43, pp. 56–67.

Rotter, J.B., Chance, J.E. and Phares, E.J. (eds) (1972), *Applications of a Social Learning Theory of Personality*, New York, Holt, Rinehart & Winston.

Rotter, J.B., Liverant, S. and Crowne, D.P. (1961), 'The growth and extinction of expectancies in chance, controlled, and skill tasks', *Journal of Psychology*, vol. 52, pp. 161–77.

Ruble, D.N. and Nakamura, C.Y. (1972), 'Task orientation versus social orientation in young children and their attention to relevant stimuli', *Child Development*, vol. 43, pp. 471–80.

Rushton, J.P., Brainerd, C.J. and Pressley, M. (1983), 'Behavioral development and construct validity: the principle of aggregation', *Psychological Bulletin*, vol. 94, pp. 18–38.

Ryff, C.D. and Heinke, S.G. (1983), 'Subjective organization of personality in adulthood and ageing', *Journal of Personality and Social Psychology*, vol. 44, pp. 807–16.

Samenow, S.E. (1984), *Inside the Criminal Mind*, New York, Times Books.

Sampson, E.E. (1977), 'Psychology and the American ideal', *Journal of Personality and Social Psychology*, vol. 35, pp. 767–82.

Schaie, K.W. (1965), 'A general model for the study of developmental problems', *Psychological Bulletin*, vol. 64, pp. 92–107.

Schaie, K.W. (1973), 'Methodological problems in descriptive developmental research on adulthood and old age', in J.R. Nesselroade and H.W. Reese (eds), *Life-span Developmental Psychology: Methodological Issues*, New York, Academic Press.

Schaie, K.W. (1974), 'Translations in gerontology – from lab to life: intellectual functions', *American Psychologist*, vol. 29, pp. 802–7.

Schaie, K.W. and Parham, A. (1976), 'Stability of adult personality traits:

fact or fable?, *Journal of Personality and Social Psychology*, vol. 34, pp. 146–58.

Scheier, M.F. (1980), 'Effects of public and private self-consciousness on the public expression of personal beliefs', *Journal of Personality and Social Psychology*, vol. 39, pp. 514–21.

Scheier, M.F. and Carver, C.S. (1981), 'Private and public aspects of self', in L. Wheeler (ed.), *Review of Personality and Social Psychology*, vol. 2, pp. 189–216, Beverly Hills, Sage.

Scheier, M.F. and Carver, C.S. (1983), 'Two sides of the self: one for you and one for me', in J. Suls and A.G. Greenwald (eds), *Psychological Perspectives on the Self*, vol. 2, pp. 123–57, Hillsdale, New Jersey, Lawrence Erlbaum Associates.

Scheier, M.F., Buss, A.H. and Buss, D.M. (1978), 'Self-consciousness, self-report of aggressiveness, and aggression', *Journal of Research in Personality*, vol. 12, pp. 133–40.

Schifter, D.E. and Ajzen, I. (1985), 'Intention, perceived control, and weight loss: an application of the theory of planned behavior', *Journal of Personality and Social Psychology*, vol. 49, pp. 843–51.

Schlenker, B.R. (1980), *Impression Management*, Monterey, California, Brooks/Cole.

Schlenker, B.R. (ed.) (1985), *The Self and Social Life*, New York, McGraw-Hill.

Schneider, D.J. (1973), 'Implicit personality theory: a review', *Psychological Bulletin*, vol. 79, pp. 294–309.

Schuessler, K.F. and Cressey, D.R. (1950), 'Personality characteristics of criminals', *American Journal of Sociology*, vol. 55, pp. 476–84.

Schur, E.M. (1971), *Labeling Deviant Behavior: Its Sociological Implications*, New York, Harper & Row.

Seidenberg, M.S. and Petitto, L.A. (1979), 'Signing behavior in apes: a critical review', *Cognition*, vol. 7, pp. 177–215.

Semin, G.R. and Manstead, A.S.R. (1983), *The Accountability of Conduct*, London, Academic Press.

Semin, G.R., Rosch, E. and Chassein, J. (1981), 'A comparison of the common-sense and "scientific" conceptions of extraversion–introversion', *European Journal of Social Psychology*, vol. 11, pp. 77–86.

Shapland, J. and Rushton, J.R. (1975), 'Crime and personality: further evidence', *Bulletin of the British Psychological Society*, vol. 28, pp. 66–8.

Sheehy, G. (1976), *Passages: Predictable Crises of Adult Life*, New York, Dutton.

Shepard, R.N. (1975), 'Form, formation and transformation of internal representations', in R.L. Solso (ed.), *Information Processing and Cognition*, Hillsdale, New Jersey, Lawrence Erlbaum Associates.

Shields, J. (1976), 'Heredity and environment', in H.J. Eysenck and G.D.

Wilson (eds), *A Textbook of Human Psychology*, Baltimore, University Park Press.

Shrauger, J.S. and Schoeneman, T.J. (1979), 'Symbolic interactionist view of self-concept: through the looking glass darkly', *Psychological Bulletin*, vol. 86, pp. 549–73.

Shweder, R.A. (1975), 'How relevant is an individual difference theory of personality ratings?', *Journal of Personality*, vol. 43, pp. 455–85.

Shweder, R.A. (1977), 'Likeness and likelihood in everyday thought: magical thinking in judgments about personality', *Current Anthropology*, vol. 18, pp. 637–48.

Shweder, R.A. (1982), 'Fact and artifact in trait perception: the systematic distortion hypothesis', in B.A. Maher and W.B. Maher (eds), *Progress in Experimental Personality Research*, vol. 11, pp. 65–95, New York, Academic Press.

Shweder, R.A. and Bourne, E.J. (1984), 'Does the concept of the person vary cross-culturally?', in R.A. Shweder and R.A. LeVine (eds), *Culture Theory: Essays on Mind, Self, and Emotion*, Cambridge, Cambridge University Press.

Shweder, R.A. and D'Andrade, R.G. (1980), 'The systematic distortion hypothesis', in R.A. Shweder (ed.), *Fallible Judgment in Behavioral Research: New Directions for Methodology of Social and Behavioral Science*, no. 4, San Francisco, Jossey-Bass.

Siegler, I.C., George, L.K. and Okun, M.A. (1979), 'Cross-sequential analysis of adult personality', *Developmental Psychology*, vol. 15, pp. 350–1.

Sinclair, I. and Chapman, B. (1973), 'A typological and dimensional study of a sample of prisoners', *British Journal of Criminology*, vol. 13, pp. 341–53.

Singer, J.L. (1976), *Daydreaming and Fantasy*, London, Allen & Unwin.

Skrypnek, B.J. and Snyder, M. (1982), 'On the self-perpetuating nature of stereotypes about women and men', *Journal of Experimental Social Psychology*, vol. 18, pp. 277–91.

Smith, E.E. and Medin, D.L. (1981), *Categories and Concepts*, Cambridge, Massachusetts, Harvard University Press.

Smith, E.R., and Miller, F.D. (1978), 'Limits on perception of cognitive processes: a reply to Nisbett and Wilson', *Psychological Review*, vol. 85, pp. 355–62.

Snow, R.E. (1977), 'Research on aptitudes: a progress report', in L.S. Shulman (ed.), *Review of Research in Education*, vol. 4, Itasca, Illinois, Peacock Press.

Snow, R.E. (1978), 'Aptitude-treatment interactions in educational research', in L.A. Pervin and M. Lewis (eds), *Perspectives in Interactional Psychology*, New York, Plenum Press.

Snyder, M. (1974), 'Self-monitoring of expressive behavior', *Journal of*

Personality and Social Psychology, vol. 30, pp. 526–37.

Snyder, M. (1979), 'Self-monitoring processes', in L. Berkowitz (ed.), *Advances in Experimental Social Psychology*, vol. 12, pp. 85–128, New York, Academic Press.

Snyder, M. (1984), 'When beliefs create reality', in L. Berkowitz (ed.), *Advances in Experimental Social Psychology*, vol. 18, pp. 247–305, New York, Academic Press.

Snyder, M. and Monson, T.C. (1975), 'Persons, situations, and the control of social behavior', *Journal of Personality and Social Psychology*, vol. 32, pp. 637–44.

Snyder, M., Tanke, E.D. and Berscheid, E. (1977), 'Social perception and interpersonal behavior: on the self-fulfilling nature of social stereotypes', *Journal of Personality and Social Psychology*, vol. 35, pp. 656–66.

Spearman, C. (1927), *The Abilities of Man*, New York, Macmillan.

Startup, M. (1985), 'The astrological doctrine of "aspects": a failure to validate with personality measures', *British Journal of Social Psychology*, vol. 24, pp. 307–15.

Stephenson, W. (1953), *The Study of Behavior: Q-technique and its Methodology*, Chicago, University of Chicago Press.

Sternberg, R.J. (1985), 'Implicit theories of intelligence, creativity, and wisdom', *Journal of Personality and Social Psychology*, vol. 49, pp. 607–27.

Sternberg, R.J., Conway, B.E., Katron, J.L. and Bernstein, M. (1981), 'People's conceptions of intelligence', *Journal of Personality and Social Psychology*, vol. 41, pp. 37–55.

Storms, M.D. and Nisbett, R.E. (1970), 'Insomnia and the attribution process', *Journal of Personality and Social Psychology*, vol. 2, pp. 319–28.

Stricker, L.J., Jacobs, P.I. and Kogan, N. (1974), 'Trait correlations in implicit personality theories and questionnaire data', *Journal of Personality and Social Psychology*, vol. 30, pp. 198–207.

Strickland, B.R. (1977), 'Internal–external control of reinforcement', in T. Blass (ed.), *Personality Variables in Social Behaviour*, Hillsdale, New Jersey, Lawrence Erlbaum Associates.

Sullivan, H.S. (1953), *The Interpersonal Theory of Psychiatry*, New York, Norton.

Swann, W.B. (1984), 'Quest for accuracy in person perception: a matter of pragmatics', *Psychological Review*, vol. 91, pp. 457–77.

Terman, L.M. and Oden, M.H. (1959), *The Gifted Group at Mid-life: Thirty-five Years' Follow-up of the Superior Child*, vol. 5 of L.M. Terman (ed.), *Genetic Studies of Genius*, Stanford, California, Stanford University Press.

Thurstone, L.L. (1947), *Multiple Factor Analysis*, University of Chicago Press.

Tupes, E.C. and Christal, R.E. (1961), 'Recurrent personality factors based on trait ratings', *USAF ASD Technical Report*, no. 61–97.

Turner, R.G. (1978), 'Consistency, self-consciousness, and the predictive validity of typical and maximal personality measures', *Journal of Research in Personality*, vol. 12, pp. 117–32.

Tversky, A. and Kahneman, D. (1973), 'Availability: a heuristic for judging frequency and probability', *Cognitive Psychology*, vol. 5, pp. 207–32.

Tversky, A. and Kahneman, D. (1974), 'Judgment under uncertainty: heuristics and biases', *Science*, vol. 184, pp. 1124–31.

Tzeng, O.C.S. and Tzeng, C.H. (1982), 'Implicit personality theory: myth or fact? An illustration of how empirical research can miss', *Journal of Personality*, vol. 50, pp. 223–39.

Vaillant, G.E. (1977), *Adaptation to Life*, Boston, Little, Brown.

Valins, S. and Ray, A.A. (1967), 'Effects of cognitive desensitization on avoidance behavior', *Journal of Personality and Social Psychology*, vol. 1, pp. 345–50.

Van Heck, G. (1984), 'The construction of a general taxonomy of situations', in H. Bonarius, G. Van Heck and N. Smid (eds), *Personality Psychology in Europe*, Lisse, Swets & Zeitlinger.

Vernon, P.E. (1972), 'The distinctiveness of field independence', *Journal of Personality*, vol. 40, pp. 366–91.

Wadsworth, M.E.J. (1975), 'Delinquency in a national sample of children', *British Journal of Criminology*, vol. 15, pp. 167–80.

Waldo, G.P. and Dinitz, S. (1967), 'Personality attributes of the criminal: an analysis of research studies 1950–65', *Journal of Research in Crime and Delinquency*, vol. 4, pp. 185–202.

Wallerstein, J.S. and Wyle, C.J. (1947), 'Our law-abiding law breakers', *Probation*, April, pp. 107–12.

Wallston, K.A., Wallston, B.S. and DeVallis, R. (1978), 'Development of the multidimensional health locus of control (MHLC) scales', *Health Education Monographs*, vol. 6, pp. 161–70.

Warburton, F.W. (1965), 'Observations on a sample of psychopathic American criminals', *Behavior Research and Therapy*, vol. 3, pp. 129–35.

Warr, P.B. (1974), 'Inference magnitude, range, and evaluative directions as factors affecting relative importance of cues in impression formation', *Journal of Personality and Social Psychology*, vol. 30, pp. 191–7.

Weiss, D.S. and Mendelsohn G.A. (1986), 'An empirical demonstration of the implausibility of the semantic similarity explanation of how trait ratings are made and what they mean', *Journal of Personality and Social Psychology*, vol. 50, pp. 595–601.

Welford, C. (1975), 'Labelling theory and criminology: an assessment', *Special Problems*, vol. 22, p. 332.

West, D.J. (1963), *The Habitual Prisoner*, London, Macmillan.

West, D.J. and Farrington, D.P. (1973), *Who Become Delinquent?*, London, Heinemann.

West, D.J. and Farrington, D.P. (1977), *The Delinquent Way of Life*, London, Heinemann.

White, P. (1980), 'Limitations on verbal reports of internal events: a refutation of Nisbett and Wilson and of Bem', *Psychological Review*, vol. 87, pp. 105–12.

Wicklund, R.A. (1975), 'Objective self-awareness', in L. Berkowitz (ed.), *Advances in Experimental Social Psychology*, vol. 8, pp. 233–75, New York, Academic Press.

Wicklund, R.A. (1978), 'Three years later', in L. Berkowitz (ed.), *Cognitive Theories in Social Psychology*, New York, Academic Press.

Wiggins, J.S. (1973), *Personality and Prediction: Principles of Personality Assessment*, Reading, Massachusetts, Addison-Wesley.

Wiggins, J.S. (1979), 'A psychological taxonomy of trait-descriptive terms: the interpersonal domain', *Journal of Personality and Social Psychology*, vol. 37, pp. 395–412.

Wiggins, J.S. and Broughton, R. (1985), 'The interpersonal circle: a structural model for the integration of personality research', in R. Hogan and W.H. Jones (eds), *Perspectives in Personality*, vol. 1, pp. 1–47, Greenwich, Connecticut, JAI Press.

Winslow, R.W. (1969), *Crime in a Free Society*, Belmont, California, Dickenson.

Wishner, J. (1960), 'Reanalysis of "impressions of personality"', *Psychological Review*, vol. 67, pp. 96–112.

Witkin, H.A. and Berry, J.W. (1975), 'Psychological differentiation in cross-cultural perspective', *Journal of Cross-cultural Psychology*, vol. 6, pp. 4–87.

Witkin, H.A. and Goodenough, D.R. (1977), 'Field dependence and interpersonal behaviour', *Psychological Bulletin*, vol. 84, pp. 661–89.

Witkin, H.A., Goodenough, D.R. and Karp, S.A. (1967), 'Stability of cognitive style from childhood to young adulthood', *Journal of Personality and Social Psychology*, vol. 7, pp. 291–300.

Witkin, H.A., Dyk, R.B., Faterson, H.F., Goodenough, D.R. and Karp, S.A. (1974), *Psychological Differentiation: Studies of Development*, Hillsdale, New Jersey, Lawrence Erlbaum Associates.

Witkin, H.A., Lewis, H.B., Hertzman, M., Machover, K., Meissner, P.B. and Wapner, S. (1972), *Personality Through Perception: An Experimental and Clinical Study*, Westwood, Connecticut, Greenwood Press.

Wohlwill, J.F. (1970), 'The age variable in psychological research', *Psychological Review*, vol. 77, pp. 49–64.

Wohlwill, J.F. (1973), *The Study of Behavioural Development*, New York, Academic Press.

Wolfgang, M.E., Figlio, R.M. and Sellin, T. (1972), *Delinquency in a Birth Cohort*, Chicago, University of Chicago Press.

Woodruff, D.S. and Birren, J.E. (1972), 'Age changes and cohort differences in personality', *Developmental Psychology*, vol. 6, pp. 252–9.

Wootton, B. (1959), *Social Science and Social Pathology*, London, Allen & Unwin.

Wyer, R.S. (1970), 'Information, redundancy, inconsistency, and novelty and their role in impression formation', *Journal of Experimental Social Psychology*, vol. 6, pp. 111–27.

Wyer, R.S. and Srull, T.K. (1984), *The Handbook of Social Cognition*, vols I and II, Hillsdale, New Jersey, Lawrence Erlbaum Associates.

Wylie, R.C. (1974), *The Self-Concept*, vol. 1, Lincoln, Nebraska, University of Nebraska Press.

Wylie, R.C. (1979), *The Self-Concept*, vol. 2, Lincoln, Nebraska, University of Nebraska Press.

Wymer, W.E. and Penner, L.A. (1985), 'Moderator variables and different types of predictability: do you have a match?', *Journal of Personality and Social Psychology*, vol. 49, pp. 1002–15.

Yochelson, S. and Samenow, S.E. (1976), *The Criminal Personality*, vols I and II, New York, Jason Aronson.

Zimbardo, P.G., Cohen, A., Weisenberg, M., Dworkin, L. and Firestone, I. (1969), 'The control of experimental pain', in P.G. Zimbardo (ed.), *The Cognitive Control of Motivation*, Glenview, Illinois, Scott Foresman.

Zuckerman, M. (1974), 'The sensation-seeking motive', in B. Maher (ed.), *Progress in Experimental Personality Research*, vol. 7, pp. 79–148, New York, Academic Press.

Author index

Subject index

Achievement Motive, 16
actor component, 196
adolescence and life-span research, 235–40
age as a dependent variable, 217–18
age changes, interpretation of, 231–9
ageing, 9, 211
aggregation, 89–92
analysis of variance, 83, 85, 88
anxiety, 48, 55, 84
ascending reticular activating system (ARAS), 53, 56
Authoritarianism, 16
autonomic nervous system (ANS), 53, 54

behaviour: age differences as inherent characteristics of, 217–18; and Cattell's theory, 67; consistency in, 2, 72–97, 192; criminal, 252–3; and database for multi-trait theories, 41–3; deviant, 249–52; FD-I and, 26; as a function of both person and situation, 83; as a function of reinforcement, 28; immediate behaviour ratings and implicit personality theory, 142–53; and reattribution studies, 170; self-observations of, 173–5; and single-trait theories, 16; situationism and, 81–3;

specification equation, 67; and social labelling theory, 265
Beunreuter Personality Inventory, 222
Big Five personality factors, 69–70, 158–9

California Test of Personality (CTP), 228
categories, traits as, 202–4
Cattell's personality theory, 58–67, 67–8, 224, 225; and criminal personality, 257; cf. Eysenck's personality theory
children: childhood experience and adult personality, 218–20; study of gifted children, 220
cognitive algebra, 129
cognitive models of trait integration and inference, 130–3
cohorts, 211, 212–18
conditioning, 54–5
consistency, 2, 72–97; four types of, 72–6; meaning of, 72; Mischel's attack on personality theorist's perspective, 76–81; new approaches to, 89–96; situationism and, 81–3
constructivist position, 8–9, 196–206; and criminal personality, 280; dynamic nature of, 197–200; implications of, 200–5; and life-span research, 209–10, 230–48